# LERMONTOV'S *A HERO*
# *OF OUR TIME*

*A Critical Companion*

18/09/02

Павлу

За все, что ты
делаешь для наших
студентов (и не только
тех в этом издании.

Лёва

D1707756

# LERMONTOV'S *A HERO*

# *OF OUR TIME*

## *A Critical Companion*

### Edited by Lewis Bagby

Northwestern University Press

The American Association of Teachers

of Slavic and East European Languages

Northwestern University Press

Evanston, Illinois 60208-4210

Copyright © 2002 by

Northwestern University Press.

Published 2002. All rights reserved.

Printed in the United States of America

10 9 8 7 6 5 4 3 2 1

ISBN 0-8101-1680-4

**Library of Congress Cataloging-in-Publication Data**

Lermontov's "A Hero of our time" : a critical companion / edited by

Lewis Bagby.

    p.  cm.

    ISBN 0-8101-1680-4 (pbk. : alk. paper)

    1. Lermontov, Mikhail Yur'evich, 1814–1841. Geroi nashego vremeni. I. Bagby,

Lewis, 1944–

    PG3337.L4 G49 2001

    891.73'3—dc21

2001001122

THIS VOLUME IS DEDICATED TO MY MENTOR, COLLEAGUE,
AND FRIEND, JOHN MERSEREAU, JR., AND TO THE
STUDENTS OF RUSSIAN AT THE UNIVERSITY OF WYOMING.

# Contents

# Acknowledgments

I would like to express my appreciation to Susan Harris of North-western University Press for the invitation to compile this volume of critical works on Mikhail Lermontov's novel, *A Hero of Our Time*. Her patience with my schedule of ever-changing professional obligations has made it possible for me to complete the project within, if not a reasonable, then at least a feasible amount of time. Her offer has made it possible for me to do something we know is essential to the development of our students' capacities – applying their linguistic skills and cultural understanding to real-world tasks. It has been a pleasure to solicit the aid of recent students of Russian at the University of Wyoming to translate the excerpts contained herein. They include Matthew Feeney, Lisa Holte, Katrina Jones, Victoria Klein, Matthew Micheli, Dawn Moser, and Joseph Peschio, many of whom are now pursuing advanced degrees in Slavic studies as well as international careers connected with Russia. Special thanks go to my former students, Kurt Kelly, Bryce Krug, Matthew Lamont, and Benjamin Whitfield for translations, which, for lack of space, could not appear here.

I would also like to thank Susan Layton, of the Centre d'études du monde russe, sovietique et post-sovietique, who accepted my offer to write on the question of ethnicity in the novel. She is the foremost Slavic scholar on the literary representation of the Caucasus, and her contribution here provides insight into this thorny issue in Lermontov's novel. Professor Jane Costlow, Bates College, has taken up the difficult issue of women in the novel. Having reviewed the critical literature in Russian and English on Lermontov's novel, I was surprised by a relative lack of feminist treatments. Costlow's contribution fills the void admirably.

Professor Andrew Swensen, Brandeis University, accepted the task of translating one of the more challenging works of criticism that appeared in 1840. S. O. Burachok's scathing review required a steady hand and a deep understanding of the period and the issues surrounding the novel, and Dr. Swensen provided both. My colleague, Joseph Krafczik, University of Wyoming, translated the entirety of Vladimir Fisher's seminal "Lermontov's Poetics," only a small portion of which appears herein. I am indebted to him for his fine work.

Of some regret was my inability, due to space limitations, to include three items of some note: (1) Lermontov's letters from 1837 to 1841, the period of his certain entry into the literary arena; (2) his first experiment in developing an early variant of Pechorin (see Guy Daniels's translation of "Princess Ligovskaya," in which Pechorin's precursor appears); and (3) comments on Lermontov and his novel by nineteenth-century Russian authors from Gogol to Chekhov. Many of these items may be accessed, however, at the web address, http://www.uwyo.edu/lermontov.

It would be possible, of course, to catalogue a great wealth of material that might have been included in this volume of translations. There is, necessarily, much more missing of value than is present. Nevertheless, the work contained herein provides the reader with a fair representation of the types of discourse that have surrounded Lermontov's novel since its initial publication, particularly the first responses of 1840 and 1841. These earliest critical works appear here for the first time in English.

I wish, also, to thank my family, Donna, David, and Ryan, for their constant support in all my endeavors. And to the contributors and translators for this volume, I express my gratitude for their hard work and patience. For any errors, oversights, or infelicities, I assume full responsibility.

LEWIS BAGBY, UNIVERSITY OF WYOMING

# Note on Transliteration

A slightly modified version of the Library of Congress system of Russian transliteration is used. When an individual of Russian origin is well known in the West under a conventional form, that orthography is used.

I     INTRODUCTION

# Mikhail Yur'evich Lermontov and *A Hero of Our Time*

LEWIS BAGBY

## A Brief Biography

Mikhail Lermontov (1814–41) is considered the second most important Russian poet of the nineteenth century, after Alexander Pushkin (1799–1837). This opinion, held by critics in Russia and abroad, is of no small consequence, for Lermontov's verse is held up against the poetic achievements of many accomplished poets of the Golden Age of Russian verse.[1] Lermontov's poetry is recited to this day: it is on the lips of both national figures and provincial educators in the Russian Federation. What is remarkable about Lermontov's credited verse is that it was almost entirely written between the time he was twenty-three and twenty-seven. Adding piquancy to the stature of his aesthetic accomplishment is the woeful fact that he was killed in a duel.

Lermontov's poetry holds a special position in Russian culture, but his importance also derives from the one novel he published in his lifetime, *A Hero of Our Time*. The novel took the public by storm in 1840 and has continued to disturb, challenge, and excite readers and critics since that time. It has been praised as the first novel of "psychological realism" in Russian prose and as a critique of the repressive times in which Lermontov lived. Lermontov's life coincided with the notorious historical period when political, economic, and social ideas had to go underground, surfacing indirectly in works of art rather than in public forums or in the public media that the police and censor controlled for content. *A Hero of Our Time* is one such work, a seminal one at that.

Lermontov stands as a key figure in Russian culture of the second quarter of the nineteenth century. His small but significant mature poetic output, the tragic circumstances of his death, the role he played in society, his continual affront to government, and his contribution to Russian prose through the publication of *A Hero of Our Time* earned him this place.

It was a complex time in which he lived. Tsar Nicholas I's tyrannical reign was a troubled era when over ninety percent of the population was living in conditions of poverty, when a large percentage of the peasant population was virtually enslaved, when power, land, and wealth were amassed in very few hands, and when the country had yet begun to recover from the trauma of the Decembrist revolt that occurred in 1825 on the first day of Tsar Nicholas I's rule.

On that December day, a group of bright, radical military officers attempted to install a constitutional form of government by rallying the rank and file troops of St. Petersburg to forestall the Senate's swearing allegiance to Nicholas I. The revolt was a fiasco, ending when over one hundred officers were tried, convicted, and exiled to Siberia and the Caucasus. Six principal organizers were hanged. December 14 set a paranoic tone for Tsar Nicholas I's rule, although he might have been the tyrant he was in any case.

Lermontov was born on October 3, 1814, approximately eleven years before the Decembrist revolt. He would have known of it as a child but become more familiar with it as a cadet in St. Petersburg. In his brief life, he met with several of the Decembrists when he was exiled in the Caucasus. His life was connected adversely with the tsar, his court, and secret police – not only during the years of Lermontov's greatest literary output (which placed him in the eye of the censors as well as the court and police) but also while he was being schooled and trained for military duty when he was a youth.

———

Before tracing the details of Lermontov's biography in greater detail, it is important to acknowledge the difficulties that occur in attempting to reconstruct his life. The historical record is very slim. Although the reader has his poems, dramas, and prose, Lermontov left few letters, notebooks, diary pages, or drafts.[2] Memoirs about his life were penned many years after his death, when archetypal images of Lermontov's persona already prevailed. In treating his biography, it becomes difficult to differentiate fact and fiction. This is the case for a variety of reasons, some of which belong to Lermontov himself; others to his friends, acquaintances, and enemies (and problems associated with their memoirs); and others to the interpretive means at our disposal 160 years after Lermontov's death.

Lermontov created smokescreens, manipulating the presentation of his self in a way that ultimately blocked it from view. For example, in a moment of despair, he once wrote to Sofia Bakhmeteva, a close friend, that "the poetry of my soul has died." Then he added, "If I had started writing to you an hour earlier, perhaps I would have written something entirely different; every moment I have new fantasies."[3] We might conclude from this remark that constant internal movement defines Lermontov. But it may also be accurate to say that Lermontov created the image of a contradictory, yet heroic, character and that he did so in order to remain outside the grasp of those who tried to define him. There are historical reasons why memoirists cannot always be trusted either. During the first several decades of the nineteenth century, it was normative to equate literature with life. It is to be expected that Lermontov acquired the habit of his generation, particularly among the ultraromantics, to fashion himself by aesthetic means. The public would have viewed him in the same manner.

The equation of his art with his person has long dominated critical discourse about him. For example, Ivan Turgenev delivers the following description of Lermontov:

There was something ominous and tragic in Lermontov's appearance: his swarthy face and large, motionless dark eyes exuded a sort of somber and evil strength, a sort of pensive scornfulness and passion. His hard gaze was strangely out of keeping with the expression of his almost childishly tender, protruding lips. His whole figure, thick-set, bow-legged, with a large head on broad, stooping shoulders, aroused an unpleasant feeling; but everyone had at once to acknowledge its immense inherent strength. It is, of course, a well-known fact that he had to some extent portrayed himself in Pechorin. The words, "His eyes did not laugh when he laughed," from *A Hero of Our Time*, etc., could really have been applied to himself.[4]

Turgenev's words sound more like literary cliché, as in the physiological sketch in the "Maksim Maksimych" chapter of *A Hero of Our Time*. But there is also the chance that Turgenev's description is accurate and provides an adequate depiction of Lermontov's social image. Whether that projection was a game Lermontov played for the benefit of society or whether it was authentic is difficult to ascertain. In any case, Turgenev's record of Lermontov maintains the practice of equating literature and life in synchrony with the times.

That mode of apprehension has not disappeared. In his 1982 biography of Lermontov, John Garrard writes, "The symbiotic relationship between love and suffering is, of course, a favorite Romantic paradox, but for Lermontov it was much more than a literary device. He was unlucky in love and believed that he always would be: fate had ordained it" (6–7). As with Turgenev's testimony, Garrard's description may be a judicious interpretation of the man, but we note that art and fiction are woven together in it.

Other memoirs of Lermontov confuse the issues because the source of information sometimes proves unreliable. Ekaterina Sushkova's memoirs are a case in point. Lermontov had fallen for her when he was seventeen years old, but she did not reciprocate his feelings. Several years later he sought his revenge, courting her publicly – much to her newfound delight – then dropping her suddenly and viciously. As one might expect, Sushkova's recollections of Lermontov are neither flattering nor entirely objective, even if they contain useful information.

When the historical record seems more certain, another problem can emerge. In recounting Lermontov's life, it is not uncommon to interpret his life in a deterministic manner. One such pitfall is illustrated by the circumstances of his early life. Lermontov was born to Maria Mikhailovna Arsen'eva and Yury Petrovich Lermontov. Maria was the only child of Elizaveta Alekseevna Arsen'eva (née Stolypin, a family of great fame, position, and wealth). Yury Petrovich, several years Maria's senior, lived on a small, rather undistinguished, estate. Elizaveta Alekseevna was not pleased with her daughter's fascination with this dashing, young, retired officer who was known for his libertine ways and small pocketbook. In 1812, when the couple married against the mother's wishes, there was a falling out of the kind one encounters in stories and novels of the time. The pair lived briefly in Moscow until they could persuade Arsen'eva to receive them in her home. She seems to have been willing to do so because Mikhail had been born.

In 1817, when Mikhail was not quite three years old, his mother, Maria, died of consumption. Arsen'eva immediately sought to take control of her grandson's upbringing. She bought Yury off with a large payment, apparently threatening to disinherit the child if Yury were to interfere with raising the boy. Yury removed himself from the family altogether. Over the next fourteen years, he saw his son two times that have been attested – once in 1827 and again in 1828. Yury died of consumption in 1831 when Lermontov was seventeen.

From this series of tragedies, and the widely acknowledged fact that his grandmother saw to his every whim, it is reasonable to conclude that Lermontov was destined to be sad, lonely, isolated, and even manipulative of those he loved. Such a reading, as compelling and logical as it appears to be, may be a neat, compact, and aesthetically balanced story; but it may not be accurate.

Another example of Lermontov's biography, which might result in a deterministic assessment, derives from the behavior of his maternal grandmother, Madame Arsen'eva. She sent him to good schools, lobbied for his release from punishment when he misbehaved, worked successfully to have him placed in the Imperial Guard Hussars, and helped him gain release from two of his exiles. On three occasions she took him to the northern Caucasus when he was still a young boy, and she indulged his "dreamy, willful, self-centered, and impulsive"[5] nature – including the precocious urge to copy out others' poems and compose his own. Lermontov's lifelong dependence upon his grandmother and her smothering concern are part of many biographical descriptions of his ambivalence toward life, love, fate, and death. Although such assessments may appeal to a twentieth-century sense of psychological inevitability, these readings may not be valid, for they cannot be reinforced by demonstrable causal links.

Because of problems associated with a relative dearth in the Lermontov archives, with Lermontov's propensity to project images of himself that may only belong to his persona, and with the confusion of literature and life in the memoirs of the period, the "facts" of Lermontov's life remain contingent. Consequently, the reader must be aware of the type of discourse the critic engages when reviewing Lermontov's biography. With these caveats in mind, it is possible to attempt to separate fact and fiction in Lermontov's life.

Lermontov's grandmother raised him as best she could, which was substantial in material terms. She made certain that competent French and English tutors were available. When he reached thirteen, she enrolled him in the best school for the nobility in Moscow. There he enjoyed visiting his large extended family, from which a cousin was selected each summer to visit the family estate in Tarkhany to keep Lermontov company. Later he attended military school in St. Petersburg.

Lermontov was not physically attractive. He had bowlegs and was somewhat bent, physical features that worsened when, as a cadet, he attempted a gambol on horseback that backfired and left him with a broken leg that produced a limp. Lermontov, however, was an impressive individual by other measures. Even as a youth, he was an accomplished painter, vocalist, pianist, and violinist. His poetry, though callow, showed moments of genius. His still famous "Angel" was written when he was but sixteen.

The sensitivity Lermontov displayed in some contexts seems to have developed a shadow side – he could also be self-conscious, capricious, even bilious. His grandmother spent much of his twenty-seven years bailing him out of trouble. He seems to have delighted in annoying those he disliked with aggressive and inconsistent behavior. He assaulted his interlocutors' and audience's intellectual and emotional comforts. As a result, memoirs of Lermontov range from vitriol to affection. Although the Karamzin family, famous in court and in the literary world, enjoyed Lermontov's company and appreciated his talent, others could not tolerate him.

Tsar Nicholas I and his chief of the secret police, Count Alexander Benckendorf (Madame Arsen'eva's relative) exiled Lermontov to the Caucasus three times for egregious infringements that must have dumbfounded Lermontov's supporters and friends. For example, Lermontov insulted the tsar's daughters at a masked ball. He fought a duel, a practice that was outlawed at the time, and – what is worse – he fought it against Ernest de Barante, the son of the French ambassador. When a disagreement arose about the way Lermontov comported himself during the duel, he again challenged de Barante from his prison cell. He published poems like "The Death of a Poet" (1837) that attacked high society for its pretenses and moral bankruptcy. (In this poetic commemoration of Alexander Pushkin, he lambasted society for its part in Pushkin's death.) He thumbed his nose at the authorities in the capital. Lermontov was society's bad boy, and he appears to have favored the role.

When in 1832 Lermontov transferred from Moscow University to St. Petersburg and found that he could not receive credit for work already completed and would have to begin his university education all over, he decided to enroll instead in the prestigious School of Cavalry Junkers and Ensign of the Guard. He lived the flamboyant life of a military man, drinking, wenching, and pulling pranks. He put it indirectly to Maria Lopukhina in a letter of August 4, 1833: "The time of my dreams has passed; the time for believing is long gone; now I want material pleasures, happiness I can touch, happiness that can be bought with gold, that one can carry in one's pocket like a snuff-box, happiness that beguiles only my senses while leaving my soul in peace and quiet!" (Garrard, 17).

By 1834, at age twenty, he was assigned to the Life Guard Hussars. He was commissioned cornet and stationed at Tsarskoye Selo, a prestigious assignment. For a few years, he lived in the social whirl of St. Petersburg, simultaneously enjoying its fruits and castigating the duplicities of high society. But in 1837 much changed. His poetic career began in earnest and he became famous for his poem on Pushkin's death. He appeared regularly in print and experimented in writing prose. (He did not complete a society tale, "Princess Ligovskaya," in which a precursor of the later Pechorin makes an appearance.)

His Pushkin poem was circulated in manuscript. Because of its content, he was arrested and interrogated. During Lermontov's interrogation, in an act he considered cowardice, he faulted his friend, Svyatoslav Raevsky, for the latter's part in the circulation of the poem. As a result, Raevsky suffered a more severe punishment than did Lermontov. Raevsky was sent to the north for two years to serve in a lowly clerk's position. Perhaps in exchange for his confession, or due to his grandmother's efforts (if not for both reasons), Lermontov was not even demoted. He was transferred instead to the Nizhegorodsky Dragoon Regiment in the Caucasus, but he never reached his assignment. First, after leaving St. Petersburg, he stayed on in Moscow for close to a month, then he stopped to take the waters in Stavropol in order to cure influenza and rheumatism. From there he was transferred to the hospital in Pyatigorsk, where he remained for the summer.

Throughout the journey, he was surrounded by friends and relatives who were in charge of his circumstances. He met several Decembrists serving in the ranks for their part in the failed revolt, and he kept good company in Pyatigorsk society. He was sent to join a military expedition in August, and this forced him to travel to Anapa on the Black Sea by way of Taman. The expedition was canceled, and he was sent back to Stavropol. By October he was transferred to Novgorod, and in April 1838 he was reassigned to the Life Guard Hussars at Tsarskoye Selo. Thus, Lermontov's first exile ended up being a long holiday in the Caucasus. During that time, Lermontov produced a good deal of poetry, completed several paintings of its landscape and peoples, and prepared chapters for publication that would eventually form part of *A Hero of Our Time*.

In 1838 he became friends with important members of the intelligentsia, most notably the famous court poet Vasily Zhukovsky and the distinguished romantic poet Prince Peter Vyazemsky. Lermontov was a constant visitor to the Karamzin family literary salon. But he continued to lead a dual life – carousing on the one hand, and pursuing a serious literary career on the other.

At the end of 1839, he was promoted from cornet to lieutenant, but soon he provoked leading society with his callous disregard of the tsar's daughters, his duel, and his poetic challenge to high society. He was exiled a second time to the Caucasus, on this occasion to the Tenginsky Infantry Regiment (a demotion from the Life Guard Hussars).

Assuming the leisurely pace of his first exile, Lermontov left St. Petersburg in May and stopped in Moscow, where he met Nikolai Gogol and renewed his friendship with Prince Vyazemsky. By June he arrived in Stavropol, from where he was sent to the Grozny Fortress. This was not his official assignment but one the local command issued for him.

Lermontov distinguished himself in one battle after another, the most prominent in July 1840 at the river Valerik (after which his famous poem is named). Had he behaved well, he would have been awarded a gold saber "for courage." Unfortunately, Lermontov could not remain constant for the length of time it normally took to recommend someone for an honor and have the case disposed.

In January 1841 Lermontov was given a two-month pass to return to St. Petersburg. Upon his arrival in February, he did not report immediately to his commanding officer, as was required. Instead, he went to a ball, a particularly grievous breach for someone still serving under the conditions of punishment. This act of disobedience provoked an official examination of the circumstances under which he had been nominated for military commendations. It was then discovered that, in the spring, he had not reported to his regiment as ordered but had been reassigned to fight in expeditions he was not intended to see. Furthermore, it was discovered that he had over-stayed his leave of absence in St. Petersburg by more than a month. Consequently, he was summarily ordered to leave the capital and return to the Tenginsky Infantry Regiment.

In April Lermontov began a third leisurely trip to the Caucasus. He fell ill again on the journey south, which necessitated a stay in Pyatigorsk to take the cure. In June Tsar Nicholas I signed an order that he conduct *frontovaia sluzhba* (literally, "front duty") in the south. Many scholars have assumed that this meant frontline duty, in the thick of battle where the Tenginsky Regiment was located. It was an inhospitable location where the infantry and officers were suffering massive losses. It has been argued, however, that *frontovaia sluzhba* at that time meant "reserve battalion duty," not "frontline service."[6] Thus, the notion that Tsar Nicholas I was intent on destroying Lermontov personally is not believed today, reams of Soviet scholarship notwithstanding. In fact, it would have been well below the dignity of the tsar, tyrant though he was, to have engaged in behavior so unbecoming the Tsar of All the Russias.

Lermontov enjoyed his round of activities in Pyatigorsk in the company of a distant relative, a Stolypin with the nickname "Mongo." He fed on his notoriety as social misfit, his fame as a poet second only to Pushkin, and his success with the second publication of *A Hero of Our Time*.

But he did not endear himself to Nikolai Martynov and others.[7] In the salons of polite Pyatigorsk society, Martynov dressed as a native Circassian, wore a long sword, affected the manners of a romantic hero cut from the cloth of Lermontov's own Grushnitsky. Lermontov teased Martynov mercilessly. There had also been mis-understandings between their families in the past (Garrard, 30–31). When Martynov could no longer stand the slights and insults, he challenged Lermontov to a duel and, on July 15, 1841, killed him. This skeletal summary of Lermontov's biography indicates why it has become common to equate the man with his persona and his persona with his art. He led such a wild, romantic life, fulfilled so many Byronic features (individualism, isolation from high society, social critic, and misfit), and lived and died so furiously, that it is difficult not to confuse these manifestations of identity with his authentic self.

There are indications, however, that Lermontov was only beginning to understand himself when he died. This idea is predicated on the notion that he could only have depicted Pechorin as clearly as he did through having gained an objective, critical perspective on his hero's behavior, patterns of thought, and beliefs. Who Lermontov had become, however, or was becoming, remains unclear. Lermontov, like many a romantic hero once closely examined, remains as open and unfinished an individual as his persona seems closed and fixed. Much the same can be said of his novel.

## *A Hero of Our Time*

Upon first reading, Lermontov's novel appears to have little depth. It consists of stock romantic characters and episodes. Thematic concerns about Pechorin's generation, the role of fate in the individual's life, the romantic hero, and his loves, sufferings, and isolation seem quite commonplace. Yet to this day, the novel elicits significant critical response, the best of which continues to unearth new information about the text, to generate challenging perspectives on the novel's subtleties, to dispel prejudices about the work (like those above), and to find layers of complexity the novel's surface seems to preclude.

Without reviewing in advance the scholarly work contained in this volume, suffice it to say that *A Hero of Our Time* represents a major aesthetic accomplishment, and it does so from a variety of perspectives. Its utilization of stock romantic genres from which to develop a "realist" novel is rather ingenious. Its chronological reordering of events necessitates a forward and backward, rather than linear, approach to reading. Its system of parallel images, repetitive lexical items, repeated plot elements, and recurring character types reinforce the forward and backward apprehension of the text, urging the reader to recall and bring together elements of similarity in an attempt at pattern formation the novel appears otherwise to lack. Its social system of "insiders" and "outsiders" becomes so knotted with each successive chapter that it is difficult to establish a "society" that might be considered normative or dominant and out of which some larger social meaning might be generated. Its apparent separation of "savages" and "civilized," too, dissolves in a way that challenges the ethnic divisions a reader might bring to the text beforehand.

D. S. Mirsky may have summed these features up most generously:

> [T]he perfection . . . of [Lermontov's] style and narrative manner can be appreciated only by those who really know Russian, who feel the fine imponderable shades of words and know what has been left out as well as what has been put in. Lermontov's prose is the best Russian prose ever written, if we judge by the standards of perfection and not by those of wealth. It is transparent, for it is absolutely adequate to the content and neither overlaps it nor is overlapped by it.[8]

Vladimir Nabokov, who thought well enough of the novel to translate it (together with his son), feels quite differently about Lermontov's stylistic achievement:

> In attempting to translate Lermontov, I have gladly sacrificed to the requirements of exactness a number of important things – good taste, neat diction, and even grammar (when some characteristic solecism occurs in the Russian text). The English reader should be aware that Lermontov's prose style in Russian is inelegant; it is dry and drab; it is the tool of an energetic, incredibly gifted, bitterly honest, but definitely inexperienced young man. His Russian is, at times, almost as crude as Stendhal's in French; his similes and metaphors are utterly commonplace; his hackneyed epithets are only redeemed by occasionally being incorrectly used. Repetition of words in descriptive sentences irritates the purist.[9]

Both Mirsky's and Nabokov's assessments are correct, at least as far as they go. Nabokov is right – stylistic faults do occur within the text. What he does not acknowledge, however, is that, as in Dostoevsky's prose, utterance belongs to the author's characters, not to the author. Consequently, it is difficult to fault Lermontov for the way his three narrators speak and write, because their style suits Lermontov's purposes. For him the languages of the novel's narrators serve two purposes – to depict Pechorin through distinct narrators and to display simultaneously those narrators' states of mind. This is as true of Pechorin-as-narrator as it is of Maksim Maksimych and the traveling narrator of "Bela," "Maksim Maksimych," and the "Introduction to Pechorin's Journal." It is one of the text's great accomplishments to demonstrate that the "how" and "what" of the story cannot be separated. Thus, if *A Hero of Our Time* is "the presentation of a realistic portrait of a contemporary type,"[10] it also represents graphically the means by which that portrait is delivered up.

In addressing the stylistic means Lermontov utilizes to body forth the content of his novel, it becomes clear that its component parts cannot be easily separated. The layers of narrators, the achronological sequence of the chapters, the later insertion of the "Author's Introduction" (1841), the independent publication of the novel's first chapters in the 1830s (apparently without Lermontov knowing they would eventually become part of a larger work) form a composite that is difficult to treat in pieces, that is, unless one reintegrates them subsequently. Lermontov's genius is that he does not permit us to completely untangle the novel without doing it a disservice. As a case in point, Nabokov realizes the limitations of his assessment of Lermontov's style and ultimately must acknowledge that "when we start to break the sentence . . . into its quantitative elements, the banalities we perceive are often shocking, the shortcomings not seldom comic; but, in the long run, it is the compound effect that counts, and this final effect can be traced down in Lermontov to the beautiful timing of all the parts and particles of the novel" (xix).

The more one ponders *A Hero of Our Time*, the more one marvels at its ingenious design. Time in the novel, its parallel structures, multiple voices, metatextual references, and ironies comprise overarching features of the novel that subsume its component parts and elevate it to a high aesthetic level. It may be worth examining these elements, not for what they say individually about the novel's construction but to gain a sense of how they work together to create what Nabokov calls the novel's "compound" or "final" effect.

There are several forms time takes in *A Hero of Our Time*. First, there is the time in which the work was created, through which it evolved, and finally reached a canonical form. Lermontov published "Bela," "Taman," and "The Fatalist" before he conceived of a way to integrate these texts into the larger work that also includes "Princess Mary," "Maksim Maksimych," "The Introduction to Pechorin's Journal," and, in 1841, the "Author's Introduction." Second, there is the temporal sequence in which we encounter the novel. We begin with "Bela" and conclude with "The Fatalist." Third, there is the chronological time of the text considered as a whole. This specific time element consists of several immanent forms, which we shall examine in more detail.

Chronological, or linear, time begins with the chapter "Taman." In it Pechorin travels in 1830 from St. Petersburg to the Caucasus via Taman on the Black Sea. Approximately two years later, Pechorin takes a military leave of absence in Pyatigorsk, where "Princess Mary" is set. He courts Mary, befriends Dr. Werner, conducts an affair with Vera, belittles and eventually humiliates Grushnitsky, makes enemies of a group of officers, and eventually kills Grushnitsky in a duel. In the fall of 1832, Pechorin, undergoing punishment for his part in the duel, is placed under Maksim Maksimych's command at a fortress in Chechnya. There the events of "Bela" occur. In December 1832 Pechorin visits a Cossack settlement where Vulich challenges fate and is murdered, and where Pechorin captures the Cossack who has killed Vulich. These events occur in "The Fatalist." Pechorin then returns to the fortress, where, in the spring and summer of 1833, the Bela abductions and murder occur. That winter Pechorin departs for Georgia and then returns to St. Petersburg. Approximately four years later, in 1837 or 1838, Pechorin travels by way of the Caucasus to Persia. On the road he happens to meet Maksim Maksimych, whom he slights. These events are recounted in "Maksim Maksimych." Angered and hurt by Pechorin's indifference toward him, Maksim Maksimych delivers the notebooks, which he had been keeping for Pechorin, to the traveling narrator of the "Bela" and "Maksim Maksimych" chapters. In 1838 (possibly 1839), while returning from his travels in Persia, Pechorin dies. The traveling narrator uses Pechorin's demise as an opportunity to publish the materials he has both collected and composed under the title *A Hero of Our Time* (1840).

To summarize, the chronological sequence of the novel is as follows: "Taman," "Princess Mary," "Bela"/"The Fatalist"/"Bela," and "Maksim Maksimych." When we consider the entire text, however, this sequence becomes more complex. For example, the "Introduction to Pechorin's Journal" adds an additional time element, one belonging to fictionalized metatime. This temporal dimension indicates something other than the object of focus (Pechorin and his time) and alludes to the subject, the traveling narrator, who has put that object into focus for us in the first place. When we examine the temporal world he brings to the novel, we come to appreciate the novel's achronological sequence of chapters as belonging to him – it is the temporal order through which he has become familiar with Pechorin.

As the traveling narrator imposes his subjective temporal experience upon his readers, we begin to suspect that he may have done more to alter the novel's content than simply reorder its chronology. Proof of this lies in his reworking Kazbich's song into Russian verse form. Thus, through Lermontov's injection of the traveling narrator's temporal orientation into the novel, we become sensitized to a problem that runs throughout the text – its instability as a source of reliable information. We are forced to question the degree to which both the traveler and Maksim Maksimych might have contaminated the novel's content.[11] As soon as we allow this possibility, the object of our focus (character and plot) recedes, and we become less sure of what we can know in final terms about Pechorin and those around him, including the narrators.

In the case of the "Author's Introduction," a further metatextual leap is taken, one that complicates the temporal arrangement of the text even more and exposes the "Introduction to Pechorin's Journal" as a model of metatextuality, not the real coin. It was only with the second edition of *A Hero of Our Time* that this introduction appeared. It subsequently became canonical and has been included in most (although not every) edition since the second was published in 1841. Through the introduction, a nonfictional temporal dimension enters the text, one belonging to the author rather than to his characters and fictionalized narrators.[12] Nevertheless, the author's time frame is fairly coterminous with those of Pechorin and the traveling narrator, all together representing the time period 1830 to 1841. Thus, the novel contains chronologies that span three distinct rhetorical levels. First there is Pechorin's biography (a fiction), followed by the traveler's achronological ordering of the text (a metafiction), and Lermontov's time beyond the novel (the metatext).

To summarize, time in *A Hero of Our Time* functions as something other than a matter-of-fact, or everyday, temporal experience. The novel's achronological order, imposed on it by the traveling narrator's experience, serves Lermontov's purposes, specifically, to gradually expose Pechorin to the reader's direct gaze. Thanks to these temporal structures, we encounter Pechorin through three narrative filters. Maksim Maksimych tells his story about Pechorin to the traveling narrator, who tells it to us. These are the events of 1832 to 1834 that involve "Bela" and "The Fatalist." Then, in 1837 and 1838, the traveling narrator observes Pechorin directly and passes his impressions on to the reader in "Maksim Maksimych" and "The Introduction to Pechorin's Journal." Finally, the reader assesses Pechorin through Pechorin's own words about himself as represented in "Taman," "Princess Mary," and "The Fatalist" (1830–34). Not that all filters have been removed from the novel by the time we reach "Pechorin's Journal." On the contrary, here the psychological element becomes most profound, for the filter that remains in the text is Pechorin's own mind – his penchant to fool himself.[13]

As the unusual temporal shapes of the text move sequentially from the early 1830s to 1841, there is a coincidental movement from fiction to reality. In Lermontov's introduction, the relationship of fiction to reality is raised in four distinct dialogical steps. First he rejects the notion that there is a connection between the two. Then he reconnects art and life, but only under specific conditions. Dissatisfied with the implications of his second assertion, Lermontov modifies his stance yet again. In a final maneuver, he advances an image over rhetorical argument to summarize his idea of the novel.

In his first move, Lermontov specifically chides his readers for seeing his portrait in Pechorin's, but more generally, for mistaking a real person for a fictional one. Lermontov remarks, "What an old and paltry jest."[14] Here he severs the link between fiction and reality, at least in terms of biography. Pressing this point even harder, he shames readers for their subjective approach to art: "With us [Russians] the most fantastic of fairy tales would hardly escape the reproach of being meant as some personal insult" (2), he remarks in the pugilistic manner typical of the introduction.

In his second move, Lermontov modifies his argument, indicating that his fiction nevertheless has implications for real life: "since you [readers] have believed in the possibility of so many tragic and romantic villains having existed, why can you not believe in the reality of Pechorin?" (2). He responds to his own rhetorical query by arguing that Pechorin makes his readers uncomfortable. Hence their denial of any validity contained in the narrative: "there is more truth in this character than you would desire there to be. . . ." (2). Lermontov deliberately utilizes the words "reality" and "truth" to confuse the issue he had just clarified in relation to himself. Reality and fiction may be distinct ontological realms, and authors may differ from their dramatis personae, but life and art can and do interact.

Lermontov's third step is to argue that reality and fiction connect through art's traditional role to educate and enlighten real readers. He cites his critics, for example, who have stated in articles appearing in 1840 that "morality gains nothing" from the example Pechorin sets his readers. Lermontov responds, "I beg your pardon" (2). His sarcasm suggests that there indeed is a lesson contained within the novel, and a moral one at that. For Lermontov that lesson requires readers to receive "caustic truths" about themselves and their society, truths he claims, by inference, to have delivered up in *A Hero of Our Time*.

Because Lermontov has stressed that there is contact between fiction and life in regard to the ethical issues his novel raises, he, by inference, becomes the bearer of the novel's didactic message. But Lermontov refuses to hold the high moral ground: "do not think after this that the author of this book ever had the proud dream of becoming a reformer of mankind's vices. The Lord preserve him from such beknightedness!" (2). He will not represent himself as a voice of moral suasion (which would not fit his image as social misfit).[15] Lermontov eliminates the point of contact between fiction and reality he had just advanced – its didactic purpose. This leads to a final dialogical move in his quest for a definition of how art and life interact. He suggests that, as a social and historical type, Pechorin represents a point of contact between the two domains. Lermontov states that he "merely found it amusing to draw modern man such as he understood him, such as he met him – too often, unfortunately, for him and you" (2). As he states elsewhere in his introduction, Lermontov has drawn Pechorin as a portrait, "but not of a single individual" (2). He is a composite taken, as we have seen, from daily life of the period from 1830 to 1841. But where Lermontov states that this type is composed of "all the vices of our generation in the fullness of their development" (2), he can make no similar moralistic claim now that he has dismissed his role as author-moralist. Rather, Lermontov demotes the issues Pechorin represents to a physical level, shifting the burden of the contact between reality and fiction from ethics to physiology: "Suffice it that the disease has been pointed out; goodness knows how to cure it" (2). Lermontov moves from a position he considers untenable (author as moral arbiter) to one with which he is more comfortable – author as image maker, or, Pechorin as a disease.

In suggesting that Pechorin is an illness infecting society, Lermontov turns from one kind of discourse (specifically, his four-step dialogical argumentation) to the use of a metaphor through which the relationship of fiction to reality can be represented. Here we must not let the image of "disease" arrest our attention. Better to notice that a figure of speech has been elicited as Lermontov's final step in developing his idea of the novel and its relation to reality. The plasticity images possess, employed rhetorically, guarantees that Lermontov can achieve several ends simultaneously, but without being committed to them in final terms. Through the "disease" image, the novel's moral dimension can be secured, but without reducing the whole novelistic enterprise to it, without defaming Lermontov as preacher, and without making Pechorin a mere antihero. The novel is more multifaceted and open-ended than these reductionist ideas allow.

We have observed how the discourse on fiction and reality emerges out of an examination of the temporal dimension of the novel. This indicates in one way the degree to which discrete parts of the text are interconnected. Another way to appreciate the interconnectedness of the novel's elements is through examining the use of parallelism in the development of scenes, characters, plot events, and even the structure of the text itself. In *A Hero of Our Time*, the constructive principle undergirding much of the text is "parallelism," which operates in prose narratives when phenomena are repeated across real or apparent divisions the author establishes in his text. It follows from the constructive principle operative in Lermontov's novel that if there is one introduction, there will be another. If there is one narrator, there will be at least one other. If there is one perspective from which we view events, there will be yet others as well. If there is one rejection scene, there will be others. If there is a master/victim relationship in one chapter, it will be duplicated elsewhere by other characters in the novel. If there is violence inflicted on an innocent or naive character, it will be inflicted on yet other such types. If an innocent turns out to be less than that, so will others elsewhere in the text.

To explore one example, rejection scenes occur frequently in *A Hero of Our Time*. Of major importance in the second chapter is the moment when Pechorin holds out his hand indifferently to Maksim Maksimych, a man who would warmly embrace his old comrade. There, too, is Pechorin's rejection of Bela after he has won her heart, or Pechorin's manipulation of Princess Mary, whom he rejects in one of the final scenes of the chapter in her name. All these scenes are of one piece in regard to Pechorin's personality.

But there are more rejection scenes than Pechorin's case elicits. Yanko, in "Taman," rejects the blind boy who serves him. But there is a difference registered here. Pechorin is the narrator in this instance. He describes the scene in which the child weeps for having been left alone to fend for himself.[16] From Pechorin's pen, the rejection is played out for its full sentimental value:

> "And what about me?" said the blind lad in a piteous voice [to Yanko]. "What use are you to me?" was the answer . . . he put something in the blind lad's hand, saying, "Here, get yourself some gingerbread." "Is that all?" said the blind lad. . . . Yanko got into the boat. . . . For a long time, the white sail glanced in the moonlight amid the dark waves; the blind lad kept sitting on the shore, and presently I heard something resembling a sob, and indeed, the blind little fellow was crying. He cried for a long time. . . . I felt sad. (79)

The curiosity that emerges from the repeated scenes of rejection, from the interplay of manipulators and victims, is that we see many sides of Pechorin's personality simultaneously. Not that he merely plays these two roles himself. For example, we also observe his capacity for compassion. But through Pechorin's description of Yanko's effect on the blind boy, Pechorin models for the reader appropriate responses to his effect on his own victims – Bela, Mary, Maksim Maksimych, and others.

Furthermore, through the contrast made possible by the comparison of rejection scenes in the novel, particularly in relation to Yanko and Kazbich, Pechorin undergoes a transformation, a "decivilization" that is the counterpoint to the compassion he shows elsewhere. Like Yanko, Kazbich, and Azamat, Pechorin sees people as temporary chattel and as means toward selfish ends. All three engage in abductions or thefts of one sort or another, either of people or of goods. For example, Pechorin, Azamat, and Kazbich in their own ways doom Bela to a violent death – Pechorin by enticing Azamat to steal Bela for him in exchange for Kazbich's horse; Azamat by valuing the horse more than his sister; and Kazbich by avenging himself on them by killing Bela (and her father).

Rejection scenes are integrally linked to hierarchical relations in the novel and to the violence inflicted upon innocents (or apparent innocents). Yanko is master of Undine and the blind boy. Undine outdoes Pechorin. Pechorin masters all the Russian characters in the novel. Kazbich subdues Bela's and Azamat's family. (At another level, the traveler's narrative supersedes Pechorin's – he publishes the journal Pechorin did not wish to see in print.)[17]

*A Hero of Our Time* is meant to challenge readers, not to comfort them with easy thoughts about the novel. This is as true in the "Author's Introduction" and the traveling narrator's "Introduction to Pechorin's Journal" as it is in the "compound" or "final" effect the novel produces through its five chapters. The degree to which ethical sensitivities are challenged, social mores assaulted, violence viewed as a means of resolving conflicts, and injustice served up to any number of victims suggests how deeply Lermontov was committed to saying something new about important matters in Russian literature. He successfully confuses readers about identities in the novel, about the nature of the word and its adequacy to encompass reality, about the nature of values in the various communities the novel represents, about the individual's capacity to seek meaning in a world that is anything but stable, and about the responsibility people must assume for their actions, speech, beliefs, and aspirations.

With such complex issues at stake, Lermontov could hardly have created a "society of readers" capable of receiving *A Hero of Our Time* in a manner that equated with all the riches it holds. For this reason the present volume has been published – to bring together a representative sample of critical works that indicate the novel's range and display how response to the novel has evolved since 1840 when reviews of it first appeared in the press.

## The Critical Literature on *A Hero of Our Time*

The articles and materials contained here have been selected for a variety of reasons, not the least of which is their quality, their impact on the novel's reception, or their historical value. The articles contained in the first section represent four distinct forms of response to Lermontov's text. First is Vissarion Belinsky's seminal treatment of the novel in an article published in 1840. It set the tone for much of the debate that has followed. His article expressed a radical opinion to counter the negative press the novel had received from some in the conservative camp. Because of the extensiveness of Belinsky's article, which runs five times the length of the excerpt here, only key portions of his analysis are introduced. Most of the theoretical argumentation has been eliminated. Another key essay on Lermontov included in this section was written by B. M. Eikhenbaum in 1948. The Soviet period produced a vast amount of Lermontov criticism, not all of which is useful. But Eikhenbaum provided great insights into Lermontov's art. His *Lermontov* has been published in English in a translation by Ray Parrott and Harry Weber, and readers are encouraged to refer to it to gain insight into Lermontov's poetry and drama. But Eikhenbaum's ground-breaking articles on *A Hero of Our Time* have not appeared in English previously; one of these is introduced here.

Two articles were commissioned for this volume. They are included in the first chapter. Susan Layton's study treats ethnic identity in *A Hero of Our Time* and delivers a wealth of information pertinent to the times and the literary representation of the Caucasus. Jane Costlow's article analyzes women in the novel, a topic heretofore left untreated.

Missing from the first section is Viktor Vinogradov's highly rewarding essay "The Style of Lermontov's Prose" and V. A. Manuilov's overwhelming number of works on the text, from book-length studies, including an annotated volume that discusses the minute detail of each chapter, to his *Lermontov Encyclopedia* and innumerable articles produced over the course of an entire career. The sheer volume and very nature of the latter's work is not conducive to excerpts and, thus, has necessitated its exclusion here. And in Vinogradov's case, the analysis of Lermontov's stylistic registers in *A Hero of Our Time*, for all its insights, is difficult to render in an adequate English form. This is because Vinogradov treats in detail, for example, the peculiarities of Maksim Maksimych's speech, which defy translation sufficient to support an appreciation of his analysis.

It has been decided, too, to exclude all work in the English language that can be obtained through libraries, either directly or through interlibrary loan. For these works, readers are referred to the bibliography. Of particular note are the books, monographs, and articles by John Mersereau, Jr., John Garrard, Andrew Barratt and A. D. P. Briggs, Richard Peace, William Mills Todd, C. J. G. Turner, and Vladimir Golstein.

The second chapter represents twentieth-century Russian and Soviet criticism of the novel. N. Kotlyarevsky's book-length study of Lermontov (1909), as antiquated as it might appear to be today, is valuable for at least one reason. He was one of the first to advance a cogent argument refuting the assumption that Lermontov was Pechorin. Despite Lermontov's disclaimer in his introduction to the novel, it was entirely normative to equate the two throughout the last two centuries. Kotlyarevsky argues effectively that Lermontov had surpassed his Pechorin by the time the novel was completed.

From the pre-Soviet period, too, V. Fisher's seminar article on Lermontov's poetics (1914) is included, specifically those portions that treat, in large measure, common elements of Lermontov's poetry that recur in *A Hero of Our Time*.

Sergei Durylin's study of the novel (1940) represents something of a milestone in its attempt to restore the story to its historical context. His analysis of the ethnic theme in the text is useful in providing information that supports Susan Layton's study of ethnicity in the novel. A small portion of Emma Gershtein's work on Lermontov's career (his relations with high society, Nicholas I, and his ministers, as well as on Lermontov's novel and death) is included in this volume. It should be noted, however, despite the wealth of historical information contained in her research, Gershtein's dogged attempt to prove Nicholas I's malice toward Lermontov has proven more ideological than authoritative.

To represent more recent Soviet criticism, V. Levin's examination of Pechorin's famous monologue or "confession" to Princess Mary provides an example of close reading of parallel phenomena in Lermontov's novel.

The third section of this volume provides critical articles and commentaries by Russian critics from 1840 and 1841. Because Lermontov was keen on responding to his critics in his 1841 "Author's Introduction to the Novel," it has been deemed wise to include all substantive responses to *A Hero of Our Time* from this period, none of which has appeared previously in English.

It is hoped that the diversity of critical texts contained here will stimulate the reader to utilize the bibliography to explore in more detail the riches *A Hero of Our Time* contains.

NOTES

1. David Powelstock, "Living into Language: Mikhail Lermontov and the Manufacturing of Intimacy," in *Russian Subjects: Empire, Nation, and the Culture of the Golden Age* (Evanston, Ill., 1998), 297–324.

2. See Mikhail Lermontov, *Polnoe sobranie sochinenii* (Moscow, 1934–37), 5:425–574.

3. John Garrard, *Mikhail Lermontov* (Boston, 1982), 15.

4. Ivan Turgenev, *Turgenev's Literary Reminiscences*, trans. David Magarshack (New York, 1959), 176.

5. Marc Slonim, *An Outline of Russian Literature* (New York, 1958), 38.

6. Helen Michailoff, "The Death of Lermontov (The Poet and the Tsar)," *Russian Literature Triquarterly* 10 (1974): 290.

7. Lawrence Kelly, *Lermontov: Tragedy in the Caucasus* (New York, 1977), 167–68.

8. D. S. Mirsky, *A History of Russian Literature from Its Beginnings to 1900* (New York, 1958), 163.

9. Vladimir Nabokov, introduction to *A Hero of Our Time*, by Mikhail Lermontov (New York, 1958), 12–13. All subsequent citations from the novel are taken from the Nabokov translation and are noted in parentheses throughout this volume.

10. John Mersereau, Jr., *Mikhail Lermontov* (Carbondale, Ill., 1962), 76.

11. Andrew Barratt and A. D. P. Briggs argue the point about Maksim Maksimych's reworking of reality in *A Wicked Irony: The Rhetoric of Lermontov's "A Hero of Our Time"* (Bristol, 1991), 19–23.

12. This claim must remain conjectural pending a reading of the introduction's ironies. See M. Gilroy, *The Ironic Vision in Lermontov's "A Hero of Our Time,"* no. 19 (Birmingham, 1986).

13. There is yet another filter operating just outside the text. The traveling narrator does not publish all of Pechorin's notebooks, only the three pieces of "Pechorin's Journal." If we can believe the traveler, there is a wealth of additional material that could have been selected for publication. What it may or may not say about Pechorin's character, or his development between 1834 and 1837, is unknown.

14. Mikhail Lermontov, *A Hero of Our Time*, trans. Vladimir and Dmitri Nabokov (New York, 1958), 2.

15. In addition, he simultaneously guards Pechorin from the impulse to finalize him as a type, that is, as an antimodel from whom ethical principles might be extracted by the exercise of reverse logic.

16. This scene is related to the dead-horse scene, where Pechorin weeps, rejected soul he claims himself to be at that moment, if only for an instant.

17. To complicate, if falsely, the moral issues the novel raises, Pechorin's success comes with the complicity of his victims. Many of Pechorin's defenders, in fact, blame his victims in order to exonerate him; Bela is a savage, Mary, a spoiled rich girl, and Grushnitsky, an annoying fake.

# A Hero of Our Time

VISSARION BELINSKY

Translated by Joseph Peschio

[We] . . . shall directly state our main thesis – that the distinguishing characteristic of Russian literature is the sudden flash of strong and even great artistic talent, and, with a few exceptions, the reader's eternal [complaint]: "There are many books, but nothing to read." Mr. Lermontov's talent belongs to a group of strong artistic talents that have unexpectedly appeared amidst this emptiness. . . . Of [current talent] only Kol'tsov[1] promises a life that does not fear death; although his poetry is not important today, it is nevertheless a noteworthy event. None of those who appeared with him and after him can be placed on the same level with him, and he long stood a good distance above all others. Then suddenly a new bright luminary has risen on the horizon of our poetry and immediately turned out to be a star of the first magnitude. We are talking about Lermontov, who appeared as an unknown in the 1838 "Literary Supplement to the Russian Invalid" with his *poema*, "A Song about Tsar Ivan Vasilevich, His Young Bodyguard, and the Valiant Merchant Kalashnikov" ["Pesnja pro Tsarja Ivana Vasilevicha, molodogo oprichnika i udalogo kuptsa Kalashnikova"], and since 1839 has continued to appear regularly in "Notes of the Fatherland."[2] His *poema*, despite its great artistic merit, complete originality, and extraordinariness, did not attract the broad public's special attention and was noted by only a few. Yet each of his minor works aroused general and intense enthusiasm. Everyone saw something completely new and original in them; everyone was struck by the power of inspiration, the depth and intensity of feeling, the elegance of invention, the vivaciousness and the sharply palpable presence of thought in artistic form. Leaving comparisons aside for now, we shall presently note only that, with all his depth of thought, energy of expression, and diversity of content (in which he hardly need fear competition), the form of Kol'tsov's poems, despite their artistic quality, is always the same, always singularly artless. Kol'tsov is not just a *folk* poet. No, he is above that, for as much as his *songs* are comprehensible to any plebeian, his *meditations* are inaccessible to any of them. But at the same time, he cannot be called a national poet, for his powerful talent cannot exit the vicious circle of folk ingenuousness. This is an ingenious plebeian, in whose soul arise questions peculiar only to people developed by science and education, and who poses these deep questions in the form of folk poetry. Consequently, he is not translatable into any language and is understood only at home and only by his compatriots. "A Song about Tsar Ivan Vasilevich, His Young Bodyguard, and the Valiant Merchant Kalashnikov" demonstrates that Lermontov is capable of rendering the phenomena of immediate Russian life in a folk-poetic form that is peculiar to him alone. Other works by him, equally suffused with Russian soul, nonetheless exhibit the universal form of poetry that, not ceasing to be national, is accessible in any age and any country.[3]

When two poems in the first two volumes of "Notes of the Fatherland" (1839) aroused so much public interest in Lermontov and secured him the reputation of a poet from whom big things were to be expected, Lermontov suddenly [surprised us] with a prose story "Bela." This surprised everyone all the more pleasantly because it revealed still more the strength of the young talent and demonstrated his diversity and versatility. In the story, Lermontov displays the same talent as in his poems. From the first, one was able to note that this story came not exclusively from a desire to interest the public with its favorite kind of literature, not from a blind urge to do what everyone does, but from the same wellspring from which his poems have come – a deep, creative nature that is foreign to any motive but inspiration. Lyrical poetry and the story of contemporary life have come together in one talent. The unification of these apparent opposites is not a rarity in our time. Schiller and Goethe were lyric poets, novelists, and playwrights, although the lyrical element always remained predominant and prevalent [in their work]. "Faust" itself is a lyrical work in dramatic form.

The poetry of our time is mainly the novel and the drama, but lyrical verse remains a common element of poetry anyway because it is a universal element of the human soul. Nearly every poet begins with lyricism just as every nation begins with it. Walter Scott himself shifted to the novel from lyrical epic poems. Only the literature of the United States began not with lyricism but with Cooper's novel, and this phenomenon is as strange as the country in which it occurred.[4] Perhaps this is because North American literature is a continuation of British literature.

Our literature also presents a completely exceptional case. We are simultaneously undergoing all the stages of European [development], which evolved over a period of time in the West. Our poetry remained mostly lyrical, at least until Pushkin, who engaged lyrical verse for a short time and soon switched to the *poema*, and from that [genre] to the drama. As a full representative of the spirit of his times, he also made an attempt at the novel that appeared in "The Contemporary" (1837). Six chapters (with the beginning of a seventh) were printed from his unfinished novel *The Blackamoor of Peter the Great [Arap Petra Velikogo]*. The novel's fourth chapter appeared in *Northern Flowers* [in 1829].

Pushkin began writing stories only in the last years of his life. But it is evident that his real forte was lyrical verse, the story in verse (*poema*), and the drama, for his prose efforts are by far unequal to his poetic efforts. His best story, "The Captain's Daughter," with all its enormous merits, cannot compare in any way with his narrative poems and dramas. It is no more than a superior belletristic work with poetic and even artistic details.[5] His other stories, especially "The Tales of Belkin" [1831], belong exclusively to the belletristic arena. It may be that this is the reason that the novel, begun previously, was not finished.

Lermontov is equally proficient in prose and poetry, and we are certain that, as he develops artistically, he will proceed directly to drama.[6] Our proposition is not arbitrary. It is based as much on the fullness of dramatic movement noted in Lermontov's stories as on the spirit of the present age, which is especially propitious for the unification of all forms of verbal art in one person. The latter circumstance is very important, for the art of any people also has its own historical development in consequence of which the character and career of a poet are defined. Perhaps if Pushkin had come on the scene later and been preceded by someone similar to himself, he would have been as great a novelist as he was lyricist and playwright.

"Bela" was both a separate, finished story and a segment of a larger composition, [and in this way it was] similar to "The Fatalist" and "Taman," which were subsequently printed in "Notes of the Fatherland." They now appear together with "Maksim Maksimych," "Introduction to Pechorin's Journal," and "Princess Mary" under one title – *A Hero of Our Time*. This common name is not the author's caprice; in the same way, it should not be concluded from the title that the stories contained in these two books[7] are the narratives of a certain man, to whom the author tied the role of narrator. In all the stories there is one theme, and this theme is expressed in one character who is the hero of all the narratives. In "Bela" he is a mysterious type. The heroine of this story is all before you. But the hero – it is as if he has taken an assumed name so that he will not be recognized. Because of his behavior in "Bela," you involuntarily make suppositions about some other [implied] story, an alluring, mysterious, and gloomy story at that. And then the author [i.e., the traveling narrator] immediately unveils it to you during the meeting with Maksim Maksimych, who told him the story about Bela. But your curiosity is not satiated, only more agitated, and the story of Bela remains for you all the more mysterious. At last, Pechorin's journal is in the author's hands. In the introduction to the journal, the author alludes to the theme of the novel, but it is an allusion that only further arouses your impatience to get acquainted with the hero of the novel. The hero of the novel appears in the highly poetic narrative "Taman'" as an autobiographer, but the mystery only grows more alluring from this, and there is still no solution. Finally, you come to "Princess Mary" and the fog dissipates, the mystery is solved, and the primary idea of the novel, momentarily dominating your entire being, sticks with you and haunts you like a bitter feeling. Finally, you read "The Fatalist," and although Pechorin is not the hero but only the narrator of an occurrence to which he was witness, and although you do not find one new feature in it that would have completed the portrait for you, you understand him still more (strange thing!), think about him more, and your feeling grows still more gloomy and melancholy. . . .

――――

What a frightful man this Pechorin is! Because his restless soul demands action, his activity seeks sustenance, and his heart is greedy for the advantages of life – for this the poor girl must suffer! "Egoist, monster, scoundrel, an immoral man!" strict moralists will perhaps scream in unison. It is your right, gentlemen. But what are you fussing about? Why are you angry? Indeed, it seems to us that you are out of place, that you have sat down at a table set [for someone, but] not for you. . . . Do not approach this [Pechorin] too closely, do not fall upon him so rashly. He will glance at you, grin, and you shall be judged, and on your embarrassed face all shall read the verdict. You anathematize him not for vices – there are more of them in you, and in you they are blacker and more shameful – but for his daring freedom, for the frankness with which he speaks. . . . You allow a man to do anything he pleases, to be anything he wants, you eagerly forgive him insanity, lowliness, and depravity, but you demand moral maxims from him regarding how a man should think and act (and how he in reality does not think and act). . . . And your inquisitor's auto-da-fé is ready for anyone who has the noble habit of looking reality in the eye without dropping his own, of calling things by their real names, and showing himself to others not in evening dress, not in full-dress uniform, but in a dressing gown, in his room, in a solitary discussion with himself, in a tallying of the books with his conscience. . . . And you are right: show yourself before people just once in your shameful negligee, in your soiled nightcaps, in your tattered dressing gowns, and people will turn away from you with disgust, and society will expel you. But this man has nothing to fear. There is the mysterious awareness in him that he is not who he seems even to himself, and that he exists only in the present. Yes, there is an intensity of spirit and a power of will in this man that you lack. In his very vices something great flashes, like lightning in black clouds; and he is marvelous even in those moments when human feeling rises against him. . . . His is a different intention, a different path than yours. His passions are storms that cleanse the spirit; his delusions, no matter how horrible they are, are the sharp illnesses in a young body that fortify it for a long and healthy life. These are deliriums and fevers, not the gout, rheumatism, and hemorrhoids from which you, poor dears, so pointlessly suffer. . . . Let him slander the eternal laws of reason, placing the loftiest happiness in rich vanity; let him slander human nature, seeing in it only egoism; let him slander himself, taking aspects of his spirit for his total development and confusing youth and manhood. . . . Let him! . . . There will come to pass a solemn moment, and contradiction shall be permitted, the struggle shall end, and the scattered sounds of the soul shall flow together into one harmonious chord!

———

One thing is clear and certain to us: without storms there can be no fertility, and nature languishes; without passions and contradictions, there can be no life, no poetry. Provided only that in these passions and contradictions there were reason and humanity, their results would lead a man to his goal; but judgment is not ours. Each man's verdict is in his own dealings and in their consequences! We must demand reality as it is from art, for, no matter what it is, this reality, it tells us more, teaches us more than all the fabrications and homilies of the moralists.

But, perhaps the philosophers will say, why draw a picture of disgraceful passions instead of captivating the fancy by depicting gentle sensations of nature and love, touching the heart and preaching to the mind? That is an old tune, gentlemen, as old as "Shall I go out to the river, look at the quick . . ."![18] The literature of the eighteenth century was mostly *moral* and *rational*. It had no stories other than *contes moraux* and *contes philosophiques* [moral and philosophical songs]. But these moral and philosophical books corrected no one, and the century was nonetheless mostly *immoral* and *depraved*. And this contradiction is very understandable. The laws of morality are in the nature of a man, in his sense, and for this reason do not contradict his doings. But he who feels and acts in accordance with his senses says little. Reason does not compose or invent the laws of morality but is only aware of them, accepting them from the senses as "givens," as *facts*. And because of this, *sense* and *reason* are not opposed and not hostile to one another but related, or to put it better, identical elements of the human spirit. But when a person is either denied a moral sense or is ruined by poor upbringing or a disorderly life, then his *reason* composes its own laws of morality. We are saying *reason* and not *mind*, for the mind is the self-conscious entity that provides the sense of a subject and substance to thought, whereas *reason*, lacking real substance, by necessity resorts to arbitrary structures. This is the downfall of *moral reasoning*, and this is the reason for contradictions between the words and actions of literary moralists. Reality is nothing to them. They pay no attention to what is but merely advance a notion of what and how things should be. These erroneous philosophical bases gave birth to false art long before the eighteenth century, art that depicted some kind of imaginary reality and created some kind of imaginary people. Indeed, are the settings of Corneille's and Racine's tragedies the earth and not the air, their characters people and not marionettes? Do these *tsars, heroes, confidants*, and *messengers* belong to a particular age or country? Has anyone since the creation of the world spoken a language similar to theirs? The eighteenth century bore this rational art to the limits of awkwardness. It took extreme measures to make art into an inside-out reality and made from it a *dream*, which still finds its knights of la Mancha [Don Quixote] in a few kind old men of our time.

———

Our age abhors this hypocrisy. It speaks loudly of its sins but does not take pride in them. It bares its bloody wounds and does not hide them under the beggar's rags of pretense. It has understood that an awareness of its sinfulness is the first step toward salvation. It knows that real suffering is better than imaginary happiness. For it, utility and morality are in truth alone, and truth is only in the real, that is, in that which is. Because of this, the art of our age is the reproduction of rational reality. The mission of our art is not to present events in a story, novel, or drama in concordance with a *preformed objective* but to develop them in concordance with the *laws of rational inevitability*.

———

"Perhaps a few readers will want to know my opinion of Pechorin's character. My reply is the title of this book. 'But this is a wicked irony!' they will say. I do not know." And so that is the primary theme of the novel. Indeed, after this, the whole novel may be considered a cruel irony, because a large part of the readers will probably exclaim, "Some hero!" "But in what way is he bad?" we dare ask you.

> But why on earth does he inspire
> So harsh and negative a view?
> Is it because we never tire
> Of censuring what others do?
> Because an ardent spirit's daring
> Appears absurd or overbearing
> From where the smug and worthless sit?
> Because the dull are cramped by wit?
> Because we take mere talk for action,
> And malice rules a petty mind?
> Because in tripe the solemn find
> A cause for solemn satisfaction,
> And mediocrity alone
> Is what we like and call our own?[9]

You say in response that there is no faith in him. Marvelous! But is that not really the same as blaming a beggar for having no gold?

He would be happy to have it, but it does not come easily to him. And anyway, is Pechorin really happy about his faithlessness? Does he really pride himself on it? Has he not suffered from it? Is he not prepared to pay with his life and happiness for this faith, for which his hour has not yet struck? You say he is an egoist? But does he not really despise and hate himself for this? Does he really not thirst for a pure and guileless love? No, this is not egoism. Egoism does not suffer, does not blame itself, but is satisfied and happy with itself. Egoism does not know torment; suffering is the lot of love alone. Pechorin's soul is not rocky ground but earth made barren by the heat of an inflamed life. Let suffering break it up and abundant rain water it – and it will bear resplendent flowers of heavenly love.

It has grown painful and sad for this man that everyone dislikes him – and who is this "everyone"? Empty, insignificant people who cannot forgive him his superiority over them. And his readiness to stifle false shame, the voice of social honor, and insulted pride when, in return for acknowledgment of the slander, he was ready to forgive Grushnitsky, the man who just now shot at him and shamelessly awaited an uncharged shot from him? And his tears and sobbing in the deserted steppe next to the body of a dead horse? No, all this is not egoism!

"But," you say, "what of the cold efficiency and systematic calculatedness with which he seduces a poor girl, not loving her, and only in order to laugh at her and occupy his idleness with something?" That is true, but we were not thinking of justifying him in such actions or of setting him forth as a model or a high ideal of the purest morality. We only want to say that one must see the man in a man, that ideals of morality exist only in classical tragedies and the moralistic, sentimental novels of the last century.

In taking the moral measure of a man, one must take into account the circumstances of his development and the sphere of life into which he was placed by fate. In Pechorin's thinking, there is much that is false; there is perversion in his sensations. But this is all redeemed by his rich nature. His, in many respects, nasty present promises a wonderful future. . . . You are charmed by the quick movement of a steamboat and see in it a great victory of the spirit over nature? Then you want to deny any merit in it when it crushes careless people who have fallen under its wheels, crushes [them like] grain. Does this not mean you are contradicting yourselves? The danger of a steamboat is a result of its inordinate quickness; its vice comes from its virtue. There are people who are revolting in all the irreproachability of their behavior because it is a sign in them of lifelessness and weakness of the spirit. Vice is disgraceful in great people; but, once punished, they move your soul. This punishment is a victory of moral spirit only when it comes not from the outside but as a result of the vice itself, as a negation of the individual's personality, in justification of the eternal laws of a violated morality.

The author [i.e., traveling narrator] of the work under our examination, describing Pechorin's appearance when they meet on the highway, says this about his eyes:

> In the first place, they never laughed when he was laughing! Have you observed this bizarre trait in some people? It is either the sign of a wicked nature or of a deep and constant melancholy. From behind half-lowered lashes, they shone with a kind of phosphorescent glitter, if I can put it thus. It was not the reflection of the soul's glow or of an effervescent imagination; this was a gleam akin to the gleam of smooth steel, dazzling but cold; this glance, while not lingering, was penetrating and oppressive, it left the disagreeable impression of an indiscreet question and might have appeared insolent had it not been indifferently serene. (57)

Do you agree that, like these eyes, the whole meeting scene of Pechorin and Maksim Maksimych shows that if this is vice, then it is not at all exultant, that one must be born for the good to be punished so harshly for evil? The triumph of the moral spirit over noble natures is far more striking than over scoundrels.

Yet this novel is not at all a cruel irony, although it may very easily be taken for irony. This, in fact, is one of those novels:

> In which our age is well displayed
> And modern man himself portrayed
> With something of his true complexion –
> With his immoral soul disclosed,
> His arid vanity exposed,
> His endless bent for deep reflection,
> His cold, embittered mind that seems
> To waste itself in empty schemes (Falen, 176).

"Some contemporary man!" exclaimed one moralistic "composer" explicating or, more accurately, lashing out at the seventh chapter of *Eugene Onegin*.[10] Here we consider it pertinent to note that any contemporary man, as a representative of his age, no matter how bad he is, cannot be bad in truth, for there are no bad ages, and no one age is better than another. This is because it is a necessary point in the development of humanity and of society.

Pushkin asked himself about his Onegin:

> That dangerous and sad pariah,
> That work of heaven or of hell,
> That angel . . . and proud fiend as well.
> What was he then? An imitation?
> An empty phantom or a joke,
> A Muscovite in Harold's cloak,
> Compendium of affectation,
> A lexicon of words in vogue . . .
> Mere parody and just a rogue? (Falen, 177)

And with this very question he *solved the riddle and found the word*. Onegin is not an *imitation* but a *reflection*, one created not by the poet's fancy but in contemporary society, which he depicted in the person of the hero of his novel in verse. The rapprochement with Europe must have been the particular means of reflection in our society – and Pushkin caught this reflection in the character Onegin with the instinct of a great artist. But Onegin for us is already the past, and the past is irrevocable. If he were to appear in our time, you would have the right to ask, with the poet:

> Is he the same, or is he learning?
> Or does he play the outcast still?
> In what new guise is he returning?
> What role does he intend to fill?
> Childe Harold? Melmoth for a while?
> Cosmopolite? A Slavophile?
> A Quaker? Bigot? – might one ask?
> Or will he sport some other mask?
> Or maybe he's just dedicated,
> Like you and me, to being nice? (Falen, 198)

Lermontov's *Pechorin* is the best answer to these questions. This is an Onegin of our time, *a hero of our time*. The dissimilarity between them is far smaller than the distance between the Onega and the Pechora.[11] Sometimes in the very name that a true poet gives his hero there is a rational inevitability, although perhaps one unseen by the poet himself.

From the point of view of artistic execution, there is no comparing Onegin and Pechorin. But, if Onegin is higher than Pechorin in an artistic sense, Pechorin is higher than Onegin in idea. However, this advantage lies with our time and not with Lermontov. What is Onegin? The French epigraph to the *poema* serves as his best characterization, the best interpretation [of him]: "Suffused with vanity, he possessed more than this a particular pride which called forth a uniform indifference in deeds good or ill – the consequence of a feeling of superiority perhaps merely illusory." We think that this superiority in Onegin is not one bit imaginary, because he "respected feelings vicariously" and that in "his heart there was both pride and direct honor." In the novel he is a man whom upbringing and life in high society have killed, who is tired of everything, bored with everything, . . . and whose entire life consists of [yawning everywhere].

Pechorin is different. This man does not bear his sufferings indifferently or apathetically. He chases after life furiously, searching for it everywhere. He bitterly indicts himself for his delusions. Personal questions incessantly are raised [to consciousness] in him, disturb him and torment him, and he seeks their solutions in reflection. He investigates every movement of his heart and examines each of his thoughts. He makes himself the most curious object of his observations and, attempting to be as sincere as possible in his confession, he not only frankly acknowledges his true shortcomings but also invents nonexistent ones or falsely interprets his most natural actions. Just as Onegin is expressed fully in Pushkin's characterization of contemporary man, Pechorin appears wholly in these lines by Lermontov:

> By chance we love, by chance we hate, but will
> Not give ourselves to hate or love entire,
> Until a strange decay and chill
> Consume us, though our blood's on fire.[12]

*A Hero of Our Time* is a melancholy meditation on our time, like the meditation with which the poet so nobly, so energetically renewed the world of poetry and from which we have taken these four lines.

But as regards form, the depiction of Pechorin is not entirely artistic. However, the reason for this is not the author's shortcoming but that the character depicted by him, as we have already alluded in passing, is so close to him that he was not able to distance himself from him and objectify him. We are convinced that no one can see in our words a desire to present the novel as Mr. Lermontov's autobiography. Schiller was not a bandit, but he expressed *his ideal* of a man in Karl Moor.[13] Varnhagen von Ense put it marvelously when he said that one might view Onegin and Lensky as similar to Johann Paul Friedrich Richter's brothers, Walt and Vult [of the unfinished *Flegeljahre*, 1804–5], that is, as a rupture in the poet's very nature; or that consequently he may have embodied the duality of his self in these two fictional characters.[14] The idea is correct, yet it would be very awkward to search for common lines between the lives of these characters and the life of the poet himself.

That is the reason for Pechorin's uniqueness and the contradictions in which the depiction of this character becomes tangled. To represent this character correctly, one would have to distance himself from [Pechorin] completely, stand above him, and view him as something completed. But this, we repeat, is not the case in the depiction of Pechorin. He remains hidden from us and is the same incomplete and unresolved being as he appears to us at the beginning of the novel. Hence the novel itself, striking in its awesome unity of *sensation*, is not at all striking in its unity of *theme* and leaves us without any of the insight that involuntarily arises in the reader's imagination when reading an artistic work and becoming engaged in it. This novel displays an astonishing *zamknutost'*[15] but not in some lofty artistic sense, which is conferred on a creation through a unity of its poetic idea, but the kind that comes from a unity of poetic sensation, with which it [enraptures] the reader's soul. There is something unresolved in it, as if something reticent (as in Goethe's "Werther"),[16] and because of this, there is something ponderous in the impression it makes. But this shortcoming is, at the same time, also a merit of Mr. Lermontov's novel. All contemporary social questions raised in poetic works are the same: a cry of suffering but a cry that eases suffering, too.

———

"Princess Mary," taken as a separate story, is less artistic than all the others. Of the characters, Grushnitsky alone is a truly artistic creation. The captain of the dragoons is incomparable, although he appears in the shadows as a character of lesser importance. But the female characters are the most weakly depicted of all, for the subjectivity of the author's perspective is particularly reflected in them. Vera's character is especially elusive and vague. This is more probably a satire of a woman than a woman. Just when you begin to become interested in her and charmed by her, the author immediately frustrates you [by providing] some sort of arbitrary pronouncements. Her relations with Pechorin are like a riddle. Sometimes she seems to you a deep woman, capable of boundless love and loyalty and of heroic self-denial. Sometimes you see in her only weakness and nothing more. Particularly appreciable in her is the lack of feminine pride and a feeling of feminine dignity, which do not hinder a woman from loving heatedly and selflessly, but which hardly ever allow a truly deep woman to tolerate the tyranny of love. She loves Pechorin but marries (her second time) an old man, apparently for money. Having betrayed one husband for Pechorin, she betrays yet another, but more likely from weakness rather than from some overwhelming passion. She adores in Pechorin his lofty nature, but there is something servile in her adoration. In consequence of all this, she does not elicit strong involvement from the author and slips past in his imagination like a shadow.

Princess Mary is depicted more successfully. She is neither a stupid girl nor an empty one. Her attitude is a bit idealistic, in the childish sense of this word. It is not enough for her to love a man to whom she is drawn by her feelings; it is absolutely necessary that he be unhappy and wear a thick, gray private's greatcoat. It was very easy for Pechorin to seduce her. All it took was to seem incomprehensible, mysterious, and to be impudent. There is something common between her attitude and Grushnitsky's, although she is also incomparably higher than he. She allowed herself to be deceived. But when she saw herself deceived, she, like a woman, felt her insult deeply, succumbed as a victim, suffering silently, but without degradation – and the scene of her last meeting with Pechorin elicits strong sympathy and fills her image with a flash of poetry. Nevertheless, there is also something somehow left unsaid about her, the reason for which is again that her rivalry with Pechorin is not judged by the kind of outside observer the author should have been.

However, in spite of this shortcoming in artistic quality, the entire story is penetrated through and through with poetry and filled with the highest interest. Every word in it is so significant, the paradoxes themselves are so instructive, every situation is so interesting and depicted so vividly! The story's style is sometimes a flash of lightning, sometimes the blow of a broadsword, sometimes pearls scattered over velvet! The primary idea is so close to the heart of any thinking and feeling person that *anyone*, no matter how dissimilar his

situation to those presented in the story, sees in it the confession of
his own heart.

In the "Introduction to Pechorin's Journal," the author says in
passing: "I have put in this book only that which refers to Pechorin's
sojourn in the Caucasus. There still remains in my possession a fat
notebook wherein he narrates all his life. Some day it, too, will be
presented to the judgment of the world, but for the present there
are important reasons why I dare not assume such a responsibility"
(64). We thank the author for this pleasant promise, but we doubt it
will be fulfilled. We are strongly convinced that he has parted forever from his Pechorin. We are confirmed in this conviction by
Goethe's acknowledgment that, having written "Werther," which
was the fruit of a difficult spiritual condition, he was freed from it
and was so far from the hero of his novel that it was strange for him
to see the fiery youngster come from his own mind . . . Such is the
noble spirit of the poet that, through strength of character, he sun-
ders the bonds of any limitation and flies to new, living phenomena
of the world, to creativity full of glory. In objectifying his own personal suffering, he frees himself from it. In translating into poetic
sounds his spirit's dissonance, he enters anew into his native sphere
of eternal harmony.

If Mr. Lermontov does fulfill his promise, then we are certain that
he will present not the old and familiar Pechorin, about whom he has
already said everything, but a completely new one about whom
much remains to be said. Perhaps he will show him to us reformed,
acknowledging the laws of morality (probably not to the delight but
to the great disappointment of our moralists). Or perhaps he will
make him acknowledge the rationality and grace of life but only so
that he can assure himself it is not for him, so that he can see that he
has expended much energy in the terrible struggle with it, has become cruel [by the effort and because he] cannot make that rationality and grace his own. But it may also be that the author will make
Pechorin privy to the joys of life, make him a victorious conqueror of
life's evil. But, either way, in any case, reconciliation will come only
through a woman, whose [value] Pechorin stubbornly disbelieves,

founding [this conclusion] not on reflection of any sort but on his bad experiences [with women] in his life. . . .[17]

NOTES

Reprinted from V. G. Belinskii, "*Geroi nashego vremeni,*" *Polnoe sobranie sochinenii,* 13 vols. (Moscow, 1953–59), 4:193–270.

1. Aleksei Vasil'evich Kol'tsov (1809–42), a Voronezh cattle dealer who began publishing folk-oriented verse in 1831, with Belinsky's help.

2. Belinsky, evidently, was not aware that Lermontov's first appearance in print was in 1830.

3. Since Lermontov's poems will soon come to light in a special book, we shall speak of them in more detail at another time in a special article [Belinsky's note].

4. Belinsky judged America severely.

5. For the duration of his career, Belinsky undervalued Pushkin's prose.

6. Since they were not published during the poet's lifetime, Belinsky was unaware of the dramas Lermontov worked on in the thirties.

7. The first (1840) edition appeared in two volumes.

8. Refers to Iu. A. Neledinskii-Meletskii's poem "A Song."

9. From the ninth stanza of the eighth canto of Pushkin's *Eugene Onegin,* trans. James Falen (Carbondale, Ill., 1990), 199.

10. An allusion to Bulgarin's review of the seventh chapter of *Eugene Onegin.* Bulgarin, quoting the same lines as Belinsky, wrote: "These lines are very remarkable. Truth be told, this is a very pitiful idea of contemporary man – but what to do? We shall bow to fate!" (*The Northern Bee* [1830] no. 35).

11. These two north-flowing rivers run parallel to each other.

12. From Lermontov's "Duma" ("Meditation," 1838).

13. The hero of Schiller's drama, "The Robbers" (1781).

14. Belinsky here quotes nearly word for word from Varnhagen von Ense's article "A Foreigner's Reaction to Pushkin" ["Otzyv inostrantsa o Pushkine," in Katkov's translation].

15. *Zamknutost'* is a central term of Belinsky's organic aesthetics. It has no English equivalent and might be understood as a meeting of several interrelated notions: independence, self-integration, self-sufficiency. In some respects, the term refers to the universe the text creates independently of other systems, a universe of relationships that is integrated unto itself artistically.

16. Refers to *The Sorrows of Young Werther* (*Die Leiden des jungen Werther*), Goethe's sentimental novel of 1774, which was supposedly inspired by an unfortunate love affair.

17. For Belinsky's full text in translation, go to: http://www.uwyo.edu/lermontov.

# A Hero of Our Time

## B. M. EIKHENBAUM

Translated by Lewis Bagby

The idea for writing *A Hero of Our Time* and the history of its composition remain obscure. Neither Lermontov's personal letters nor memoirs about him attest to anything [of interest] about the novel. But some notion as to its central idea and composition may be generated through an analysis of the stories themselves. Before the publication of the novel as a whole, three of its chapters were published in *Notes of the Fatherland*: "Bela" (1839, No. 3), "The Fatalist" (1839, No. 11), and "Taman" (1840, No. 2). "Bela" appeared with the subtitle "From an Officer's Notes on the Caucasus." It contained, likewise, a suggestion that there would be more to follow. This possibility is suggested at the end of the tale when the [traveling narrator] describes his farewell meeting with Maksim Maksimych: "We did not expect ever to meet again, and yet we did meet, and if you like, I'll tell you about it; it's quite a story" (49).

When "The Fatalist" appeared, it lacked a subtitle altogether, but the publisher made the following remark: "With particular satisfaction we take this opportunity to inform our readers that M. Iu. Lermontov in the near future will publish a collection of his stories, both those previously published and those which have not appeared in print. This will be a new, beautiful gift to Russian literature." From these words alone we cannot necessarily conclude that the future "collection of stories" would turn out to be a complete "composition" (as it is put on the cover to the first edition), not to mention a novel. But the author's foreword to "Bela" precedes "The Fatalist," and this establishes a direct structural link between the two [tales]: "The story presented here comes from Pechorin's notebooks, which Maksim Maksimych passed on to me. I cannot hope that all readers might remember both of these two names, so unforgettable to me. I, therefore, consider it necessary to recall to you that Maksim Maksimych is the same good old officer who had told me the Bela tale, published in No. 3 of *Notes of the Fatherland*, and that Pechorin is the very same young man who had stolen Bela. I am presenting the excerpts from Pechorin's notebooks in the exact same form in which I received them." We might add that the attentive reader could very well notice for himself that the narrator and the hero of "The Fatalist" are none other than Pechorin, for at the tale's end we read: "After my return to the fort, I related to Maksim Maksimych all that had happened to me" (194) and so forth. It should be noted, too, that in the foreword to "The Fatalist," Pechorin linked his personage with that of the [traveling narrator] in "Bela," thus lending a documentary, or memoir-type tone to the meeting with Maksim Maksimych narrated there. As concerns "Taman," it was printed in the 1840 edition with a brief editorial remark: "This is yet another excerpt from Pechorin's notebooks, that is, the Pechorin of 'Bela,' published in issue No. 3 of *Notes of the Fatherland* for the year 1839."

———

*A Hero of Our Time* is a cycle of tales collected around one dramatis persona. This is of key import in differentiating this "composition" from all manner of similar collections and cycles of the 1830s in Russian literature. In order to develop such a psychologized cycle and to make it artistically convincing, it was necessary to move away from the routine devices of previous story cycles and to discover a new means that could motivate the story cycle in an entirely natural manner. Lermontov did just that, and he accomplished this feat by differentiating his traveling narrator from the hero and by laying out the cycle in a peculiar chronological sequence, a sequence, moreover, that could motivate not only the shift from one narrator to another (something already accomplished previously by Bestuzhev) but gradually provide familiarization with the life and personality of the hero. From the very first features of character we encounter as readers, but at two removes (the traveling narrator of

"Bela" passes along Maksim Maksimych's story to us), we readers receive a direct description, one conveyed by the traveling narrator directly on the basis of his chance observation [of Pechorin in "Maksim Maksimych"] ("on the highway," as it is put in the foreword to "Pechorin's Journal"). Following this rather fluid preparation of the reader's sensitivities, the possibility of judging the hero for oneself on the basis of his own notes is presented to us. Belinsky had noted that parts of the novel had been laid out in accordance with an internal necessity and that "despite its chronological disruptions, it is impossible to read it in any other sequence than that dictated by the author himself. Otherwise, one would read only two quite remarkable tales and a few wonderful stories, but not a novel."[1]

It should be added that the life of the hero is given not only in fragments (as the traveling narrator points out in his foreword to the journal) but through a complete destruction of a normal chronological order, or, better put, through the intersection of two chronological movements. One of those movements advances directly and logically: from the first meeting with Maksim Maksimych ("Bela") to the second one a day later. Then, after some time has passed, the traveling narrator, having learned of Pechorin's death, publishes the latter's notes. This is the chronology of the [traveling narrator] – the successive history of the traveling narrator's (and with him, the reader's) acquaintance with the hero himself.

The other movement represents the chronology of events, from "Taman" directly to "Princess Mary," in that Pechorin arrives at the spa, apparently, after participating in frontline action (remember that in "Taman" he is an officer on his way to the front). But between "Princess Mary" and "The Fatalist" we must insert the Bela story inasmuch as Pechorin has come under Maksim Maksimych's command at the fortress after his duel with Grushnitsky ("It is now a month and a half already that I have been in the fort of N. Maksim Maksymich is out hunting" [159]). The traveling narrator's meeting with the hero described in the piece "Maksim Maksimych" occurs five years after the events narrated in "Bela" ("It will soon be five years," the junior captain says), and the reader learns about that meeting before encountering the journal. The reader also finds out about the hero's death before reading about his adventure with the "undine," Princess Mary, and so forth, and he does so in the foreword to the journal. Nor should we forget *how* we receive that shocking bit of news: "I learned not long ago that Pechorin had died on his way back from Persia. This news gladdened me very much. . . ." (63).

We have before us, then, a dual composition, so to speak, one which, on the one hand, creates the necessary novelistic impression of duration and plot complexity, and, on the other, conveys readers into the hero's private world and develops the possibility for motivating in a natural way the most complex and difficult elements – the traveling narrator's meeting with the hero himself and the untimely (from a plot perspective) announcement of the latter's death. All this was entirely new for Russian prose of the 1830s. It was not merely some narrow or formal experiment. It was, in fact, born of [Lermontov's] desire to narrate "the history of a human soul" and to put before readers, in Belinsky's expression, "a burning, contemporary question about the inner man" (267). In order to accomplish this, it was necessary to use all devices available to him from prior example for linking discrete stories and for the development of plot but to do so by assigning them new functions and by effecting internally logical means by which to motivate these new functions.

Apollon Grigoriev had it right: "Those elements, which rage so widely in 'Ammalat-bek' and in the endless 'Mulla Nur' [by Bestuzhev-Marlinsky], you enjoy in Lermontov's [*A Hero of Our Time*] because of the strong, guiding hand of the artist. . . ."[2] Thus, it was necessary (for a fluid development of the hero) to put the first information we receive about Pechorin into the mouth of a unique narrator, of a man well-informed and of good will, but tangential to the hero by dint of upbringing and [character]. This required a Maksim Maksimych. In the hands of any other author of the 1830s, however, Maksim Maksimych would have remained in the role of primary narrator for the remainder of the novel. Lermontov went to great lengths to solidify Maksim Maksymich's place in the novel and to render his motivating function less noticeable. Verisimilitude and authenticity in motivating information is one of the artistic achievements of *A Hero of Our Time*. Because of it, the "romantic" situations and scenes familiar to the reader from the literature of the time (both Russian and Western) acquire a completely natural, "realistic" hue. The simplicity with which Lermontov achieves the integration of the old material works quite effectively when assayed against the background of such an unusual rendering of Pechorin's personality, which retains elements of the "demonic." The dual composition of the novel is reinforced by the dual pyschology and stylistic registers of Russian life.

———

In order to solve the aesthetic challenges the novel posed for him, Lermontov had to resolve a most essential question related to the novel's structure: how might the interior life of the hero be displayed for the reader? Would it be by means of a self-revelation (in the confessional vein) or through third-person narrative? All the more important, given Lermontov's wish to motivate in a natural and convincing way [the novel's component parts], each of these two modes has its advantages and its deficits. The first mode, the confessional, opens up wide terrain for the hero's self-analysis and self-justification, and it also permits the use of irony as well as others' criticism or judgment of him. But it also delimits the world to the hero's subjective apprehension of it. This either renders the author's position indeterminate or forces the reader to examine the hero's portrait as Lermontov's own self-portrait. The second mode, third-person narrative, would introduce external material into the narrative, any "reality" – except, of course, the "history of a soul," which could only be divulged (and then only in part) with the aid of a series of conventional and even naive forms of motivation (such as eavesdropping, chance encounters, and so forth). These would weaken the work's [verisimilitude] and destroy its artistic illusion. A third mode, one by which the author's narrative could be effected outside any motivational structure (that is, in the voice of an omniscient personage, who, as it were, hovers over the dramatis personae), came into the literary canon later, when the novel had torn itself away from the short-story form and had reached out to drama (such that the narrative voice was reduced to a mere "remark making" function). This mode was not available to Lermontov, particularly because the novel had been invented not as a complete narrative whole but as a cycle of discrete tales. How could Lermontov's reader obtain an image of the hero both from the latter's own revelations ("subjectively") and also from an exterior point of view ("objectively")?

Such were the fundamental formal (generic and stylistic) problems Lermontov had to resolve as he worked on *A Hero of Our Time*. It goes without saying that, coincidentally, a set of formal problems arose associated with the development of plot. Since the novel was to consist of separate stories, this would mean that the hero and the history of his soul would be presented not wholly and sequentially but in fragments. And, given this fact, there would be no necessity in presenting his history (parents, childhood, adolescence, youth, and so on), as it had been done, for example, in [Lermontov's unfinished novel] "Princess Ligovskaya." Nor would there be any need to wind the novel up with the hero's death or with an oh-so-touching epilogue in which the hero's delightful old age in the bosom of his family would be described. What was necessary was something entirely different: that each fragment would be entirely substantive and expressive, sufficiently so that each would open up [for the reader] the hero's emotional conflicts and inconsistencies, the ones that constitute the "disease of the century," the "ruination" of the passions (ruined, moreover, by society), and debased heroism. In other words, it would be necessary to depict the hero in diverse situations – not only positive ones but in negative ones as well; not only in intimate but in public circumstances. Or, to put it yet another way, the stories comprising the novel's "cycle of tales" would have to be disparate both in the genres they would represent and in the range of characters depicted in them.

To create the type of "personal" novel in which *A Hero of Our Time* was cast, the problem of the surrounding order acquired particular importance. No one could be on an equal footing with the hero or acquire supremacy over him. He would have to have enemies and perhaps only one friend. In addition to this, of course, in his life and behavior it would be absolutely necessary for the "ailment of the heart" and the fits of "empty passion" (ending in disillusionment and senseless revenge) to be made absolutely clear. This was so terribly important, in fact, that most every story of the cycle would have to consist of a love intrigue.

But even these do not exhaust the list of elements Lermontov would have had to tackle early on in order to bring his novel to a successful, effective, and convincing fruition. Pushkin could enjoy the privilege of not worrying that his Onegin might suddenly appear silly to the reader or might trespass the lofty border separating tragedy from comedy. Even Tatiana had entertained that frightening thought:

> What was he then? An imitation?
> An empty phantom or a joke,
> A Muscovite in Harold's cloak,
> Compendium of affectation,
> A lexicon of words in vogue. . . .
> Mere parody and just a rogue?[3]

Lermontov had greater cause to fear such a remark about his hero, for Pechorin's character played a more difficult role and carried a greater risk as a "hero of [his] time" who could not fulfill his "high calling" in life. How could Lermontov protect him from the horrific danger of suddenly appearing silly or insignificant?

We can say that the danger that threatened the image of Pechorin came from the reader's side but also from the literary context itself, for that context included at the time a wholesale flight from so-called "Byronism" and so-called "romanticism" and so-called "loftiness of soul," not to mention from [romantic] "heroism," inasmuch as it had already been crushed by historical circumstance. But Lermontov considered it his historical obligation or mission to show a young Russian man not as a Khlestakov [from Gogol's "The Inspector

General"] but as a being of strength and of great passions and noble aims in life, with "phenomenal promise for a substantial future," to cite a comment from "Princess Ligovskaya." Not only Onegin but Chatsky [of Griboedov's *Woe from Wit*] were in Lermontov's mind while he composed *A Hero of Our Time*. "When I was young I was a dreamer," says Pechorin. Let him be numbered among those "miserable descendants, who roam the earth without convictions or pride" (188). Even this admission elevates him over the Onegins of the world, for an Onegin would never have let the word "conviction" enter his mouth.

———

If it was necessary to set up Grushnitsky as a parody of one of Pechorin's sides, then it was necessary also (for the same overall purpose) to set up another character [Werner] to reflect Pechorin's ironic side. This would remove the possibility of the readers or critics assuming such a position themselves. After Werner shows up in the novel, no one could accuse the author of favoring his hero. Recall that Werner himself is called Mephistopheles by Pyatigorsk youngsters. If along with Grushnitsky Pechorin may be seen as a demon masked as a Guards Officer, then along with Werner he is something of a Faust, for his words, after his first meeting with Vera, resound with Goethe's voice: "Could it be that youth with its beneficial storms wants to return to me again. . . . And yet it's absurd to think that in appearance I am still a boy: my face is pale but still fresh-complexioned, my limbs are supple and svelte, my thick hair curls, my eyes sparkle, my blood is ebullient" (106).

These two personages, Grushnitsky and Werner, are quite sufficient for the portrayal of Pechorin within the limits of his "journal," but still [more was required]. One of the fundamental and principal developments in the new novel that differentiated it from those preceding it consisted of the objective representation of the hero – objective not only in the sense that it would not be confined merely to the "confessional" mode (as it had been in Musset's *Confessions of a Child of the Century*) or merely to the memoir genre (as, for example, in Constant's *Adolph*) but in the sense that there would no longer be the conventional author-narrator who, for whatever reason, knows every step his hero takes and even every thought that passes through his mind. In the new novel, things would have to be presented in such a manner that the author himself would acquire his knowledge of the hero from others' mouths, a position for an author that, indeed, is quite strange and paradoxical but one that had the capacity to possess no small degree of verisimilitude for the reader and that could be quite convenient for a writer seeking to motivate his fictional material effectively. It is for this reason that Maksim Maksimych appears in the role of narrator and that "Bela" represents the first story to appear in the novel, a story that mixes two distinct genres [the travelogue and the tale of the Caucasus], one motivating the other, one impeding the progress of the other and thus creating tension.

One had to have been courageous in 1838 to write a tale, the action of which occurs in the Caucasus, particularly one that would appear at first glance to be no different from those many preceding it, as indicated in the formulaic subtitle "From an Officer's Notes of the Caucasus." More than one reader, not to mention critic, would have despaired: "Enough of these officers and this crazy Caucasus!" Without even mentioning the flood of Caucasus poems and epic tales that had inundated Russian literature in the 1830s, sketches of the Caucasus, "evenings at the Caucasian spas,"[4] tales of the Caucasus in prose, and novels of the same had become the done thing.

The tale "Bela" appears against this background, even under the subtitle "From an Officer's Notes on the Caucasus." It must be noted, however, that Pushkin's "Journey to Arzrum" served Lermontov, it would seem, as a main point of departure. By juxtaposing his text to it, he created a hybrid genre of the travelogue by combining it with an interpolated dramatic novella. Or perhaps it is just the opposite: Lermontov spliced the "dramatic" (or adventure) novella onto the travel sketch and in this way not only developed a more complex plot line but simultaneously impeded its evolutionary progress. He thus developed an entirely "natural" and clever motivation for the tale ("I am not writing a tale, but travel notes" [31–32]) and defined for Russian literature an innovative role for the travel notes of the Caucasus subgenre, one that Pushkin had put the finishing touches on. This was a typical move for Lermontov. In "Bela" the travel sketch loses its former independent meaning and becomes material for the development of a new plot line, thus reanimating the genre itself. This represents a major aesthetic achievement for Lermontov.

———

Bela's tale is narrated by Maksim Maksimych but only after [the traveling narrator] has endeavored to "get some yarn out of him" (8). He narrates his tale at three distinct stages (with Kazbich's and Pechorin's monologues interpolated within them): (1) from the beginning, commencing with the words "Well, you see, I was stationed then, with my company, in a fort beyond the Terek" (10) and concluding with "We mounted and galloped off home" (19); (2) from "Well there is nothing to be done. Since I have started this story, I have to go on with it" (19) to "Yes, they were happy" (27); and (3) from "Well you have guessed" (35) to "At Kobi, Maksim Maksimich and I parted" (49). A long interlude is presented in which the author describes his becoming acquainted with Maksim Maksimych during an overnight stay in a hut on the road to Gud-Gora. There is a large pause between the second and third parts of the "yarn," in this instance filled with details about the ascent up Gud-Gora, the view of the Koyshaur Valley, the descent from Gud-Gora, the ascent up Krestovaya Mountain, the descent from it, and then another evening in a hut at the Kobi station. We must add to all of this that the real narrator or author of Bela's story is not Maksim Maksimych but the writer "traveling post from Tiflis" (3). For it occurred to [him], by his own admission, and making good use of his time while being retained in Vladikavkaz, that he "might find some diversion in writing down Maksim Maksimych's tale about Bela. Little did [he] think that it would become the first link of a long chain of stories" (50). Here we observe how complex, upon close examination, the construction of the story in fact turns out to be, especially after a first

reading when [the novel] appears to be so natural and simple
. [*legkaia*].

As a result of its construction and artistry, the genre is reanimated.
Its plot line becomes enriched by [Lermontov's] new ideas and
shades of meaning. Belinsky was quite right when he expressed
openly his surprise (this propensity for surprise is one of his most
amazing gifts as a critic): "And just what does the 'content' of the tale
consist of? A Russian officer steals a Cherkess girl, at first loves her
mightily, but cools quickly toward her. Then [Kazbich] almost steals
her away, but, finding himself in danger of being captured, he throws
her down after delivering her a fatal wound, from which she dies.
That's it! Other than the fact that there is quite a bit that is insignificant here, there is nothing poetic, nothing particularly unique, nothing too riveting. Everything is ordinary to an extreme, even out-
worn" (218). Belinsky's response is unclear and entirely too abstract:
"A work of art must be thoroughly prepared in the artist's soul before
hand, before he takes up the pen. . . . He must see before him ahead
of time the characters from whose relationships his drama or tale
takes shape. He does not cogitate, does not dissect into parts, does
not lose himself in imaginings. Everything comes from him of its
own accord and appears on the page as it perforce must" (ibid). This
position, of course, is indefensible; nor does it address the requisite
question. The artist, of course, cogitates very much, dissects very
much, and often becomes agitated, crosses out what he has written,
writes anew – and all this to tear from words and their combinations
new, fresh meanings. In verse, this process accords with rhythm and
the semantic impact on the word connected with rhythm. In prose
(particularly in the novel), this process is attained not as much by
stylistic means as by the plot-oriented constructive [*siuzhetno-
konstruktivnyi*] elaboration of the story line's [*fabula*] scheme, by the
sequencing and linkage of various scenes and episodes, and by sup-
plying a substantial and fresh form of motivation [for these ele-
ments].

In "Bela" this is accomplished with surprising mastery. The tale of
the Cherkess lass is narrated by a person who, by station in life,

personality, habits, and age, can only be an observer, no matter how closely he takes things to heart. He even "envies" Pechorin somewhat ("It vexed me to think that no woman ever loved me like that" [27]), a fact that motivates sufficiently the lyrical coloration of his [Maksim Maksimych's] tale. If his utterances are not completely in keeping with the parameters of the speech typical of a junior captain, they are nonetheless sufficiently motivated for such inconsistency by the fact that all of Maksim Maksimych's tale is transcribed by the [traveling narrator], in which case an exact replication of the former's speech would not have occurred. The fact of the matter is that Lermontov, on the one hand, had to preserve the tonal differences between the two narrators but, on the other, had to create a unity in auctorial narrative style without breaking it into distinct languages: that of the traveling narrator, of the junior captain, of the bandit Kazbich, of the boy Azamat, of Bela, and of Pechorin himself (the words of whom, in Maksim Maksimych's attestation, had "cut into his memory"). The [stylistic] task was resolved by giving each of these characters here enumerated their own distinct set of language "signals." These signals endowed the speech of each with a specific tone and coloration. Nevertheless, the work as a whole operates as the work of a single "author," that is, the one who would "get some kind of yarn" out of Maksim Maksimych and then transcribe it. In this way, this "common story to the point of banality," the tale of a Cherkess lass kidnapped by a Russian officer, is reflected through a prism that has several faults in it – thanks to which it is perceived by the reader as a spectrum of great multicolored significance.

Other than this complex narrative structure, which gives the words new shades of meaning, the story about Bela, as we have mentioned already, represents a complex generic mixture as well, one in which the adventure tale turns into a travel piece, and this travel account enters the adventure tale to break its action. This makes it something of a stair-step structure. This is accomplished in a most simple and natural way so that an impression is made that the story flows as if "under its own power, without any help by the author" [Belinskii, 220]. Only in one spot does Lermontov decide to break this illusion and permit the reader to sense the power of art at work in the story: "Yes, they were happy!" says Maksim Maksimych. "How dull!" (27) his interlocutor cries out cynically (doubtless with the reader's full sympathy). Then a slow and detailed description of the ascent and descent of Gud-Gora commences, a description made at the expense of the reader's patience but simultaneously forcing the reader, one would hope, to pay attention to each detail – something any author would ask – until that patience, at long last, is worn thin. And at this very moment with its penultimate aphorism ("and if all people reasoned more, they would be convinced that life is not worth worrying about so much" [30]), at this moment of silence in plot development, a sudden, deafening question resounds: "But perhaps you would like to know the ending of Bela's story?" (31) Who is it who puts this question? Maybe it is Maksim Maksimych asking his interlocutor [the traveling narrator]? No, this is the [traveling narrator] himself putting the question to his own readers with whom until now there has been no previous direct contact. And it is to those readers the playful answer is addressed as well: "In the first place, it is not a novella I am writing, but traveling notes; consequently, I cannot make the junior captain tell the story before he actually began telling it. Therefore, wait a while, or, if you wish, turn several pages; however, I do not advise you to do this. . . ." (31–32). In essence, this is virtually the same maneuver we see in Betuzhev's "The Test" (1831)[5] but with a difference – there the break in the action is done openly, without any motivation supplied by the genre [the society tale]. But here it acquires a more serious function – it is the result of the hybrid nature [of the story] that gives the plot a new ideational and emotional coloration.

It is precisely here, within this extended "geographical" pause, that the author of "Bela" utters one multivalenced phrase that throws another light on his personality and, consequently, on the entire novel. The descent from Krestovaya Mountain was difficult: "The horses were exhausted; we were chilled; the blizzard hummed louder and louder, just like one of our own in the north, only its savage melody was more sorrowful, more plaintive, 'You, too, are an exile,' I reflected. 'You wail for your wide spacious steppes! There you had room to unfurl your cold wings, while here you are stifled and cramped like an eagle that beats with cries against the bars of his iron cage'" (33). To whom do the words "You, too, are an exile" refer? Who is the exile here pining away for the spacious steppes? Clearly, it is the author of "Bela," who very soon (in April 1840) will repeat the remark but in reference to dark clouds: "Rush on, just as I, oh ye exiles." Thus, this "traveler to Tiflis" is a writer, not a "traveling officer," as he is usually called in works about *A Hero of Our Time*, but one who has been exiled. And he is not traveling, it would seem, to St. Petersburg, but on to Stavropol, just as Maksim Maksimych ("We seem to be fellow-travelers" [4]).

———

To all that has been mentioned about the writing profession of the narrator of "Bela" and "Maksim Maksimych," we must add that this profession is particularly well suited for solving one of the novel's most important problems: somewhere it would be necessary to paint the portrait of the hero, and more so, the "hero of our time." Such portrait painting was traditional in [the literature of the time], but, more to the point, it was an unnecessary obligation. But the task, in this instance, acquired a new and important meaning, for the story narrated in "Bela" elicits a strong interest in Pechorin as a whole personality – this, in fact, is one of Lermontov's greatest achievements here. It is significant that for the hero's portrait, [Lermontov] located a brilliantly witty and plausible motivation for it – the "traveler by post to Tiflis" becomes a writer, someone who listens to the Bela tale, transcribes it, and then comes face to face with Pechorin himself. It is entirely natural that he gazes upon [Pechorin] intently, examining every feature, observing every move of this "strange" man (to cite the captain's own description of him). And thus we have a portrait at the heart of which is an assertion about the connection between the surface appearance of the individual and his character or psyche in general, an assertion through which we ascertain linkages of the latest philosophical and scientific theories (theories that themselves served as the basis for the early development of materialist philosophy – symptomatic here is the figure of Dr. Werner). It is significant, for example, that at this time at Kazan University Professor E. F. Aristov (1806–75) published a work entitled *On the Significance of Appearances* (1846) and *On Physical Attributes* (1853). Lermontov ascertains Pechorin's psychology through a reading of his hands, gait, wrinkles, and the color of his hair versus mustache and eyebrows. The materialist basis of Pechorin's portrait is underscored in no uncertain terms in the comparison of these final details with the signs of breeding in a white horse.

Let us now turn to Pechorin's psychological portraiture. After "Bela" Pechorin remains rather enigmatic. "What a strange thing! Would you be so kind as to tell me . . . you've lived, it seems, in the capital, haven't you, and not too long ago: Is it true that all the young men there are like that?" (41), Maksim Maksimych asks the "author." His critical tone does not weaken but strengthens the enigma, introducing into it some elements of vulgar demonism. "Taman," for its part, is layered into the novel (it was originally written without being connected to the novel) as a psychological and plot-oriented "antidote" to [the disease] encountered in "Bela" and "Maksim Maksimych." In "Taman" the thin layer of naive Rousseauism, which strikes the reader of "Bela," is removed. True, in "Bela" Pechorin comes to the conclusion that "love of a wild girl [is] little better than that of a lady of rank; the ignorance and the naivete of one pall on you as much as the coquetry of the other" (40). But this can be attributed to "demonism" more than to anything substantive. In "Taman" the hero is again at it with a "wild girl," but in this instance suffers a complete fiasco and is almost killed. The "undine" is none other than a smuggler's girl, and the world of unusual bandits in fact has nothing to do with some Rousseauistic idyll of the primitive.

It is quite natural that after this fiasco, Pechorin leaves the world of the "wild girls" behind and returns to a nest that is more familiar and less dangerous to him, the world of gentry women and their daughters. The shift from "Taman" to "Princess Mary" [reflects this change of worlds]. This piece has been thoroughly analyzed already by others for its significance to the novel. Here Pechorin's character is taken up again, inasmuch as the reader becomes acquainted not only with his deeds but with his thoughts, aspirations, complaints. And all this concludes with a multivalenced "poem in prose," the meaning of which carries us well beyond the petty affairs of Princess Mary and Grushnitsky: "I am like a sailor born and bred on the deck of a pirate brig. His soul is used to storms and battles, and when cast out on the shore, he feels bored and oppressed, no matter how the shady grove lures him, no matter how the peaceful sun shines on him" (180). However, great storms and battles no longer await him. The very most he can expect is that, as so often before, he will be faced with imminent death and will escape yet again.

––––––

It is hardly surprising that the question of "fate" or "predestination" provides the theme of the novel's final tale. What *is* surprising, or, more correctly, what is more remarkable, is that Lermontov managed to get around this theme by making it the heart of a prose work of fiction. Without denying the significance of the problem itself, he takes it not in some theoretical sense ("metaphysical") but in a psychological one, as a fact of spiritual life and of mankind's behavior. And he comes to a most unexpected conclusion, unexpected, that is, for a theoretician. But it is an absolutely convincing practical conclusion nonetheless: "I like to have doubts, about everything: this inclination of the mind does not impinge upon resoluteness of character. On the contrary, as far as I am concerned, I always advance with greater courage, when I do not know what awaits me. For nothing worse than death can ever occur; and from death there is no escape!" (193–94). Fatalism here is turned on its head: if "predestination" (albeit in the form of historical necessity) in fact exists, then the consciousness of it must necessarily render a person's actions more aggressive and courageous. The question of "fatalism" is not resolved in this manner, but something else comes to light by it, specifically, a philosophical stance that does not permit a passive relationship with reality but makes one's character even more decisive and prone to act. Lermontov, by inverting the philosophical theme's import in such an artistic manner in his final story, saves it from tendentiousness, and at the same time, likewise saves his novel from a silly and banal conclusion.

"The Fatalist" plays the role of the novel's epilogue, although (as we have seen in "Taman") given the chronological sequencing of the events narrated therein, it is not the *only* epilogue. The meeting with Maksim Maksimych and Pechorin's departure for Persia occur much later in time. Additionally, the foreword to "Pechorin's Journal," inasmuch as we are informed there that the hero has died and we learn something more about his life, serves as a final epilogue in a chronological sense. But such is the power and such is the triumph of art over the logic of facts. Or, to put it differently, the triumph of plot (*siuzhet*) over story material (*fabula*). The hero's death is announced in the middle of the novel in the form of a simple biographical notation, without any details added and with a most stunning turn of phrase: "This news gladdened me very much" (63). This decision did not only free the author from the cliché of completing his novel with the hero's death but gave him the opportunity to conclude it in a major key.

Pechorin is not only saved from death in the final tale but he performs (for the first time in the novel) a courageous deed of general good to the community, one in no way connected with those "empty passions" of his. The theme of love in "The Fatalist" is excluded altogether. Thanks to the dual composition (discussed earlier) and the fragmented structure of the novel, the hero, in a compositional (plot-oriented) sense, does not perish. The novel concludes with some promise for the future – with the hero's exit from his tragic condition of idle doom ("I always advance with greater courage. . . ."). Rather than a funeral march, [we hear] congratulations for his victory over death: "The officers kept congratulating me – and indeed, there was reason enough" (193), the hero himself acknowledges.

The final conversation between Pechorin and Maksim Maksimych introduces into the novel's concluding lines an ironic note

The "fatalist" turns out to be Maksim Maksimych, not Pechorin: "However, this must have been what was assigned to [Vulich] at his birth!" (194). But his is a fatalism without any love of "metaphysical discussions." In this way at the end of the novel, the two characters come in some measure, although from completely opposite directions, to a similar view of life. [Like Maksim Maksimych], Pechorin has confessed earlier that he does not like dealing with "abstract ideas."[6]

NOTES

Reprinted from B. M. Eikhenbaum, *"Geroi nashego vremeni," Stat'i o Lermontove* (Moscow, 1961), 221–85.

1. V. G. Belinskii, *Polnoe sobranie sochinenii,* 13 vols. (Moscow, 1953–59), 4:267.

2. From "Sovremennoe obozrenie," *Vremia,* no. 10 (1862): 26. Let us recall, however, that when Tolstoy, in a conversation with S. T. Semenov, asked, "Have you read Marlinsky?" the latter responded, "No, I haven't." "Too bad. There was so much of interest [in his work]." S. T. Semenov, *Vospominaniia o L. N. Tolstom* (St. Petersburg, 1912), 80. [Eikhenbaum's note.]

See also A. A. Bestuzhev-Marlinsky, "Ammalat-bek," trans. Lewis Bagby, *The Ardis Anthology of Russian Romanticism,* ed. Christine Rydel (Ann Arbor, Mich. 1984), 212–41; Lewis Bagby, *Alexander Bestuzhev-Marlinsky* (University Park, Penn., 1995), 306–31; and Susan Layton, *Russian Literature and Empire: Conquest of the Caucasus from Pushkin to Tolstoy* (Cambridge, England, 1994), 110–32.

3. Alexander Pushkin, *Eugene Onegin,* trans. James Falen (Carbondale, Ill., 1990), 177.

4. Bestuzhev-Marlinsky penned a sketch with this title.

5. Alexander Bestuzhev-Marlinsky, "The Test," trans. Lewis Bagby, in *Russian Romantic Prose: An Anthology,* ed. Carl Proffer (Ann Arbor, Mich., 1979), 145–95.

6. For a more complete translation of the Eikhenbaum article, see http://www.uwyo.edu/lermontov.

# Ironies of Ethnic Identity

SUSAN LAYTON

Lermontov's novel features many Caucasian peoples, both in principal and peripheral roles. Most of the ethnic groups appear in "Bela," an episode set mainly at a Russian fort on the Chechen frontier of the Kumyk plain.[1] The tale of Pechorin and his "Circassian" concubine foregrounds several local characters: Bela herself, her brother Azamat, and Kazbich. In addition, as Maksim Maksimych tells this story about the past, he and the novel's master narrator come into contact with Ossetians ( a people here subject to much verbal abuse).[2] "Bela" also mentions Georgians, Armenians, Kabardinians, Shapsugs, and "Tatars."[3] In some cases, the narrator pegs a person's ethnic identity, in unflattering terms, on the basis of looks alone. Without exchanging a word with anybody in the Ossetian hut where he and Maksim Maksimych pass the night, the narrator spots a "lean Georgian" in rags (like all the other locals).[4] Similarly, as the narrator prepares to continue his journey, he sees "dirty Armenians" pulling into the posting station just as Pechorin's elegant coach arrives ("Maksim Maksimych").[5]

Lermontov's modeling of cross-cultural relations poses a dilemma for today's readers: should we examine "Bela" primarily from the standpoint of our convictions about the value of cultural multiplicity and peoples' right to national self-determination? Or should we concentrate on trying to understand what the interethnic relations meant to Lermontov? Each of these avenues has pitfalls. Any historical inquiry must take pains not to project contemporary values and attitudes back into the past. A good deal of Soviet commentary on Lermontov fell into this practice because tsarist imperialism was such an explosive issue.[6] Up to the late 1930s, Stalin regarded the Caucasian mountaineers as fighters for national liberation against

Russian aggression. But then he made an about-face to denounce the Muslim resistance movement as religious fanaticism and Asian despotism (in the person of Shamil, the imam of Dagestan and Chechnya from 1834 to 1859). Stalin and his spokesmen admitted that Russia's war against the mountaineers was cruel, but they claimed it had a good, "progressive" outcome in the long run (by spreading literacy in the Caucasus, for example). The stress on the supposedly positive outcome of the Caucasian conquest went together with propaganda about the USSR as a state where many nationalities lived happily together under communism. Evoked by the phrase the "friendship of peoples," this idea was still prevalent in Russia in Gorbachev's time.

The Russian state's changing interpretation of the Caucasian war naturally affected literary specialists' views of Lermontov's mountaineers. In 1934 the literary critic Nikolai Svirin counted Lermontov among nineteenth-century Russians who had colonialist attitudes toward the Caucasus.[7] Three years later, however, another Russian commentator claimed just the opposite, presenting "Bela" as a protest against the "bestial and merciless enslavement of Caucasian peoples."[8] Once the Soviet state pronounced the Caucasian war a harsh but necessary fight against Asian despotism, literary critics toed the official line. Sometimes they even claimed that Lermontov (and other famous writers) had anticipated the Soviet outlook. A critic of 1957 thus argued that "wild" Bela's death "symbolizes the inevitability and necessity" of Russia's colonizing the Caucasus.[9] Such interpretations of *A Hero of Our Time* remained common in Russia into the era of *glasnost*.

Given the bad example of efforts to pretend that Lermontov's thinking matched Soviet ideas about the Caucasian conquest, it is perhaps tempting to let modern knowledge alone guide our reading of *A Hero of Our Time*. If we make this choice, though, we must essentially sacrifice the intriguing question of Lermontov's intentions. The exemplary case is Peter Scotto's analysis of "Bela" as a literary manifestation of Russian colonialism vis-à-vis the Caucasian mountaineers.[10] Surely most readers would agree that Pechorin's actions and speech convey assumptions about Russia as the more civilized, "European" power destined to dominate the "Asiatic" Caucasus. Ethnic slurs in the speech of Maksim Maksimych and the master narrator also express imperialist mentalities, similar to Pechorin's. While Scotto effectively advances these arguments, he does not accuse Lermontov himself of racism nor of ethnocentric loyalty to the Russian empire. To the contrary, Scotto leaves aside the complex issue of Lermontov's own outlook.

*A Hero of Our Time* makes it particularly difficult to study the author's values because Lermontov's masterful irony distances him from his characters.[11] All the same, analysis can clarify the authorial perspective on interethnic relations in "Bela." To set a framework for examining the story itself, certain features of Lermontov's life and poetry merit introductory consideration. Lermontov developed an extraordinary sense of connection to the Caucasus during his childhood. His grandmother's nephew, Akim Khostatov, had an estate including a silk factory at Shelkozavodskaya on the left bank of the Terek between Grozny and Kizlyar. Lermontov first visited this frontier homestead when he was five years old. A second Caucasian vacation with his grandmother in the summer of 1825 included a trip to Hot Springs (Pyatigorsk's name at the time). Given the ethnic diversity of merchants and customers at Khostatov's compound, little Lermontov conceivably may have met some nice "old Chechens," as two Soviet critics speculated.[12] However that may be, Lermontov's relatives apparently told him some Caucasian folklore, and they showed him the rubble of a Kabardinian village razed by the Russian army after the inhabitants had fled.[13]

These unusual personal impressions gave the author a sense of the Caucasus as his true, spiritual home. With his painful sense of orphanhood, Lermontov approached the mountain borderland as a substitute family. The poet's lyric "The Caucasus" (1830) imagines his mother as an angel watching over him in the mountain heights. More typically, as a teenage youth, Lermontov dreamed up macho mountaineers, as though compensating for the lack of a powerful father. The tribal heroes of Lermontov's verse tales of the 1830s – "Kally," "The *Aul* Bastundzhi," "Izmail-Bey," and "Hadji-Abrek" – are all sword-swinging killers, attached to their ruggedly beautiful native realm. Never submitted for publication by the poet himself, these tales of violent tribesmen surely betrayed some adolescent relish for the so-called "oriental" savagery prominent in trashy Russian literature of the time.

Nonetheless, Lermontov's early Caucasian poems also manifest a politically interesting authorial identification with mountaineers construed as victims rather than aggressors. Similar to the writer himself, his Circassian protagonists Izmail-Bey and Selim ("The *Aul* Bastundzhi") are orphans.[14] Moreover, in an extension of the homelessness that preoccupied Lermontov early on, these tribesmen both come from villages leveled by the Russian army. "Izmail-Bey" most strikingly expresses the poet's recurrent perception of tribal victimhood. This work's third part begins with a characterization of Russian imperialism as a "Roman" drive to enslave the entire world. Although, when "Izmail-Bey" first appeared in 1843, the censor deleted this stanza, his blind patriotism permitted him to pass Lermontov's ensuing depiction of the Russian army as a "predatory beast," killing children and old people during a raid on a Circassian village.

Particularly in view of the anti-imperialist thrust of "Izmail-Bey," Lermontov's complicated (perhaps unfathomable) attitudes toward military service deserve stressing. After a two-year program at the St. Petersburg military academy, Lermontov received his officer's commission in 1834. Upon occasion, however, he showed an enormous disrespect for military decorum. In the most famous instance, he wore a toy sword at an inspection before the tsar's brother, Grand Prince Mikhail. Funny as it may sound, this prank seems to have manifested a serious alienation from the violence that soldiers commit with real weapons. Just before Lermontov took part in an expedition against mountaineers during his first exile, he fell ill. On May 15, 1837, he set off with the army, but by the end of the month, he was in Pyatigorsk on sick leave.[15] By the next spring, when his exile had ended, he was petitioning to resign from the army (a request the authorities always denied him). Thus, after a brief exposure to a hot theater of war, the poet sought to abandon the army and devote himself wholly to writing.

Despite his effort to resign from the army, Lermontov had a typically romantic, touristic enthusiasm for the wild frontier. In a letter he wrote to Svyatoslav Raevsky in the fall of 1837, Lermontov speaks delightedly of his new "Circassian" clothing and his travels – all along the line of Russian military outposts from Kizlyar to Taman and across the mountains into Georgia and other regions of Transcaucasia.[16] The letter also recounts an excitingly close call Lermontov had with Lesgin tribesmen near Kuba during a nighttime ride with an allied mountaineer. Lermontov's thirst for adventure conforms to a general tendency evident in memoirs of the era: educated Russians often enlisted in the Caucasian army in order to see the stupendous alpine country and the valiant mountaineers celebrated in writings by Pushkin and Bestuzhev-Marlinsky. Many Russian enlistees surely hoped to win medals in combat, if only to impress civilians back home (a motive young Tolstoy would attribute to himself in his diary of April 1852).[17] But such hopes easily combined with the romantic urge to use military service as a way of visiting a fascinating foreign land.

In turning now to "Bela," my analysis will try to demonstrate that the story expresses the author's resistance to colonialist beliefs about Russia's cultural superiority to the Caucasian mountaineers – a resistance in harmony with Lermontov's poetic theme of family attachment to the mountain borderland, his denunciation of the Russian empire as a slave-state sustained by a bestial army, and his desire to quit the service. This investigation will focus on the subversive implications of Pechorin's interaction with Kazbich, nineteenth-century Russian literature's most famous Chechen.[18] Lermontov's choice of Kazbich's ethnic identity has special significance. During the late 1820s and the early 1830s, some hapless Russian writers had published tales with Chechen villains in them. Furthermore, Lermontov's first exile brought him into contact with Russian commanders who considered Chechens exceptionally "vicious" (or "mean," "wicked," "evil" – the Russian *zloi*). Viewed from these perspectives, Kazbich seems a polemical figure – a character whom Lermontov used to challenge Russian prejudices against Chechens.

To test that proposition, let us now look at "Bela" with these questions in mind: if Chechens are the nastiest of the nasty "savages" (as many Russian army commanders said they were), where does that leave Pechorin? Has Europeanization really made him a better man than Kazbich? And if the fruits of civilization do *not* noticeably improve people, then what moral justification can Russia's subjugation of the Caucasus have? This is the set of politically incorrect problems that Lermontov creates by making Pechorin so despicable.

Pechorin's political incorrectness comes sharply into focus when "Bela" is read alongside third-rate literature of Lermontov's era. The intensification of Russian military operations in Chechnya and Dagestan in the late 1820s and early 1830s coincided with an influx of awful savages into Russia's literary Caucasus (Layton, *Russian Literature and Empire*, 156–74). Unlike the heroic, freedom-loving mountaineers of Pushkin and Bestuzhev-Marlinsky, these tribesmen were fiends, often brutal to women of their own countries. But Russian soldiers (usually Cossacks) were luckily on hand to try to protect the lovely tribeswomen. Always good Christians, the Russians sometimes even hoped to marry a beautiful Muslim, as long as she converted to Orthodoxy. "Bela" parodies this kind of story about Russian military men with noble feelings for Caucasian tribeswomen. Largely out of boredom, Pechorin indulges a passing erotic fantasy that destroys Bela (besides ruining her family and cheating Kazbich of his irreplaceable horse). Pechorin states more than once that he is just not the marrying kind. An ignoble egoist in his treatment of Bela, he brings about her annihilation rather than her salvation.

As a parody of patriotic love stories about Christian soldiers and beautiful Muslim tribeswomen, "Bela" appears most specifically aimed at "The Bedouin Woman," a tale set in Algeria rather than the Caucasus.[19] Published by an unknown author in the *Library for Read-*

*ing* in 1838, "The Bedouin Woman" is about the French conquest actually underway in North Africa at the time. During war against "bandit" tribes of the desert next to the snowy Atlas mountains, a disastrous love affair occurs between the heroine (Ambra) and Franz, a German officer in the foreign legion. Franz, while traveling with a military companion into the area where he first met Ambra, whom he now intends to marry, tells most of the story as a flashback. As in "Bela," descriptions of stormy weather interrupt to build suspense about the cross-cultural romance: will Ambra be waiting for Franz or not? Besides structuring the story largely as a conversation about the past, "The Bedouin Woman" also gives a central role to the hero's own writing (as *A Hero of Our Time* would do). Just after Franz dies in combat near the story's conclusion, his friend finds his diary and reads it to learn what happened during the hero's as yet unexplained, but evidently shocking, encounter with Ambra's family. The comrade then shares the information with readers, in a spirit of affectionate loyalty to the dead hero: poor Franz had found Ambra stabbed to death by her father and brothers, in revenge for her loving a Christian.

Franz's high moral character sets him apart from the average legionnaire and his commander in chief, an old French general. Unlike the hero, who yearns to marry Ambra, many Frenchmen in this story keep Bedouin concubines. The author also hints that soldiers rape women during attacks on local villages. But Franz is different. During a raid, he finds Ambra hiding in the deserted house of her father, a powerful sheik. Educated in oriental studies, Franz can speak Ambra's language and he quickly explains his wish to save her from the "coarse" soldiers under his command. The heroine instantly falls in love with him and promises to be his "slave." After wrapping Ambra in his overcoat and taking her away on his camel, Franz keeps her hidden in his tent so she will not be sent home. Throughout their life together in the army camp, the hero sticks to his moral principles. Ambra tries to seduce him, but he begs her to wait until they marry. The dream of wedlock collapses when the commander in chief learns about Ambra. The general comes to

Franz's tent and strips him of his sword, after reprimanding him for cohabiting with the daughter of a sheik (who by now is a vital French ally). Ambra is given back to her family to meet her dreadful end. Interaction between the main characters of "Bela" ironically inverts the relationships between Franz, Ambra, and the French commandant. Maksim Maksimych is the military authority figure, who confiscates Pechorin's sword to punish him for Bela's abduction. But where the Algerian tale's senior officer is a sexual menace (who probably rapes Ambra after taking her into custody), Maksim Maksimych has a fatherly attitude toward Bela. He perceives "bandit" blood in her eyes when she first spots Kazbich near the fort, and he may feel some erotic attraction to her.[20] All the same, Bela's sole sexual harasser is Pechorin, whose behavior reverses Franz's gallantry step-by-step: Pechorin has Bela kidnapped, makes her learn *his* language, regards her virginity as a challenge, and never has the slightest thought of marrying her. Like Ambra, Bela too dies by the knife of a local Muslim man. However, "The Bedouin Woman" rigidly separates Franz from the heroine's local Muslim killers. By contrast, the cruelty of Pechorin's erotic conquest inculpates him in Bela's murder.

In weaving a web of moral liability around Pechorin, Lermontov plays with a contrast in *appearances* typical of nineteenth-century stories about "refined" Europeans in the "barbaric" Orient. Pechorin is blonde, fair-skinned, and impeccably groomed, while Bela's Chechen murderer, Kazbich, has a swarthy "bandit's mug" and slovenly clothing.[21] But instead of isolating Kazbich as the savage, dark man completely different from the Russian hero, Lermontov shows how these two men resemble one another in their treatment of Bela. This sly process starts when Maksim Maksimych presents Kazbich as Bela's admirer at the marriage celebration in her father's house. Bela's interest in Pechorin makes the Russian a rival in Kazbich's eyes – an outsider who threatens to take the place in Bela's affections that the Chechen seems to want for himself. At this point in the narrative, Pechorin and Kazbich begin assuming similar roles in Lermontov's plot. Kazbich receives Azamat's offer to steal Bela in return for Karagyoz, but Pechorin steps in to accept the deal (after Maksim Maksimych relays the mountaineers' conversation). Bela comes into Pechorin's clutches bundled on a horse – the same way she will exit as Kazbich's captive. In the attempt to wear down Bela's resistance, Pechorin tries to convince her he is superior to a mountaineer like Kazbich: "You're not in love with some Chechen, are you?" he sneers (25). However, while considering himself a much better man than Kazbich, Pechorin is doing violence against Bela – a *moral* violence that corresponds to Kazbich's physical assault. The Chechen actually kills the heroine, but Pechorin already has destroyed her socially and culturally by abducting her with no intention of marrying her. Bela dies through the combined action of two men whose contrasting, ethnically marked appearances disguise their shared ruthlessness toward her.

The depiction of Bela's murder stresses Pechorin's inner savagery. In recalling the event, Maksim Maksimych says that Pechorin "let out a yell no worse than that of any Chechen" (43) when he saw Kazbich galloping away with Bela. The phrase "no worse" wickedly hints that, in general, it is hard to see any real *moral* difference between Pechorin and a lawless Chechen. Not content to unmask the nastiness beneath fair-haired Pechorin's pretensions to "European" superiority over swarthy "savages," Lermontov even implies that Kazbich is the more admirable man, ethically speaking. Kazbich, after all, comes through "Bela" with a certain spiritual integrity intact – an unwavering sense of right and wrong rooted in his own culture.

Lermontov's repeated references to Kazbich's Chechen identity may create puzzlement about the story's other ethnic indicators. Although Maksim Maksimych locates the Russian fort in Chechnya, he and Pechorin call Bela "Circassian." This was simply the term which nineteenth-century Russians commonly applied to any Caucasian mountaineer. Russians tended to relate tribeswomen in particular to the Circassian heroine of Pushkin's "The Prisoner of the Caucasus" (Manuilov, 88–89). In order to credit Lermontov for "realism," some Soviet commentators insisted that *he* knew Bela was

Chechen or Kumyk: it is Maksim Maksimych and Pechorin who fail the ethnographic test.[22] But did Lermontov know that the story's local words (*yok*, and so on) are Kumyk rather than Chechen? Apparently not, to judge by the repeated ascription of speech to Kazbich through the vague phrase "in his own language" (*po svoemu*).[23]

However, no amount of ethnographic confusion detracts from Lermontov's selection of a Chechen as Pechorin's Caucasian counterpart. To grasp the full import of Kazbich's ethnic identity, we need to examine his interestingly mixed antecedents in the Russian imagination. Chechens understandably loomed large in the mind of Russian military men at the outset of the conquest. When General Aleksei Ermolov undertook the "pacification" of the Northern Caucasus in 1818, he sought to persuade Alexander I that Chechens were the "strongest" and "most dangerous" of the local peoples.[24] In the same period, General Mikhail Orlov (then in Kishinev) privately expressed the opinion that Russia's attacking "Chechens and other peoples of this region" was such folly that he suspected Ermolov of simply trying to increase his own prestige: this "may bring great benefits to Ermolov personally, but none whatsoever to Russia."[25] A Russian traveler in the Caucasus in 1821 also remarked the Chechens' reputation for being "unconquerable."[26] This observer mistakenly supposed, however, that Ermolov had already subdued these formidable mountaineers.

While prominent in the minds of Russians on the empire's periphery, Chechens were not central in Russian literature (as they probably would have been had young Pushkin's "The Prisoner of the Caucasus" given them star billing). Even passing references, however, comprise Kazbich's literary context. The so-called "Circassian Song" of Pushkin's captivity poem evokes a Chechen ready to swim to the Russian side of the Terek.[27] The Cossack women singers seem distressed about the possible attack, but Pushkin presents such tribal incursions as daring heroism when actually enacted by a character in the poem, a Circassian mountaineer who swims across a river and kills a Cossack border guard. One of Pushkin's contemporaries, the gentleman traveler and poet Stepan Nechaev, imagined a Chechen tribesman as a bard rather than a raider.[28] By contrast to the poetic perspectives of Pushkin and Nechaev, "vicious" Chechens populate Alexander Shishkov's "Lonskoi," an unfinished poem stimulated by the author's Caucasian military service from 1818 to 1821.[29] Shishkov's Chechens all have hideous designs on Russia. Even the women thirst for Russian blood and beg departing warriors to bring back Russian skulls. Bestuzhev-Marlinsky's semianonymous story "An Evening at a Caucasian Spa in 1824" seems to mock such vampiric notions. Set in Kislovodsk, the work features a scared Russian full of fantasies about Chechens. He warns his Russian companions about "Chechens' bestiality and audacity: how they stole two ladies and their daughters away from here two years ago; how they killed a sentry on the redoubt a much longer time ago, and so on, and so on, and so forth. . . ."[30] Those final words, of course, convey Bestuzhev-Marlinsky's ironic view of the Russian's fear.

The Chechens of Lermontov's time leaned toward the demons of "Lonskoi" rather than Pushkin's romanticized raider, Nechaev's Homeric poet, or Bestuzhev-Marlinsky's scary figments of imagination. Alexander Polezhaev's poem of military exile, "Chir-Yurt" (1831), expressed friendly sentiments toward neutral (*mirnye*; peaceful) Chechens, but called rebellious Chechens an "animalistic people" – "bloodthirsty" and "recalcitrant."[31] Similar vilification occurred in "Zlomilla and Dobronrava" (1834), a tale in verse by the forgotten scribbler, P. Markov, who stereotyped the entire male population as a thoroughly "vicious" breed – the "sons of murder and pillage."[32] Markov's beautiful tribeswomen, on the other hand, are attracted to Russians.

Lermontov's poetry runs counter to Russia's dehumanizing portrayals of Chechen men and even takes a sideswipe at the key word "vicious." Lermontov's earliest Chechen overlaps completely with the dashing mountaineers of Pushkin's "The Prisoner of the Caucasus." In fact, Lermontov's poem of the same title (1828) has a bold "Circassian" jump into the Terek and come out on the other bank as a "Chechen." (Obviously, the fourteen-year-old Lermontov thought these two ethnic terms fully interchangeable.) Lermontov's

"Dzhulio" (1830) also expresses admiration for a daring Chechen. On a different note, "Izmail-Bey" (1832) features an old Chechen storyteller as the traveling author's guide. "Vicious" Chechens then suddenly invaded Lermontov's "Gifts from the Terek" (1839) and "A Cossack Lullaby" (1840), two works produced between his exiles.

Before looking more closely at these latter two poems and their relation to "Bela," the military context demands further comment. Although the exact time and place of the poems' composition is unknown, both were written after Lermontov's initial encounter with Chechen killers at the Caucasian front. Lermontov's first exile occurred when Ermolov's old comrade, General Aleksei Veliaminov, commanded the Caucasian Line. A perpetuator of Ermolov's genocidal tactics, Veliaminov had annihilated some thirty villages in Chechnya and the Kumyk plain during winter campaigns of 1830 to 1831.[33] He again rampaged in Chechnya for about three months the following year, along with General Grigory Rozen's troops. Before reaching his regiment in Georgia, Lermontov had stopped at a relative's house in Stavropol, where he met Veliaminov and other officers.[34] Furthermore, Veliaminov's new drive into the Kuban river basin was the very expedition in which Lermontov, had he not fallen ill, would have taken part from start to finish. The poet's first exile thus plunged him into Russian military circles where Chechens were considered one of the "worst," if not *the* worst of all Caucasian "savages."

"A Cossack Lullaby" and "Gifts from the Terek" evoke hostility to Chechens along the Caucasian Line but place the hate speech outside the author's voice. Both poems contain the notorious phrase "vicious Chechen," uttered by two very different speakers. In the lullaby, a Cossack mother conjures a knife-throwing Chechen as a bogeyman to make her child go to sleep. The other poem, "Gifts from the Terek," presents a "vicious Chechen" as the killer of a Cossack woman (and the Cossack man who tries to avenge her). Here the speaker is the personified Terek river, boasting about its "gift" – the woman's corpse being carried along the water down to the Caspian. Both these poems formulate a Terek-Cossack antagonism to Chechens (if only figuratively, in the river's speech). Perhaps Lermontov had actually heard such attitudes expressed when he stopped in a Cossack settlement on his way back to Petersburg. Whatever their compositional history, "A Cossack Lullaby" and "Gifts from the Terek" are Lermontov's artful transmissions of somebody else's voice, not his own.

Like these two poems, "Bela" shows us ways of speaking and thinking about Chechens that are outside Lermontov's authorial zone. Lermontov fully appreciated Chechens' exceptionally bad reputation in the Russian army. The voices of Pechorin and Maksim Maksimych demonstrate the authorial knowledge in various ways. (Maksim Maksimych, for instance, recollects the nonpacified Chechens of his fighting years as "cutthroats" and "shaggy devils.")[35] But as we have seen, Lermontov organizes "Bela" in such a manner as to suggest something that none of the characters ever recognizes: namely, that in moral terms, Pechorin is no better and in fact probably much worse than Kazbich, Chechen manhood's major representative.

Nineteenth-century responses to *A Hero of Our Time* showed that civilian readers of Russia's heartland had no particular sensitivity toward Chechens. Chechens are ever present in the experience, speech, and thought of Pechorin and Maksim Maksimych. Interestingly enough, however, Belinsky and other major critics of the time considered Kazbich a "Circassian," that all-purpose term impressed on Russian readers' minds since Pushkin's era.[36] Some members of Lermontov's audience surely had more ethnographic sophistication than others.[37] And yet, after a visit to Petersburg in 1848, the historian and army officer Arnold Zisserman complained that educated Russian civilians still tended to imagine the Caucasus as "one big fortress" under constant attack by "Circassians" or generic "mountaineers."[38]

But if insensitive to Kazbich's exact ethnic identity, commentators of Lermontov's time did not miss Pechorin's disturbing simulation of "savagery" in general. Belinsky tried hard to deny it. He sympathetically interpreted Pechorin as a man tormented by his moral shortcomings and in need of a strong, well-educated Russian woman (like

Pushkin's Tatiana) to bring out the best in him.[39] Hardly broaching Kazbich or Azamat, Belinsky hinged his argument on Bela, whom he thought too culturally backward to reform Pechorin. Despite his reading of Pechorin, Belinsky not long afterward expressed the fear that a young Russian might lapse into "Asian" depravity if he landed among Caucasian tribesmen before assimilating European culture (6:133–38). Belinsky was using the poet Alexander Polezhaev as his illustration. But Pechorin might have easily stirred the critic's anxiety about "savagery" lurking inside the educated Russian, a savagery ready to come out under suitable conditions.

While Belinsky defended Pechorin, the conservative nationalist Burachok ostracized Lermontov's hero from the civilized world.[40] In Burachok's opinion, Pechorin was not a man but a "monster," "vicious (zol) as a hungry wolf." This subhuman creature settles into a "savage's life" in Pyatigorsk and then sinks even deeper into "spiritual and physical bestiality" at Kamenny Brod. After describing Pechorin in these terms, Burachok went on to argue that the supposedly "barbaric" Caucasian peoples should beware of Lermontov's degenerate Russian aristocrat: "Barbarians!" cries Burachok sarcastically, "do not let the hero of our times into your houses!" At least two later Russian critics shared Burachok's disgust with Pechorin's "bestiality" and even called him a "pure savage."[41]

None of these indignant denunciations posed a question so evident to us today: if Pechorin is a mean animal, does he not undermine the official Russian view of the Caucasian war as a lofty civilizing mission? Imperial Russian patriots evaded this train of thought by arguing that corrupt Pechorin was a product of Western influence, atypical of his homeland's best features (features often associated with the simple heart of Maksim Maksimych). As Stepan Shevyrev put it, for example, Russia was a benevolent Christian power trying to repel a "perpetually roaring flood of mountain peoples who know nothing of the social contract."[42] A suitable slant on Russian national character and foreign policy thus made it possible to declare Pechorin wicked, without questioning the moral legitimacy of the Caucasian conquest.

But the nationalistic, imperialist capacity to neutralize Pechorin's degeneracy merely brings us back to our point of departure: how did Lermontov understand "Bela"? Prior to making a statement to the irresolvable issue, we should ponder the author's subsequent participation in heavy action as an officer in Chechnya during his second exile. As with many other aspects of Lermontov's life, combat apparently aroused contradictory feelings in him. Writing in French, with a studied nonchalance, Lermontov told Maria Lopukhina near the end of 1838 that boredom had driven him recently to ask for a transfer to the Caucasian front: "I requested transfer to the Caucasus: request denied. They will not even let me get killed." However, when Nicholas I did in fact exile Lermontov to the north Caucasian combat zone two years later, the poet fell into a depression and told friends he "would be trying to find death as soon as possible."[43] After arriving in the Caucasus, Lermontov conducted himself in a manner strikingly consistent with Pechorin's convictions about predestination ("The Fatalist"). Contemporaries remember the writer mounted on a white horse, leading his men into battle with reckless abandon at the Valerik River in Chechnya in July 1840. After the bloody clash, Lermontov wrote to his friend Aleksei Lopukhin that he had "developed a taste for war" as a gamble with death. This statement simultaneously conveyed the poet's fatalistic readiness to die, once he was forced into heavy action, and his relish for testing himself against his era's standard of military heroism.

Lermontov's same letter to Lopukhin exhibits an inner division as a text in search of the best way to write about carnage. In Pyatigorsk for recuperation by that time, Lermontov recalled his tour of duty: "We were in combat every day. One battle that was particularly hot lasted six hours. We had only 2,000 infantry, and they had nearly 6,000. We fought with bayonets the whole time. Thirty of our officers and three hundred men from the ranks were killed, while the other side left six hundred bodies on the field – that's good, it seems. Just imagine: the ravine where this fun took place still smelled of blood an hour after the battle." This passage begins with an arithmetical dispassion appropriate for a military communiqué but then introduces ironic, colloquial inflections (how "good," what "fun"). These two different types of language suggest authorial uncertainty about what tone to strike. The military censor was peeking over Lermontov's shoulder, of course.[44] But independently of outside pressure, the writer appears to have been testing his voice for a literary performance. In what key might he pitch a poem about combat? How is he to fashion himself as a persona in the Chechen killing field? Will he make himself understood to his audience in the Russian heartland or else fail to bridge the gap between civilians and the remote theater of war?

Lermontov's poem "Valerik" (1840) would tackle these aesthetic and ethical issues in a manner that sustains the irony of Pechorin's being "no worse" than any Chechen. The epistolary "Valerik" moves along several axes at once: the imperial Russian campaign against Chechen resisters; war's incomprehensibility to distant civilians; and tensions between masculine and feminine experience (the poet's addressee is a high-society woman who broke off a love affair with him).[45] While too complex to explore here, "Valerik" reaches a concluding vision of war as senseless slaughter, agonizingly evident in the pristine mountain setting. Prior to Lermontov, other Russian writers had contrasted tranquil landscape to the violence of war (examples are Vasily Zhukovsky's lyric "The Anniversary of Borodino," Bestuzhev-Marlinsky's Caucasian *recits de voyage*, and Polezhaev's narrative poem "Erpeli"). "Valerik," however, squarely situates the authorial persona among the warmongers who are violating a beautiful, bountiful world. Whether Russian or Chechen, all the "bloodshedders" in this poem are "beasts" (a reprise of the imperial army as a "predatory beast" in "Izmail-Bey"). "Valerik" thus presents war as an eruption of barbarism with no national frontiers. And yet, despite the grim insight, the author drops a hint of the human potential for cross-cultural accommodation by pairing himself with a Chechen *kunak*, Galub, at the poem's end. If not a full-fledged plea for international brotherhood, this element of Russian-Chechen comradeship harmonizes with Lermontov's "My Homeland" (1841), a famous poem that disavows various forms of patriotism, including national "glory purchased with blood."

Lermontov's poetry can never tell us beyond all doubt how wittingly he conspired with Kazbich against Pechorin. But Lermontov's disaffection with the monstrous Chechens (of Russian warmongers' descriptions) gives us good grounds for reading Kazbich as a polemical disrupter of the ideology of a "European" mission to "civilize" Caucasian mountaineers.[46] The moral scales of ethnic difference tip in Kazbich's favor, as the plot builds to Bela's death. The result is a literary time bomb, craftily set to explode in the face of Russian anti-Chechen propaganda, whenever and wherever it may arise. The Chechen wars of our time have undoubtedly heightened our sensitivity to the ironic ethnic politics of "Bela." However, to identify Kazbich's subversive relation to Pechorin is not to "read in" something not there. The provocative interchange between these two characters has always been present, waiting for readers who could fully liberate it, instead of denying it or cramping it with opinions about Pechorin's un-Russianness. Lermontov speaks from an era whose historical, cultural specificity we must make an effort to penetrate. But with our postcolonial assistance, he in turn escapes his time to reveal new riches of meaning in his novel.[47]

NOTES

1. V. A. Manuilov, *Roman M. Iu. Lermontova Geroi nashego vremeni* (Moscow-Leningrad, 1966), 80. The Kumyk plain is now Dagestan. Like Chechens, Kumyks are Sunni Muslims (with some Shiites in Derbent and Makhachkala); see Ronald Wixman, *The Peoples of the USSR. An Ethnographic Handbook* (New York, 1984), 43–44, 115–16. Russians derived "Chechen" from the name of a village where they first encountered the people who called themselves the "Nakhchuo" ("God's people"); see M. Ia. Ol'shevskii, "Kavkaz s 1841 po 1866," *Russkaia starina* 79 (July 1893): 90; and Moshe Gammer, *Muslim Resistance to the Tsar, Shamil and the Conquest of Chechnia and Daghestan* (London, 1994), 18.

2. Northern Ossetians are Eastern Orthodox, while southern Ossetians are Sunni Muslims; see Wixman, *Peoples*, 151–52.

3. Prior to the 1860s, when most of the Adyghe ("Circassian," Russian *cherkesy*) peoples migrated to Turkey, Shapsugs were the largest portion of the western peoples in this group. Kabardinians and Circassians proper constitute the rest of the Adyghe family; see Wixman, *Peoples*, 5, 45, 49–50, 88–89, 177. On Tatars, consult Wixman, 186–87. Maksim Maksimych illustrates a nineteenth-century Russian tendency to extend "Tatar" to Caucasian Muslim tribes.

4. On the pervasive impotence of Georgian men in Russian letters, consult Susan Layton, *Russian Literature and Empire, Conquest of the Caucasus from Pushkin to Tolstoy* (Cambridge, England, 1994), 204–11.

5. The quoted detail has its realistic side, as stressed by John Mersereau, Jr., in *Mikhail Lermontov* (Carbondale, Ill., 1962), 100. However, Russian literature's scarce Armenians are notably unheroic, as illustrated by Pushkin's "Tazit" (1829).

6. On the relevant shifts in Soviet ideology, see Konstantin F. Shteppa, "The 'Lesser Evil' Formula," in *Rewriting Russian History*, ed. C. E. Black (New York, 1956), 107–17; and Lowell R. Tillett, "Shamil and Muridism in Recent Soviet Historiography," *American Slavic and East European Review* 20 (April 1961): 253–69.

7. N. Svirin, "Russkaia kolonial'naia literatura," *Literaturny kritik*, no. 9 (1934): 77.

8. T. Voitik, preface to separately issued "Bela" (Moscow, 1937), 9.

9. Mikhailova, *Proza Lermontova* (Moscow, 1957), 245. See also Agil' Gadzhiev, *Kavkaz v russkoi literature pervoi poloviny XIX veka* (Baku, 1982), 18–20; and B. S. Vinogradov, *Kavkaz v russkoi literature 30-kh godov XIX veka. Ocherki* (Grozny, 1966), 102.

10. "Prisoners of the Caucasus: Ideologies of Imperialism in Lermontov's 'Bela,'" *Publications of the Modern Language Association of America* 107, no. 2 (1992): 250–56.

11. See Lewis Bagby, "Double-Voicing in Lermontov's *A Hero of Our Time*," *Slavic and East European Journal* 22 (1978): 265–86.

12. B. S. Vinogradov and M. D. Chentieva, "Lermontov i nash krai," in *Lermontovskii sbornik, 1818–1964*, ed. B. S. Vinogradov et al. (Grozny, 1964), 17–19.

13. S. A. Andreev-Krivich, *Lermontov. Voprosy tvorchestva i biografii* (Moscow, 1954), 73–76, 87–89; and M. Iu. Lermontov, *Sobranie sochinenii v chetyrekh tomakh* (Moscow, 1983–84), 2:521–23.

14. While studying at Moscow University (1830–32), Lermontov may have met the artist Pyotr Zakharov, a Chechen war orphan brought to Russia at the age of three and raised as the ward of Pyotr Ermolov (the general's brother); see Vinogradov and Chentieva, "Lermontov i nash krai," 26–27; and Manuilov, *Roman M. Iu. Lermontova*, 79–80.

15. S. N. Malkov, "Voennaia sluzhba," in *Lermontovskaia entsiklopediia*, ed. V. A. Manuilov (Moscow, 1981), 86–87.

16. Parenthetical citations refer to Lermontov, *Sobranie sochinenii*. Lermontov wrote this letter in French.

17. L. N. Tolstoi, *Dnevnik*, in *Polnoe sobranie sochinenii*, 90 vols. (Moscow, 1928–58), 46:158–59.

18. For recent stress on Pechorin's problematic behavior among the mountaineers, see Richard Gregg, "The Cooling of Pechorin: The Skull beneath the Skin," *Slavic Review* 43 (fall 1984): 287–98; Iu. M. Lotman, "Problema Vostoka i Zapada v tvorchestve pozdnego Lermontova," in *Lermontovskii sbornik*, ed. I. S. Chistova et al. (Leningrad, 1985), 5–22 (esp. 14–15: Pechorin's yelling as a Chechen); and my *Russian Literature and Empire*, 213–19.

19. N. P., "Beduinka. Byl'," *Biblioteka dlia chteniia* 31 (1838), ch. 2, otd. 3:131–56. See detailed analysis in Susan Layton, "Lermontov in Combat with *Biblioteka dlia chteniia*," *Cahiers du Monde russe* 4 (octobre-decembre 1994): 792–98.

20. Andrew Barratt and A. D. P. Briggs, *A Wicked Irony. The Rhetoric of Lermontov's "A Hero of Our Time"* (Bristol, England, 1989), 21–22.

21. Compare the discussion of tension between the "external debasement" and "internal poeticization" of Kazbich as a "child of nature" in Mikhailova, *Proza Lermontova*, 227–29. Maksim Maksimych gives Kazbich a "mug" (*rozha*) (Lermontov, *Sochineniia*, 4:16, 33).

22. R. F. Yusufov, *Dagestan i russkaia literatura kontsa XVIII i pervoi poloviny XIX veka* (Moscow, 1964), 210. Durylin argues that even though Bela is a "princess," she is Chechen, a people that had no nobles (*Geroi nashego vremeni M. Iu. Lermontova*), 49–54.

23. *A Hero of Our Time*, trans. Vladimir Nabokov and Dmitri Nabokov (New York, 1958), 200 n. 33.

24. A. P. Ermolov, report to Alexander I (May 20, 1818), in *Dvizhenie gortsev severo-vostochnogo Kavkaza v 20-50gg. XIX veka. Sbornik dokumentov*, ed. V. G. Gadzhiev and Kh. Ramazanov (Makhachkala, 1959), 24.

24. Orlov's letter to A. N. Raevskii (October 13, 1820), cited in M. O.

Gershenzon, *Istoriia molodoi Rossii* (Moscow-Petrograd, 1923), 28. Orlov concluded that Russia should try to spread "enlightenment" among the mountaineers instead of unleashing war against them.

26. I. Eikhfel'd, "Kavkazskaia doroga," *Otechestvennye Zapiski* (1821), 294.

27. Pushkin, *Sobranie sochinenii*, 3:101, 110. The two ethnic groups appear similarly interchangeable in Pushkin's letter to his brother of September 24, 1820.

28. S. D. Nechaev, "Vospominaniia," in *Poetry 1820–1830-kh godov*, 2 vols. (Leningrad, 1872), 1:107.

29. A. A. Shishkov, "Lonskoi," *Opyty 1828 goda* (Moscow, 1828), 4–5.

30. A. A. Bestuzhev-Marlinskii, *Sochineniia v dvukh tomakh* (Moscow, 1958), 1:289. Published in 1830, this story was signed "A. M."

31. A. I. Polezhaev, *Stikhotvoreniia i poemy* (Moscow, 1981), 169–70.

32. P. Markov, *Zlomilla i Dobronrava – devy gor, ili vstrecha s kazakom* (Moscow, 1834), 9.

33. Gammer, *Muslim Resistance*, 53, 58, 325 n. 84; and John Shelton Curtiss, *The Russian Army under Nicholas I* (Durham, N.C., 1965), 158. Curtiss observes that Chechens were "one of the most peaceful of the Caucasian peoples" until Russia attacked them, 163.

34. A. V. Popov, *Lermontov na Kavkaze* (Stavropol, 1954), 41.

35. Maksim Maksimych's hostile recollection of rebellious Chechens may bring to mind Lermontov's generalized sketch of old-time Caucasian army men in "The Caucasus Veteran" ("Kavkazets"), first published in 1929 (4:145). Remarks on "Kavkazets" appear in Helena Goscilo, "Lermontov's Sketches," *Canadian American Slavic Studies* 14 (spring 1980): 31–35.

36. On Kazbich and Azamat as embodiments of "Circassian national spirit" (cherkesskaia narodnost'), see V. G. Belinskii, *Polnoe sobranie sochinenii*, 13 vols. (Moscow, 1953–59), 4:208.

37. Consider Alexander Bulgakov's letter to Pyotr Viazemsky (July 31, 1841): "Lermontov has been killed – not by a Circassian, nor a Chechen, but by a Russian in a duel," in *M. Iu. Lermontov v vospominaniiakh sovremmenikhov*, ed. V. E. Vatsuro (Moscow, 1989), 460.

38. A. L. Zisserman, *Dvadtsat piat' let na kavkaze* (St. Petersburg, 1879), 1:328–29.

39. Belinskii, *Polnoe sobranie sochinenii*, 4:204–14, 236–38, 263–70.

40. S. O. Burachok, "Razgovor v gostinoi," *Maiak* (1840): 212–23.

41. A. Galakhov in *Russkaia kriticheskaia literatura o proizvedeiiakh M. Iu. Lermontova*, ed. V. A. Zelinskii, 2 vols. (Moscow, 1897), 2:152; and N. V. Shelgunov, *Delo* (1868), quoted in E. E. Naidich, "Geroi nashego vremeni' v russkoi kritike," in *Roman M. Iu. Lermontova 'Geroi nashego vremeni'*, ed. B. M. Eikhenbaum and E. E. Naidich (Moscow, 1962), 181–82.

42. S. Shevyrev, "*Geroi nashego vremeni*," in *Moskvitianin* (1841), ch. 1, no. 2, 518, 520, 533–38.

43. Alexander Herzen, cited in *Lermontov v vospominaniiakh*, 8–9.

44. A letter that Lermontov sent to Lopukhin from Grozny in the latter half of October 1840 reported that "describing the expeditions is forbidden": Lermontov, *Sobranie sochinenii*, 4:451.

45. Analysis of "Valerik" appears in Layton, *Russian Literature and Empire*, 222–29.

46. On the British tradition, see Paul Fussell, *The Great War and Modern Memory* (New York, 1977), 231–69.

47. On the notion of liberating authors from the "captivity of time," see M. M. Bakhtin, *Speech Genres and Other Late Essays*, trans. Vern W. McGee, ed. Caryl Emerson and Michael Holquist (Austin, 1986), 5–7; and Caryl Emerson, "Bakhtin and Women. A Nontopic with Immense Implications," in *Fruits of Her Plume. Essays on Contemporary Russian Women's Culture*, ed. Helena Goscilo (Armonk, N.Y., 1993), 15–17.

# Compassion and the Hero:
# Women in *A Hero of Our Time*

JANE COSTLOW

*La grande question dans la vie, c'est la douleur que l'on cause, et la
métaphysique la plus ingénieuse ne justifie pas l'homme qui a déchiré
le coeur qui l'aimait.*
— Benjamin Constant, *"Adolphe"*

He is a figure whom, surely, it is easy to hate. ("I hate you,"
says Princess Mary – her last words in the novel – and we sympa-
thize.)[1] Exquisitely adept at manipulations of gesture and feeling;
consumed with the desire for power – not so much in its brute
physical sense, as in its psychological manifestations; prey to on-
slaughts of boredom that seem to drive his more sadistic undertak-
ings, his games with the lives of others; he is a man who "understands the vampire" (145), a figure of phallic destruction who gives
us the nihilistic inverse of romanticism's myth of masculine gener-
ativity and genius. Destructive of all he comes in contact with
(women, sentimental soldiers, horses), he is a sadist of the heart, a
man emblematic of Mario Praz's observation that it's but a tiny step
from the demonic stance of Byronic malaise to the cruelties of the
eighteenth-century libertine de Sade.[2] He lays arrogant claim to
the powers of prediction (the plot of sentiment: he knows it all
before), yet is himself "blinded" – unable either to see truly what's
around him,[3] or to know himself. He claims to be driven, in fact, by
what has been *foreseen* for him by an old crone/soothsayer. As readers our vision of him is unsettled by the novel's generic and narrative
motley: travel notes, diary, multiple narrators, convoluted chronology. Endlessly playing different versions of himself, Pechorin comes
into focus only to shift again in his own words or others'.

How then might we bring into focus the women in this novel? Who are they, if not pawns in a larger game of honor played by men? "I look upon the sufferings and joys of others only in relation to myself as on the food sustaining the strength of my soul" (123). The vampiric male draws sustenance from the nourishment of women, not what women make of themselves (Mary's algebra, her reading)[4] but their raw materials: their emotional and bodily life. What to make of those women, how to make them more than ciphers – and how will reading *them* affect our understanding of *him?*

Looking into the distance, Maksim Maksimych sees "Something white" (43) slung across the back of a Circassian horse, something indistinguishable at first in this quickly drawn sketch of a brigand on horseback. What he sees is something white, something stolen, dead or dying, slung across a horse – something his gaze can't make out. What he sees is Bela: the woman's name denotes whiteness – purity but also blankness, the blankness of the blind boy's eyes in "Taman,"[5] the blankness of a psyche that seems shaped only by desire for that which will destroy it. Pechorin's other victim is "Vera": her name too is evocative, this time of faith – a faith that risks everything, that is lost (175), that seems blind to the faults of its object. The women of the novel are victims, save for the smuggler/undine of "Taman," a sea creature who is the vampire's match, capable of emasculating her prey – psychically, if not physically. It is she who is true sovereign of the watery realm to which Pechorin wants to flee ("I am like a sailor born and bred on the deck of a pirate brig. . . ." [180]); she controls the depths; the sailor rides the surface at her bidding. If Mary is a princess of drawing room and empire, the *undine* of "Taman" is princess of the deep, the figure who would draw Pechorin to watery death (water – element of flight, seduction, and death).

Bela, Vera, undine, Mary: these women are way stations on the hero's journey nowhere, figures who enable questions about how male and female inhere in the novel. We may indeed view the novel as a central document in the testament of nineteenth-century masculinity, representing the hussar code of hypertrophied honor and sexual rapacity. Tolstoy, Dostoevsky, and Chekhov were later to parody and condemn that code, but Lermontov's version is more equivocal, more anguished, more extreme. We sense the presence in Pechorin of Lermontov himself – despite all the qualifying distances of narrative transmission. We sense the agony of Lermontov's own short-lived struggle with the world of military academies, the rituals of mysogyny and drunkenness.[6] The novel's power and its prominence in the literary canon derive not from that biographical stream of angst, however. They derive rather from the poet's ability to render that private drama in near-mythic form, to create a narrative that is fascinatingly complex, that has resonance and suggestiveness far beyond Lermontov's own life story.

In this essay, I work toward understanding Lermontov's women – Pechorin's women, really – struck by the fact that, among other things, the dramas he unfolds for us bear uncanny resemblance to struggles of psyche and gender in our world. I undertake this reading by focusing on three different aspects of the novel. First, I address "the woman reader" in Pechorin's diary – a reader he invokes, reviles, yet seems to need. Who is the woman reader in this narrative – and how can she respond to the categories of Pechorin's sketch of her? Second, I examine the four women who are "heroines" for this hero: who are Bela, the undine,[7] Mary, and Vera? Finally, I return to Pechorin, his journey, and the issue of masculinity in the novel. This approach to the women in Lermontov's novel is not, strictly speaking, character analysis but an exploration of characters in their thematic and textual contexts. I aim here to wed our reading of the novel's women to a reading of Pechorin himself and to questions of meaning and masculinity that are at the novel's heart.

———

How is a woman to read this novel – a novel that to a large extent depends on the reader to make sense of the perplexities and perversions of its central hero? In the "Author's Introduction," Lermontov contends that readers' reactions are stubbornly at odds with his intentions – yet his own intentions are wrapped in layers of irony that could frustrate even the most assiduous reader.[8] "Perhaps some readers will want to know my opinion of Pechorin's character" (64). In the absence of that opinion, we are left to our own devices – registering Maksim Maksimych's shift from apologia to hurt feelings; the anonymous narrator's catalogue of physiologically based conjectures;[9] Pechorin's own extensive litany of aphorism, bitterness, and disclaimer; and the professions of hatred and submission that issue from women who love him. The novel counts on those readers, appeals both to our sympathy and our righteous indignation. But what readers is it appealing to? Are they male or female? And just how does that matter?

The readership envisioned by the "Author's Introduction" is both the "young and naive" *publika* that fails to understand nondidactic prose, and the "gentlemen" (*milostivye gosudari moi*) who suspend belief when reading Gothic fictions but feel that Pechorin "can't be as bad as all that" (2). The public here is "provincial," a reader who misses innuendo and subtlety of discourse, who needs a proverbial thrashing to get the point. While *publika* entails a feminine pronoun, the boorish reader imagined seems more male than female – but categorized primarily by his membership in that class of philistine Pechorin later predicts become "peaceful landowners, or drunkards" (84). They are representatives of that settled, married life that is anathema to Pechorin's vision of himself, the very life from which he relentlessly flees.

Women readers – readers as women – come in for a different kind of anathema and ridicule. Pechorin devotes one of his journal entries (June 11) to anatomizing the female mind, with a brief aside on women readers. The passage might keep an analyst going for weeks – it ranges from mocking parody of women's supposed illogic to the recording of "advice" given Pechorin by Dr. Werner (the closest Pechorin comes to a "friend"),[10] advice that consists of urging him to spurn women like the enchanted forest of Tasso's *Jerusalem Liberated* (142). The list of women's characteristics is extensive, if unflattering: jealous, vicious in rivalries of the heart, paradoxical of mind, illogical, lacking in "heart," quick to become indignant, easily duped by poets' flattery (of which of course Pechorin offers none). When the imaginary feminine reader of his pages cries out "Slander!" we are ready to agree.

While this passage from Pechorin's journal does not exhaust the novel's pronouncements on women, it states at least some of them with particular explicitness and poses directly the novel's "problem" for the woman reader. Pechorin claims in this passage both to love women and to have overcome his fears of them, but the novel as a whole surely proves the opposite. So how do we as women readers position ourselves vis-à-vis this text? As readers we are closeted with someone nearly as offensive as Dostoevsky's Underground Man, someone whose trajectory through the novel is defined in large part by forms of ruthless "toying" with women. Do we keep it all at arm's length (a strategy that the narrative sequence presumably works against, since we're drawn progressively more deeply into the texture of Pechorin's mind)? Do we imagine that these women are *not like us,* since the lives of women in the early nineteenth century were so different (has the psychology of abuse and submission changed that much?)? Or do we enter with some mixture of compassion and revulsion into the conflicting mass of impulse and need that is Pechorin? He himself suggests that *this* might be a "woman's way of reading," since women submit "easily" to compassion (128). Much of the work of the novel seems in fact to lie in the direction of eliciting compassion for a man who so revolts us – who seems so little worthy of it. And to the extent that Lermontov identifies compassion with women (not just in Pechorin's asides, but in a figure like Vera), then the reader he seeks is, perhaps, a woman.

What it means to read as a woman is neither simple nor something with which we may have much experience. We have learned to read Lermontov – and Pechorin – without paying the women much due. To come to grips with "women" in the novel entails seeing them through several filters: in the eyes of the men who see them from within the text and then at one further remove – for floating above the issue of Pechorin's view of women is the question of Lermontov's attitude toward his hero. In what follows, I want to look carefully at each of the novel's central women and then finally to grapple with the question of how women function in the novel as a whole. If Lermontov's novel draws us into a fundamentally masculine perspective on women, then what is the tale it tells of men's relationships to women? Can we use Lermontov's irony – that "weapon" evolved by "modern education" (1) – to our own ends, using the portrait of Pechorin to indict the culture it reflects? One is rightly wary of ideology, if it is ideology that condemns men's writing about women out of hand; but then compassion is a precious gesture of the heart and should not be given lightly – nor, necessarily, against oneself.

———

While much critical ink has been spent on considering the significance of narrative – as opposed to chronological – sequence in the novel, the narrative progression of women in the tales is more crucial to our task. That progression – Bela, the undine, Mary, Vera – begins in the binary opposition (in the stories "Bela" and "Taman") of innocence and evil, "whiteness" and chiaroscuro, the powerless and the powerful, the disembodied and the bodily. Each story takes one woman, and Pechorin's encounter with her, as its focus. The portrait of Pechorin himself differs radically in each story: in "Bela" he is a jaded officer amusing himself with an "exotic" woman; in "Taman" he is a naive greenhorn who is others' pawn; in "Bela" he controls; in "Taman" he is controlled; in "Bela" he can dress the part of a native; in "Taman" he is an awkward outsider; "Bela" is marked by his "chilling" smile of indifference to the woman's death; "Taman" is marked by *his* fear and others' indifference to him.

From the binary opposition of Bela and the undine, *Hero* moves on to a more complex structure in "Princess Mary": here there are two women, of similar social stature, both Russian, whose lives intertwine with Pechorin's. And while the contrast between the two is not as stark as that between Bela and the undine, there are significant differences, which revolve around the issues of sincerity, love, and loyalty. Where Mary is presented to us as a creature of society, vulnerable both to flattery and to romantic rhetoric, and as someone whose affections can be easily changed, Vera is true to her name:

Faith. Her love for Pechorin – won in circumstances to which we are not privy – is marked by constancy despite her understanding of his true nature (173). She is, tellingly, presented to us more frequently in solitude – and of all the novel's women, she is granted that rare indulgence: words of her own. When we read her letter to Pechorin at the story's end, we hear from her in a way we have heard from no other woman in the novel.[11]

Lermontov's novel traces, then, a trajectory from blank innocence through feminine danger to an articulate constancy of heart (which the hero nonetheless disdains). While it may be, as Barbara Heldt suggests, that Russian heroines of this period are "underdescribed,"[12] I think we can take even these meager descriptions as significant and capable of being (re)read.

Bela enters Maksim Maksimych's tale as she is literally drawn out from his pseudoethnographic account of an "Asiatic" wedding, an account that both disappoints Orientalizing fantasy ("I had a far better opinion of Circassian women," quips Pechorin [12]) and trades in tales of the exotic. Bela enters the tale singing – but the words cannot be taken in any simple sense as expressive of her self. She sings Pechorin a "compliment" – presumably, at the bidding of her father – in the form of a conventional verse that is both praise and admonition: "He stands like a poplar among [our young warriors], but it is not fated that he should grow and blossom in our garden" (13). In her performance Bela is a kind of ventriloquist's dummy, speaking for the father and the father's culture who are showing her off, the father who – had Pechorin not intervened – would have had trading rights for the daughter.

"Bela" has all the ingredients of an exotic tale: horse thieves, rugged countryside, and a beautiful native woman. Bela herself is repeatedly compared to a mountain gazelle (13, 24); an object of at least two men's desire, she is both easily stolen and in the end easily won over by Pechorin's gifts and grandstanding; once she's been transferred from one owner to another, she's remarkably loyal – reminiscent, in fact, of Kazbich's loyal, beautiful horse, the one he won't take Bela in exchange for.[13]

Bela sings words that have been given to her; is imagined as a beautiful, loyal but will-less animal who is readily available. She is at first a pawn in a complex rivalry between Pechorin, Kazbich the bandit, and Azamat, Bela's brother. Kazbich wants Bela too (13), but he wants his horse more, and so Pechorin (all-knowing, all-seeing, a malevolent deity) can play their desires off against each other. He can also encourage Azamat to become "a man," using the rhetoric of machismo to encourage the boy's theft of his sister: "You're not interested? Well, as you wish! I thought you were a man, but you're still a child; it is too early for you to ride a horse" (20). When Azamat falls to Pechorin's ploy, he returns with "a woman lying across his saddle, her hands and feet tied" (21), a posture that Lermontov will return to in the account of Bela's second abduction: Maksim Maksimych and Pechorin see a horseman "flying at full speed, holding something white across his saddle" (43).

What do we make of this portrait (or is it the merest silhouette) of a woman, the attributes of whiteness, in her name and in this metonym, the linking of the woman to the horse (something we'll return to in "Princess Mary")? Bela is defined by this whiteness – as purity and virginity, perhaps: that which hasn't been touched by another man, that which signifies potential of ownership, that which can be sullied.[14] But it is also the whiteness of blankness, of no color, of nothing: no words, no desire, no story. The whiteness that can serve as the "blank page" for man's – men's – desires, onto which they can write their narrative of tedium and will.[15] Bela becomes the blank page onto which Pechorin's confession of world weariness can be written, as he spins for Maksim Maksimych the tale of his life, an apologia, supposedly, for his crass treatment of Bela (39–41). But the pathos of Bela's death makes Pechorin's reaction seem wholly vicious, so that no apologia will do: Bela's death is also the "blank page" onto which is projected the face that Maksim Maksimych sees: tearless, laughing after death (45, 48). We finish the story with the image of a moral monster.

If Bela emerges from the genre of exotic, "Orientalizing" tales, the heroine of "Taman" comes straight out of Gothic, those fictions "frightful and hideous" that the "Author's Introduction" suggests we willingly believe (2). While its setting and genre are strikingly different, the undine of this story is first described as a "white figure," (68) oddly evoking Bela's whiteness, her ephemerality – as though some feminine Ur-spirit had migrated from one story to the next. In fact, though, the undine and Pechorin's encounter with her couldn't be more different from Bela. If "Bela" narrates men's sexual and cultural power over women, "Taman" presents the opposite. Where Kazbich and Pechorin join inadvertent cause in thieving women, it is Pechorin who is victim of thieving in "Taman." And if "Bela" narrates, allegorically, imperial power victorious over (and destructive of) a feminized other, in "Taman" the power of empire is vulnerable to its shadowy borderlands.

The undine is a creature of those shadowy borders: she comes and goes as if out of nowhere, appearing first to the ear, only later to the eye; her song (unlike Bela's!) speaks of an incantatory pact with the elements; her eyes possess magnetic power; she speaks in riddles, she uses her physicality to entice and then nearly overwhelm Pechorin. To the modern reader, the undine evokes a drama almost banal in its familiarity: the attribution to women of sexual power over men and their use of sex as a "weapon" to unman them. The pistol that gets tossed overboard in "Taman" is Pechorin's weapon, easily readable as a phallic appendage. The undine, through her alliance with primitive forces (the moon and sea, both of which have strong traditional associations with the feminine) is able to control and emasculate Pechorin. If she is essentially "unknowable" (as her riddle-responses to Pechorin's questions suggest), it is not the unknowability of Bela – which derives from an absence of color or features. It is rather the unknowability of chthonic forces that control our lives – those very forces, perhaps, that Pechorin understands as "Fate."[16]

What is striking in this story is just how much it reverses the position of power and chilly masculinity that Pechorin occupies in "Bela." The motif of thieving – one link between the two stories – is instructive here. As noted above, there is an obvious, if somewhat surprising, parallel between Pechorin and Kazbich in "Bela": both

engage in acts of theft; both are implicated – though Pechorin perhaps more so – in Bela's death. Even Pechorin's desire to "pass" for a
Circassian might seem like a kind of Kazbich-envy, evidence of his
infatuation with this figure who represents rude machismo power.[17]
Masculinity in this story is defined by Pechorin and Kazbich: to be a
man is to take what one wants, i.e., to steal. The thing stolen is made
into an object, will-less, less than human. Women and horses play
similar roles in this narrative, as "that which can be desired" or "that
which can be stolen." Shall we designate them as *feminine*, in a syntax
of power and pawns?

How odd, then, to encounter Pechorin in the next story in precisely that syntactic function, with minor modification. Billeted with
smugglers, he is no longer the one who can do the stealing. And
when he tries to desire (and to act on the desire), it turns out he's
been had. Here *he* is the victim of theft – and assault – and the things
that are taken from him in both acts of aggression are metonymies of
phallic identity: his pistol is tossed overboard in his struggle with the
feline/serpentine undine (77); when he returns to his room, what's
gone are his traveling box, a sword, and a Dagestan dagger. These
are all emblems of his masculinity – not just of his phallic power
(sexual or martial) but of his mobility. The traveling box is the
attribute of the "military man on the move" (80), the gauge of imperial power and prerogatives. But this is also – as we realize in all the
stories – Pechorin's (and Lermontov's?) essential definition of masculinity: a man moves on. Whether imaged as the "miserable descendants" of the ancients who roam without conviction or pride (188);
or as the heroic sailor scanning the horizon for a brig – men travel,
and that ability to leave everything behind defines their freedom and
their maleness. The Pechorin of "Taman" is a man without a way to
move, a sailor without a ship, a "holder . . . of a road pass" who loses
his traveling box. Pathetic, unmanned, impotent, and stuck. Uncan-
nily like a woman.[18]

I will leave for the moment the issue of the larger significance of
this story, its narrative of masculinity engulfed by a "serpentine"
woman and its rendering of masculinity in terms of stalled motion.

We will want to return, however, to the anxieties it registers – and to the way those anxieties resurface in Pechorin's encounters with the novel's other two women, Mary and Vera.

"Princess Mary" gives us two women characters, not one, and the correspondingly greater complexity of this story issues both from their relationships with male characters and with each other.[19] Some of the dynamics of this story we recognize from those that precede it: male competition for a woman who is ultimately abandoned; a woman's easy gullibility; the rhetoric of ennui, disdain – and fear – in response to the feminine. Mary and Vera are relatives – however distant – of Bela and the undine, more way stations on Pechorin's strange and destructive journey.

One might view Mary and Vera as chips off a similar block, with whatever distinguishes them a matter more of temporality than essence:[20] Vera might have been Mary in an earlier segment of Pechorin's destructive amorous life. But Lermontov is clearly at pains to distinguish the two, and indeed his "doubling" of the feminine in this tale introduces subtle grades of difference. Both women are representatives of high society, women about whom Pechorin has previously had something to say: he admits in "Bela" to having loved "fashionable belles" (40) and in "Taman" to having been "toyed with" by them (75). In "Princess Mary" there will be both love and toying.

While we might draw up a list of characteristic features of Mary and Vera, both physical and psychological, Pechorin's diary is arguably less concerned with giving us portraiture than with relaying multiple ways of seeing. The tale is, in fact, obsessed – among other things – with metaphors of sight, metaphors that pertain directly to how women are "seen." Dominant among such metaphors are two that characterize, respectively, Pechorin's and Grushnitsky's "ways of seeing": the lorgnette and the rapturous gaze.

The "insolent lorgnette" (90) is added in this tale to Pechorin's arsenal of psychic weapons. He regards (in this case, Mary) in order to dissect, to take apart, "pour mépriser": his account of Mary's eyes and teeth ("I like this kind of lusterless eyes: they are so soft, they seem to stroke you. . . . And her teeth, are they white? This is very important. . . .") elicits Grushnitsky's indignant retort: "You talk of a pretty woman as of an English horse" (88).[21] His lorgnette enables him to sit at a distance – to see without being seen – to spy – to pierce the distance. When Grushnitsky's "gang" appears on the street carrying lorgnettes and plotting Pechorin's death, they have only taken up the "hero's" weapon (136). Emblematic of distance and control, Pechorin's lorgnette bespeaks his "materialism," his tendency (as Grushnitsky puts it) to "see in everything the nasty side" (117). This is the gaze on which he prides himself, the gaze he directs at women: "it is not in a fit of annoyance and vanity that I try to tear from [women] that magic veil, through which only an experienced gaze penetrates. No, all that I am saying about them is only a result of 'The mind's cold observations, / The mournful comments of the heart'"(142).[22]

Grushnitsky, on the other hand, is characterized by a wholly different metaphor of sight. Where Pechorin sees women as English horses, Grushnitsky sees them as "angels," as ethereal, unapproachable beings: "Outside the window, in a crowd of people, stood Grushnitsky, pressing his face to the windowpane and never taking his eyes off his goddess: as she passed by, she gave him a hardly perceptible nod. He beamed like the sun" (111). If Pechorin boasts to the reader of being able to "penetrate" women, to tear from them the veil, Grushnitsky is clearly closer to the groveling poets whom Pechorin reviles – the ones who have called women angels so many times that women ("in the simplicity of their souls" [141]) have believed it.

We might relate this dualism to other aspects of the narrative; Grushnitsky's vague romanticism versus Pechorin's sanguine, "objective" realism; Grushnitsky's idolatry versus Pechorin's iconoclasm; Grushnitsky's unqualified reverence and Pechorin's unerring disdain. But for our purposes here, I want to consider how these metaphors of sight correspond to a rhetoric of knowledge – and how Lermontov suggests a move beyond this dualism (angels/horses; soul/body; adored/disdained), which is circular and impotent.

"Women love only those whom they do not know" (100). Pechorin's words apply equally well to Grushnitsky and to Mary, both of whom love an image, not a person – love without knowing the one they love. Their love depends, in fact, on their not learning the truth. Pechorin's comment challenges us to ask whether his method is any better: is his "insolent lorgnette" a tool of intimacy or control? His professed philosophy of love surely suggests the opposite: "I look upon the suffering and joys of others only in relation to myself. . . ." (123); "To be always on the lookout . . . That is what I call life"(136). We are presented with a world in which love is either self-deception or a form of vampiric visual possession, spying on the other. Knowledge – if it comes – breeds hatred, not love.

The single character in the story – indeed in the novel – who challenges that truism is Vera, and I want now briefly to consider her role in the story and Pechorin's response to her. "She's of medium height, a blonde, with regular features, her complexion is consumptive, and she has a little black mole on her right cheek. Her face struck me by its expressiveness" (97). Vera is, for Pechorin, the past: she represents the power of the past over him (97), its enduring legacy, its ability to catch up with him. She also represents a realm of his life that is not marked by deception, a person who cannot be deceived (106). She is ill; she is married; she has a son; and she is loyal, somehow, to all three – son, husband, and Pechorin. She is represented more frequently than Mary in moments of solitude; Pechorin himself thinks of her longingly when he's alone. She is the only woman in the book who articulates for us her inner life; for her, painful knowledge of Pechorin's true nature does not turn her love to hate. She is a complicated mixture of submission ("you make of me what you want" [151]) and alterity (after all, she alone of the three women who love Pechorin *leaves him*). Her ability to understand and love challenges us – both in understanding her (do we – with our progressive mores – disdain such sacrifice, such compassion?) and in understanding Pechorin. For she challenges *us* to follow her in her affections: if she can still love Pechorin, despite who he is, can we too?

Pechorin's own response to Vera's love is complex and characteristic, and brings us, I believe, to the heart of his own drama of self-knowledge.[23] That drama reaches its peak in Pechorin's response to Vera's letter of farewell. "Like a madman" he tears off in pursuit of Vera, desperate to "see her for one minute," despairing at the thought of losing her forever. "Urging [his] horse mercilessly," he comes close to his aim, only to have the horse drop dead beneath him. "I remained alone in the steppe, my last hope gone; I tried to proceed on foot – my legs gave way under me. Worn out by the agitations of the day and by insomnia, I fell on the wet grass and began crying like a child" (175). Pechorin's uncharacteristic moment of despair is quickly replaced by the denigrations of his rationalizing mind; the outpouring of anguish becomes grist for his analytic mill: "Yet it pleases me that I am capable of weeping" – a statement as devastatingly chilling in its way as Pechorin's dry-eyed laugh after Bela's death. Except what has died here is, arguably, Pechorin himself.

Why does Pechorin chase after Vera with such frenzy, such violence? What does she represent that he cannot bear the thought of losing her? What does he kill in this violent destruction of the horse – a death that seems premonitory of other equine catastrophes in Russian literature: the horse who dies in Raskolnikov's dream, fantastically linked both to the brutalities of Russian life and to his own murder of the old woman pawnbroker? Or the horse who falls beneath Vronsky, emblematic of Anna Karenina herself, whose fall into passion and deceit is a death of self and of the possibility of love? Pechorin's horse dies at his own hand, and he is left – again – without means of conveyance. When he passes once more the scene of this "descent" into childlike weeping (after his final interview with Mary), he cannot look at the horse's corpse – he "sighed and turned away" (180). He must turn away; he must forget, for continuing on his endless journey depends on forgetting. What he will not look at is what he has destroyed: not Vera – for she has escaped – but his own ability to love, his own faintest remnant of the possibility of Faith (Vera).[24] For why does man "roam," wandering without conviction or pride – if not because he has lost the ability to love, the ability to respond to a heart that offers itself. In losing Vera, Pechorin loses himself, and in refusing to look at the corpse of his dead horse, he refuses to acknowledge either that loss or his own destructiveness. The man who claimed to "pierce the veil" wills blindness.

When Pechorin turns from the corpse of his horse, he turns not just physically but rhetorically: he plunges into the rhetoric of freedom and movement that sets him once again on his "journey" – *not looking back*. Werner, his "pal," had earlier warned him not to "turn back" once safely through the "Enchanted Forest" of a woman's amorous claims. Pechorin enacts that advice at the ending of "Princess Mary," turning away from the spectacle of moral death to the fantasy of endless movement, eternal possibility. The self-deception is palpable, and painful. But it brings us to our final stage in considering Pechorin and "his" women: why is he traveling?; what is he fleeing?; why will he not "turn back"?

"My soul has been impaired by the fashionable world, I have a restless fancy, an insatiable heart; whatever I get is not enough; I become used as easily to sorrow as to delight, and my life becomes more empty day by day; there is only one remedy left for me: to travel" (41). There are straightforward answers to the question of why Pechorin travels: he has been exiled for a duel (as his author was exiled for literary indiscretion); he can find no place in a society of both elegant and "unwashed" slaves. But Lermontov suggests answers that go deeper. Pechorin's movement is an obsession, a necessity, an identity; we might say, with Tennessee Williams, that he is trying to "find in motion what is lost in space"[25] – except that we are not certain what he is searching for, or if indeed his travel is motivated by quest. His is surely the inverse of pilgrimage; Pechorin's is a journey that operates on the premise that wherever you go, it is all the same, all foreknown, that there is nothing on earth that could change the shape and texture of your experience.

I have suggested that the women of Lermontov's novel are way stations on Pechorin's journey nowhere: women who represent emotional and sexual hospitality, who offer for at least a time the illusion of joining human society.[26] But if women are his way stations, we can also read women – the fear of women – as the motor of his drive to leave, to be always elsewhere. He is already leaving Bela before she dies; leaving Mary when she offers her hand in marriage; turning away from the corpse of his horse and the memory of Vera. Werner's words about women as Enchanted Forest offer a kind of palimpsest, a figure for Pechorin's *fabula:* the journeyman (who is in Tasso's text a pilgrim crusader) must struggle through the forest of monstrous femininity and keep moving. His successful passage *defines* him as hero: "woe to you if, at the first step, your heart fails you and you turn back!" (142).

Werner's allusion bears comparison with Pechorin's own philosophical musings in "The Fatalist," where the "hero" compares himself to believers of an earlier era, who saw their lives as "illumined" and guided by higher powers (188). This generation lacks such faith, suggests Pechorin, and hence it has come unmoored; its journey is not guided by any higher light; there is no celestial map. Pechorin sees himself as one who roams the earth "without convictions or pride, without rapture or fear." Tasso's crusaders, to our modern eyes, may seem misguided, but *they* knew their paths. Pechorin is driven by nothing – or by something he won't acknowledge.

"Shall I confess? When I was still a child, an old woman told my fortune to my mother. She predicted of me 'death from a wicked wife'" (149).[27] Pechorin's meditations in "The Fatalist" cast him as a quintessentially modern hero, an existentialist in Byronic dress, ennobled by perseverance despite rueful knowledge of life's unmoored absurdity. To such noble meditations we might respond with a different reading – one of a man who wanders in fear, in flight not only from women but from his own femininity: his emotional vulnerability, his need of affection.

Simone de Beauvoir, in *The Second Sex*, suggests that the male adolescent's desire to "roam" is part of his rejection of women, of the whole feminine realm. He feels shame, she writes, at suddenly encountering his mother or sisters on one of his itinerant romps with "the boys." That encounter with the feminine (with a feminine that is not available for sexual exploitation) pulls him back into the realm of immanence, vulnerability, bodily dependence.[28] He is pulled away from "wandering" and freedom. We recognize Pechorin in this account; but we also recognize in him a more complicated impulse – in his "childlike" weeping. Is this not the moment when Lermontov acknowledges the *costs* of "masculinity," the posturing of itinerant freedom, the loneliness of distances that always beckon away from human connection and companionship?

Lermontov assures us in his introduction that he has drawn in Pechorin a portrait of "modern man" as he really is. It is the women of this novel, I believe, who pose most vividly the moral claims and challenges to Lermontov's portrait; as one recent critic reminds us, "Lermontov depicts the majority of his heroines with greater sympathy than his heroes."[29] Vera, in particular, challenges his philosophy of nihilism and endless motion with the actuality of the heart, of love and knowledge paradoxically joined. In Vera, Lermontov suggests, however dimly, the possibility of a wholly different response to the "loss of faith" that Pechorin describes in "The Fatalist." Vera's compassion is a response to Pechorin's demonic irresponsibility. The answer to Pechorin's aimless wandering is precisely what he won't accept: love.

The modern woman reader may take umbrage at this vision of sacrificial, salvific womanhood. It reminds us of numerous other scenarios of nineteenth-century writing – not just Russian – in which a submissive woman redeems an alienated man and comes to represent a kind of love that he cannot live up to. But it's worth noting that if Vera loves Pechorin – and it brings her pain – she does not destroy herself for him. And it's also worth noting that Lermontov's hero is "feminized" in a moment of vulnerability that marks his most human moment. What are we to make of Pechorin? It is the novel's women who help us come to our conclusions. Are we to revile him, with Mary? To attempt to destroy him, with the undine? Or to embrace the painful balance of clear sight and compassion we sense in Vera? "I ought to hate you," says Vera – but she doesn't. And to the extent that we as readers hold back from rejecting out of hand this exemplar of modern masculinity, we follow her lead. Lermontov asks his (male) readers to recognize some part of themselves in Pechorin; but he asks those same readers to experience the catharsis of compassion, a catharsis associated here with the feminine.

I read Lermontov's portrait of this "hero of his time" – a searing portrait of the will to destruction, fear of the feminine, the bitter consequences of willed isolation – as a devastating portrait that indicts a kind of hypertrophied masculinity that is alive and well in our world, as well. We see him as (fallen) angel; we see him in moments of childlike vulnerability and despair; we watch him through our lorgnettes, like a monstrous bug beneath our anatomizing stare. Shall we view him, then, with compassion, the emotion that, no doubt, he wants least of all?

NOTES

Epigraph from Benjamin Constant, "Adolphe," in *Oeuvres* (Paris: Gallimard, 1957), 82–83 [first published 1816]. "The great question in life is the sorrow we cause, and the most ingenious metaphysics cannot justify a man who has broken the heart that loved him," Benjamin Constant, *Adolphe*, trans. Leonard Tancock (New York, 1964), 125.

1. Mikhail Lermontov, *A Hero of Our Time*, trans. Vladimir and Dmitri Nabokov (New York, 1958), 180.

2. Mario Praz, *The Romantic Agony*, trans. Angus Davidson (Oxford, 1970), 83.

3. Joe Andrew discusses the motif of sight in "The Blind Will See: Narrative and Gender in 'Taman,'" *Russian Literature* 31 (1992): 449–76. One can extend his discussion to other chapters of the novel as well.

4. "[The old princess] has great respect for the intelligence and the knowledge of her daughter, who has read Byron in English and knows algebra" (96).

5. "I lit a sulphur match and brought it close to the lad's very nose; it illuminated two white eyes" (66).

6. Akin to Pushkin's ribaldry, the "hussar poems" written by Lermontov at age twenty give us a sense of the ethos of Russian military academies of

the era. See William Hopkin, "Lermontov's Hussar Poems," *Russian Litera-ture Triquarterly* 14 (winter 1976): 36–47.

7. Since this character remains unnamed, I will refer to her throughout as the undine.

8. Owen Ulphe suggests that "Lermontov's introduction raises so much dust that it is difficult to determine where literal seriousness ends and cal-culated leg-pulling begins." See "Unmasking the Masked Guardsman: A Case-Study of the Moral Man in the Immoral Society," *Russian Literature Triquarterly* 3 (fall 1973): 270. I do not support Ulphe's strong defense of Pechorin.

9. "For all its detail, the resultant portrait is vague." See Richard Free-born, *The Rise of the Russian Novel* (Cambridge, 1973), 54.

10. As Freeborn puts it, commenting on the "author's" preface to Pechorin's Journal, "The irony . . . is that Pechorin had no friends to whom to read his journal," 56.

11. In this sense she joins the ranks of those fictional women writers whom Diana Burgin identifies: "such female stories . . . embedded in male texts, have more significance for the production of Russian literature than their fragmentary, obscure, and one-of-a-kind nature would suggest." "Ta-tiana Larina's 'Letter to Onegin,' or 'La plume Criminelle,'" unpublished manuscript.

12. Barbara Heldt, *Terrible Perfection: Women and Russian Literature* (Bloomington, Ind., 1987), 2 and passim.

13. Maksim Maksimych makes the connection explicit: "It is as if I were looking at that horse now: pitch black, legs like taut strings, and eyes no less beautiful than Bela's. . . ." (14).

14. Heldt suggests that "Bela, once sullied, must be killed" (32). Such an interpretation suggests an act of aggression (if not vengeance) not only on Pechorin's and Kazbich's parts but on Lermontov's as well.

15. Susan Gubar offers a brilliant reading of the metaphor of woman as fantasized object of men's creative projections, in "'The Blank Page' and the Issues of Female Creativity" in *The New Feminist Criticism: Essays on Women, Literature and Theory*, ed. Elaine Showalter (New York, 1985).

16. Pechorin represents these forces in his journal in the form of an elderly woman soothsayer, who predicts his death at the hands of a future wife (149).

17. Susan Layton speculates as to the psychological origins of Lermon-

tov's fascination with the "violent machismo" of his Caucasian tales in *Russian Literature and Empire: Conquest of the Caucasus from Pushkin to Tolstoy* (Cambridge, England, 1994), 136.

18. For a reading of the novel that speculates on Pechorin's own femininity, see Aage A. Hansen-Love, "Pecorin als Frau und Pferdund Anderes zu Lermontovs Geroj nasego vremeni" in *Russian Literature* 33, no. 4 (May 1993):413–70. I am indebted to Gerda Neu-Sokol for her help in reading this essay.

19. The competition between Kazbich and Pechorin, then Yanko and Pechorin, finds its female equivalent in the competition between Mary and Vera.

20. Lermontov's depiction of women in "Princess Mary" is indebted to the tradition of the society tale (*svetskaia povest'*). See Helena Goscilo, "The First Pečorin: En Route to *A Hero of Our Time*," *Russian Literature* 11–12 (1982): 129–62.

21. In another instance, Pechorin's eye dissects an elderly woman whose physiognomy becomes, in his perception, a tissue of rough skin and warts (112). Note the symmetries established with other tales: the likening of women and horses in "Bela," as well as the propensity to read psychology through physiognomy in "Maksim Maksimych."

22. Pechorin cites Pushkin (the dedication to *Eugene Onegin*) as an anchor for his cynicism, but the narrator of *Onegin* is not as hardboiled and bitter about women as is Lermontov's hero.

23. As A. Galkin puts it, Pechorin's "mad chase" after Vera is the culminating point of the novel, not the duel with Grushnitsky, "Ob odnom simvole v romane M. Iu. Lermontova 'Geroi nashego vremeni'," *Voprosy literatury* 7 (July 1991): 119.

24. Galkin writes, "But as soon as the hero begins to mock his own genuine outburst, trying to talk himself out of it, to smother his true grief with derisive and mildly cynical arguments, he loses his true self [*teriaet sebia kak lichnost'*], burying forever the 'best half of his soul'" (120). When Pechorin does remember, what he recalls reinforces his desire to forget: "True, I remember now – once, only once did I love a strong-willed woman, whom I could never conquer. We parted enemies. . . ." (105).

25. These words are from "The Glass Menagerie," another narrative about a wanderer who devastates a woman. *The Theatre of Tennessee Williams*, vol. 1 (New Directions, 1971), 237.

26. For a discussion of travel literature and gender, see Eric J. Leed, *The Mind of the Traveler: From Gilgamesh to Global Tourism* (1991).

27. This confession comes in the entry for June 14; the very next entry narrates the crucial role of a "conjurer" in Pechorin's fate.

28. Simone de Beauvoir, *The Second Sex*, trans. H. M. Parshley (New York, 1952), 136.

29. Danushe Kshitsova, "Fridrikh Nitssche i M. Iu. Lermontov" in *Studia Slavica Academiae Scientarum Hungaricae* 33 (1987): 124.

# II ❄ CRITICISM

# Mikhail Iur'ievich Lermontov: The Poet's Personality and His Work

**NIKOLAI KOTLYAREVSKY**

Translated by Matthew Micheli

From a young age, Lermontov tried to find a more capacious framework than short lyrical verses to express his [thought]. As we know, he worked out in detail poetic and dramatic forms with a special [attentiveness]. In his youth he tried to write a prose story but didn't have the patience to finish it. But in the final years of his life, Lermontov returned to prose, clearly because the psychological world of his favorite heroic type had expanded and deepened so much that it required a more detailed and free mode, both of which could be obtained more easily in [the form of a] story or novel. Four attempts to do this were cut short. The first was a sort of fantastical story, "Lugin" (1841). A bit reminiscent of Gogol's "Portrait," it was a very busy story but did not achieve anything for the moral portraiture of the main hero.

A second unfinished story was to have contained the life history of Alexander Sergeievich Arbenin (1841), the well-known hero [of Lermontov's drama "The Masquerade"]. Here we learn nothing that we didn't already know from other compositions of Lermontov's about the childhood and youth of this "Sasha," who appears to be none other than the author himself. Lermontov did not finish the novel "Princess Ligovskaya" (1836), in which he was planning on recounting the youth of the future "hero of our time," Pechorin. Finally, he wrote a story in the form of a passage, in verse, known by convention as "A Tale for Children" (1841). It is hard to catch its meaning because it stops in the very first chapter. It is a story of a gentleman's privileged upbringing. The satire is quite caustic and contains demonic motives. It also tells us virtually nothing new about the poet's worldview. Lermontov worked on all of these stories (1836–41) while working on *A Hero of Our Time*. This might explain a lack of determination that led him to abandon these other works he had started. All he wanted to say in the other works he more completely and more coherently expressed in the stories he combined under the general title *A Hero of Our Time*.

Pechorin's identity is inseparably linked, in our opinion, to the poet's. We have become accustomed to looking at the novel as a literary "last will and testament," as if it were a final confession. It was a confession, indeed, but not a final one. Two years passed between the creation of *A Hero of Our Time* and Lermontov's death. [In this interval] Lermontov in his own personal development succeeded in leaving his hero behind. He managed even to cease liking him, at least judging by what he says in the foreword to the second edition of his novel, where he wrote:

> *A Hero of Our Time*, gentlemen, is indeed a portrait, but not of a single individual; it is a portrait composed of all the vices of our generation in the fullness of their development. You will tell me again that a man cannot be as bad as all that; and I shall tell you that since you have believed in the possibility of so many tragic and romantic villains having existed, why can you not believe in the reality of Pechorin? If you have admired fictions far more frightful and hideous, why does this character, even as fiction, find no quarter with you? Is it not, per chance, because there is more truth in this character than you would desire there to be?
>
> You say that morality gains nothing from this. I beg your pardon. People have been fed enough sweetmeats; it has given them indigestion: they need some bitter medicine, some caustic truths. However, don't think after this that the author of this book ever had the proud dream of becoming a reformer of mankind's vices. The Lord preserve him from such benightedness! He merely found it amusing to draw modern man such as he understood him, such as he met him – too often, unfortunately, for him and you. Suffice it that the disease has been pointed out; goodness knows how to cure it. (2)

As we see here, the author clearly points out his intention to portray "sinful" man and commit him to the judgment of the public. The novel, however, does not bear a didactic element. It is more like a simple journal than a well thought out satire. From the very beginning, when he was working through the novel, Lermontov did not seek to show any "vices" but to simply body forth in Pechorin's realistic portrayal a single moment of his [Lermontov's] own state of mind, as he had done earlier when he had written "The Stranger," "Two Brothers," and "The Masquerade."[1]

By 1841 Lermontov had already surpassed the moment Pechorin encapsulates. We come to this conclusion merely by comparing Lermontov's state of mind in his final years with Pechorin's. In 1840 and 1841, the poet was living through a tortuous period, reworking and changing how he looked at all of the fundamental questions of life. We also know that he could not find a solid definition either for the world or for mankind and that he experienced constant self-contradictions. The process of an unceasing, critical reworking of these fundamental questions shows us that the poet had moved quite a distance from the egotistical "disillusionment" in which Pechorin was mired. For this reason Lermontov was not in any condition to continue his novel, for the subjective state of his soul no longer coincided with [Pechorin's]. For Lermontov, Pechorin became a figure of the past, although for many of [Lermontov's] contemporaries he remained real. At one time Pechorin was a favorite of the public because he gave very clear, if one-sided, answers to life's questions. But those answers required of one neither energy nor deep thought. Lermontov himself possessed [both energy and the capacity for deep thought] and consequently he could not accept Pechorin's worldly philosophy of life. You cannot, in any case, look at Pechorin's worldview as a final conclusion reached by the poet in his pondering about life, its value, and its meaning.

———

As a smart and powerful person, standing above the herd, Pechorin belongs to the very same family of demonic natures we constantly meet in Lermontov's work. [Pechorin] is related to The Demon, Arbenin, and Izmail,[2] but he represents their further development. The Pechorin type of character, however, is more natural and plausible then these others. But like them, he too cannot be called the real coin, as we now understand it. For us, Pechorin's soul is rather dark and mysterious. His inner world is not presented to us in one general and integrated picture but in fragments that allow us to look only furtively into his soul. His past is virtually unknown to us, and we are supplied no clues to his future. As with almost all of Lermontov's characters, we have represented for us a moment in [Lermontov's] spiritual life, a [brief] excerpt from a book in which an entire human life is recounted. We have some evidence that Lermontov wanted to compose a larger novel that would have encompassed a quarter century of Russian life. Perhaps *A Hero of Our Time* represents a part of that novel.

It is well known that *A Hero of Our Time* evoked strong dissenting responses from the critics. Some saw Pechorin as a smart, progressive person who had been ruined by circumstances in life. Others saw in him the fashionable dandy of high society who was quite banal and lived entirely without purpose. The source of the disagreement resulted from the vagueness of the character's image. That is because it was taken from contemporary life and placed in a realistic setting. At the same time, however, it was too generalized and conventional an image.

In the preface to the second edition, Lermontov himself recognizes that Pechorin is not a portrait of any one person. Rather he is a portrait composed of "the vices of that generation in their full development." It was impossible to combine all of these vices in one character without breaking the logic of real life, and this is why we have the controversy. Take, for example, Pechorin's deep and sincere capacity to love versus his flirting or his mockery of women. Consider too his genuine feeling of melancholy against his constant desire to display himself and effect a pose. How can we explain his ability to feel everything of beauty and at the same time his outright and complete disillusionment? Where, in one who possesses a far-from-hardened heart, did his limitless egoism come from?

Pechorin is correct in saying that he has two souls living in him. They abided in the author himself at the time he was writing the novel. Just as much as Lermontov held continually shifting views of life, it was the same with Pechorin, despite the fact that the latter always attempted to be orderly and logical in his thought and behavior.

But Pechorin differs from Lermontov in one very important way – namely, in his spiritual lassitude and the complete absence of thought about the future. Lermontov always had the future in mind and, therefore, tried to unravel life's most serious mysteries. Pechorin answered all of these questions in one fell swoop by suppressing any attempt to deal with them. He made peace with life only passively, even though he was predisposed by nature toward action. In this contradiction (between a decision he has made about life versus basic qualities of character), we are given a key to understanding this shadowy character who undoubtedly combines many of life's truths but also much poetic fantasy.

In 1839, when Lermontov wrote *A Hero of Our Time*, Pechorin's philosophy of life was completely in tune with the author's. In that year Lermontov, having returned recently from his first exile, led a dissolute life in St. Petersburg. Despite high-society diversions, his soul remained in a troubled state. That year he wrote the poems "Don't Believe Yourself" and "The Poet," works that clearly express his doubts about his personal calling. Since childhood Lermontov had suffered under the weight of constant doubts and had tried to drown them in wine and revelry. [He] might easily have come to the conclusion that the best means to fight this debilitating disease was through a complete reconciliation with life that would derive from [two sources]: passivity and an avoidance of all troubling thoughts. He embodied this woeful philosophy in Pechorin. It is understandable that the poet would soon necessarily take his hero's leave, for life impelled [Lermontov] to once again scrutinize quick and arbitrary answers to life's deepest questions. In [Lermontov] himself, Pechorin's better side quickly overcame his vices.

NOTES

Reprinted from Nikolai Kotliarevskii, *Mikhail Iurievich Lermontov: lichnost' poeta i ego proizvedeniia* (St. Petersburg, 1909), 194–99.

1. These are Lermontov dramas, all published posthumously.

2. The eponymous heroes of "The Demon" and "Izmail Bey"; Arbenin of "The Masquerade."

# Lermontov's Poetics

VLADIMIR FISHER

Translated by Joseph Krafczik

## The Process of Creation

Lermontov's artistic methods bear an extraordinary resemblance to that of a painter, who ahead of time makes little sketches in order to use them later for the full canvas. Every detail of the future painting is worked out by him in dozens of small drafts, on which he tries out the colors until they come to life. Many of these sketches remain unused in the big picture. Many combinations of colors go into the painting. But when the final product is completed, all of these preparatory works lose their meaning in the eyes of the artist and lie scattered about like so much rubbish in his studio, at least until they are picked up posthumously by his admirers and transferred to a museum where they remain memorials to his creative work.

This is what occurred with Lermontov's works. Little by little after his death, everything he left behind was published; his creative achievements were issued simultaneously with his experimental works. If we examine the latter as completed artistic works, we experience upon reading them a feeling of aesthetic dissatisfaction: defects in style and composition catch the eye right alongside the bold brush strokes of genius. But Lermontov himself did not have such works as "The Boyar Orsha," "Aul Bastundzhi," "The Lithuanian Girl" published and apparently did not intend to do so. Thus, we have no right to place on them the same high demands that, for instance, "The Novice" ("Mtsyri") meets. We must examine many of Lermontov's works as preparatory sketches, partly used by him and partly unused. Therefore, we will divide all of Lermontov's major works into *experiments* and *achievements:* the latter being far fewer in number. Of Lermontov's major works, only the following represent real achievements: "The Novice," "The Demon," "The Song of the Merchant Kalashnikov," "The Tambov Treasurer's Wife," "Valerik," "The Deserter," "Fairy Tale for Children," and *A Hero of Our Time*. All the rest, his long poems, dramas, beginnings of novels and stories, are dear to us as a part of Lermontov's legacy. Yet they do not reach the height of those standards that we have a right to set for our poet on the basis of his immortal achievements.

With only isolated exceptions, Pushkin did not use old sketches for a new work.[1] He either brought it to artistic completion or he forgot about it. For each new idea, he had new images and expressions. The form was inextricably joined to the content: the two belonged together, and after jotting down a new poem, Pushkin zealously worked on the details, inserting his pointed epithets, rounding out his expressions. The process of Lermontov's creativity is different. He has the details already in preparation – fixed expressions [locutions], epithets, antitheses. The question was where to find a place for them. In Lermontov's imagination, conceptions and plots are changeable. But the basic elements of form are repeated and seek for themselves a suitable application. In short, we observe in Lermontov a great stability of images and expressions in the presence of an instability of plots. If Lermontov's images and locutions take on the character of fixed ideas, he parts with plots without regret.

Lermontov's creative process is defined by recurring images and expressions, for which he selected subjects. A stubborn and persistent observer, he long sought colors to convey something striking to him. First, it would appear as a pale outline in his verse. The second and third time that he repeated the sketch, you look, and the lines have become more defined, the colors brighter; the painting lights up with life and suddenly shines with all the subtleties of a rainbow. Now aglow and distinct, the piece is presented to the reader. And in it, great vitality has appeared, bringing out meaning unsuspected by the poet himself.

# Images, Style, and Language

An image that affected Lermontov during childhood and that also in many ways influenced his style was the *cloud*. In this connection we encounter Lermontov's note from 1830: "I remember a certain dream; when I was about eight years old, it had a powerful effect on my soul. I was alone somewhere riding toward a thunderstorm and I remember the cloud, which was rather small and which was like a torn-off piece of a black raincoat, quickly rushed across the sky: it is so vivid to me, as if I see it now."

This cloud, truly, was always vivid in Lermontov's imagination: he filled his poems to such a degree with clouds, storm clouds, smoke, haze, and fog that to cite all these instances is not possible nor is it necessary: they are in plain view. But these clouds do not make his poetry vague: they do not obscure the sun or the night sky, which are always bright in Lermontov's work. These clouds, smoke, and fog are elusive; they roam and spend their nights in ravines; these really are not even clouds but "fragments of thunderclouds"; they disappear without a trace, fly away "merrily playing on azure," and do not remove the bright sun-filled colors from the painting. For this reason the poet likes to compare human affairs, opinions, and childhood dreams with traceless, disappearing clouds.

Clouds for Lermontov became a symbol of freedom, carefreeness, and also of homelessness. They became for Lermontov a powerful graphic device. Because of them Lermontov's landscape assumes a specific character. When he depicts mountains, he *dots* them with clouds resting on the edges of cliffs and in ravines, and he utilizes an original, often recurring expression – in Lermontov's works, the "mountains smoke" [*gory kuriatsia*]; he employs this expression widely: "in the distance an *aul* began to smoke"; "smoke is blue as it rises in the depth of the valley"; altars smoke; censers, *sakli* [Caucasian huts] and villages smoke; scorched stalks, a wound, and a ravine all smoke; fog curls in smoke.

If Lermontov in childhood developed a passion for clouds, the Caucasus supplied him in this regard with extremely rich material for observation. In *A Hero of Our Time*, he admits he long gazed at their intricate shapes. In examining Lermontov's landscapes, we come to the conclusion that clouds play an enormous role. The point being that Lermontov always depicts them in motion. Remove them from the painting, and all that remains is a majestic, yet frozen, motionless, landscape. Clouds for Lermontov do not interfere with illumination but impart to the painting movement and life. For him, they roam, drift, race, accompany the Terek, rush like a crowd to worship, embrace, weave, and wend their way to the East. Because of them the landscape comes alive.

Observing the slow, creeping movements of clouds, the poet more than once compares them to snakes: "The clouds crawl along *like snakes,* . . . entwining, hissing, like a pile of snakes . . ."; "storm clouds, building and twisting, *like snakes* . . ."; "thither glided the mists, whirling and winding, *like snakes.* . . ." Due to this association, Lermontov transfers his gaze to the *snake* and begins to observe it persistently. He observes its movements, slow, careful, and intricate, and its cunning immobility. Thus, the snake becomes one of the most important devices of Lermontovian comparison. Clouds are compared to a snake's movements, as we have already seen; more than once the poet ascribes the snake's nature to women: "She'll crawl away, like a snake"; "I comprehend your black treachery, [you] snake . . ."; "her snakelike nature kept to this path"; and in *A Hero of Our Time*, the Aragva river is compared to a snake's shining scales (3).

Up to this point, we have dealt with Lermontov's auditory and dynamic images. But the snake – a dynamic image – is visual. The *dagger* for Lermontov is "a friend, shining and cold," a symbol of resoluteness, faithfulness, and strength, which is expressed in the poems "The Dagger" and "The Poet." Lermontov enjoys comparing eyes to a dagger, as we see in the poem "The Dagger." The same feature is mentioned in regard to Pechorin's eyes: "this was a gleam akin to the gleam of smooth steel, dazzling but cold" (57).

Here we enter into the rich world of Lermontov's visual images. His imagination is very colorful; he likes bright tropical light. He does not acknowledge the halftones of the North. For him clouds never obscure the sun, for were they to block it, the artist's brush would go dry. It is curious that he declared his kinship with the storm on so many occasions but was unable to depict a thunderstorm.

In *A Hero of Our Time*, Lermontov avoided description of thunderstorms, describing only the buildup to a storm, contenting himself with the mere mention that a thunderstorm had passed (e.g., while Vera and Pechorin were in the grotto [105]). Far more willingly, Lermontov describes a blizzard or snowstorm, but once again he has no colors for it, conveying it through sounds. All snowstorms for Lermontov are especially melodious and often sing to the accompaniment of a bell. We hear them but do not see them. For example, in *A Hero of Our Time*, we find the following: "the *blizzard hummed* louder and louder, just like one of our own in the north, only its savage melody was more sorrowful, more plaintive. 'You, too, are an exile,' I reflected. 'You *wail* for your wide spacious steppes!'" (33). Here there are no colors, only melodies.

But in the sun's brilliance, Lermontov takes up the artist's brush, and before us appears a "blue and fresh morning," a "rosy evening," "the voluptuous heat of midday," which sometimes turns into "a fire of the pitiless afternoon." Not confining himself to muted shades, Lermontov achieves his light effects by detecting in the environment millions of rays of reflected light illuminated by the sun. When the sun shines, the mountains gleam, rivers, streams, and springs sparkle, and each dewdrop glitters. "How curiously I examined every dewdrop that trembled upon a broad vine leaf and reflected a million iridescent rays!" (162), [Pechorin] exclaims in *A Hero of Our Time*. Depicting the overall landscape, he gazes deeply into each dewdrop. It lights up all of nature with countless flames like a Christmas tree. He sees [gems] everywhere. Streams and mountains are *golden;* the Aragva and Kura [Rivers] wind along the edges of islands with a border of *silver;* the Kazbek mountain peak glows like the surface of a *diamond;* clouds drift like a *pearl* chain, casting pearls on the leaves; the leaves of Oriental plane trees are *emerald.* He often compares dewdrops to tears and stars; and he often compares eyes to stars. Stars are as bright as eyes, and eyes are like stars. Eyes for Lermontov always sparkle – Bela's eyes sparkle, and Princess Mary's shine.

Lermontov's settings take on a plasticity, owing to the tactile sensations that they evoke, from the rigid humps of camels with their patterned coverings to the gentle song of the undine, and from the steep banks of the river to the gentle clouds and mountain ranges. Moreover, he conveys sensations of hot and cold, oppressive and fresh air, and of comprehensive organic states: "At five this morning, when I opened the window, my room was filled with the perfume of flowers growing in the modest front garden" (81); "The sun had just appeared from behind the green summits, and the merging of the first warmth of its rays with the waning coolness of the night pervaded all one's senses with a kind of delicious languor" (161).

Lermontov is an impressionist. Lighting for him does not play an ultimate role. Rather, he selects it in a way that highlights the mood. Pechorin's despair in the steppe, when his steed has perished, is highlighted by the brilliance of the sunset. Occasionally, the poet contrasts lighting with mood. For example, "Princess Mary" begins with a description of wondrous nature, concluding with the question: "Who, here, needs passions, desires, regrets?" (82). When Pechorin goes to duel Grushnitsky, a magnificent description of the morning is given (161–62).

The simple language of thought and the noble voice of passions make Lermontov's prose incomparable and unsurpassed to this day. Of course, if we examine Lermontov's sketches, it is possible to find many language irregularities, but if we look at his results, we have to acknowledge that his language is most proper and precise, notwithstanding [an occasional lapse into cliché]. A specialist may find in Lermontov many deviations, but a nonspecialist gains an impression of living human speech.

## Forms

A poet is one who remains a poet, whatever subject he may choose, and in whatever form he may express it. Lermontov is just such a poet, and the form of his works is determined by this characteristic. In the field of drama, for instance, he did not venture beyond experiments.

Social problems were of interest to Lermontov. But for him to represent them, it would have been essential to closely scrutinize a way of life. Yet by nature our poet was too lyrical for this. In *A Hero of Our Time*, however, Lermontov frees Pechorin from everyday existence by placing him in an exotic setting. There he could delve into [Pechorin's] psychology, providing, instead of a novel, several independent tales unified in the personality of a single hero. In formal terms, *A Hero of Our Time* is not a psychological novel. The author himself, as is evident from the title and preface, attached to his work a social meaning. Consequently, it was taken as that by the critics.

The social significance of *A Hero of Our Time* is not subject to doubt, but, in form, his is not a social novel. This is because Lermontov depicts his hero outside of the social milieu that produced him and that he had to deal with. Owing to [Pechorin's] isolation, *A Hero of Our Time* for a foreign reader or for later generations retains only psychological interest. The author rejects [Pechorin's] milieu and takes an interest in the hero, placing him before the reader in a variety of [unique] circumstances. To observe [his hero] freely, [Lermontov] was not constrained by consistency or even chronology. The novel (we shall retain this label) lets us first *hear* about the hero (in "Bela"), then gives us a direct view of him (in "Maksim Maksimych"); next his diary is opened up to us. But this is contrary to the chronology. Pechorin's journal was completed by him in Maksim Maksimych's fortress and left there. Consequently, everything described in Pechorin's journal took place either immediately before or simultaneous to the Bela story.

———

We now turn to [the novel's] parts, which are only loosely joined together. The first story, "Bela," is one of those tales in which the author recounts an event related to him by chance. The author provides the story in the style of travel notes. When, after a series of descriptions of the journey, Maksim Maksimych begins his account of Bela, the author does not hesitate in several places to interrupt him to provide descriptions, depicting it all in the sequence in which it actually occurred and giving pause to the story as dictated by the conditions of the journey.

Despite the natural development of the Bela narrative, noted by Belinsky, and despite the fact that the author seasons it with remarks and observations characteristic of Maksim Maksimych's speech, Lermontov could not avoid the danger to which writers, who put their account into the mouth of one of their characters, are exposed. The account is too literary for a junior captain. In one place, Lermontov [i.e., the traveling narrator] even felt it necessary to apologize to the reader for offering Kazbich's song in verse. Furthermore, it is unlikely Pechorin would have made a confession to Maksim Maksimych, and because he could not understand it, it is even more unlikely that Maksim Maksimych would have memorized [Pechorin's] monologue word for word. That which is appropriate in a romantic poem, for example, in "The Novice," is risky in a novel.

The section [entitled] "Maksim Maksimych" is an essay. It is not as independent a piece as the other parts of the novel. It relies on what precedes it and acts as a basis for what follows. "Taman" and "The Fatalist," however, represent clear narrative accounts, as it was understood by Chekhov, who was particularly enchanted with "Taman." The author here is an observer modestly concealed behind his characters. Especially in "Taman," [Pechorin] provides no rationales, offers no explanations, and imposes nothing on the reader. He only paints, assuming readers to be sufficiently subtle judges to make up their own minds. Chekhov also aspired to this kind of artistic objectivity. We do not know the past of the smugglers; we do not know their state of affairs. But through a few carefully dropped hints, we ourselves should be able to expand on the picture provided even though we do not know more than the author. We are granted complete freedom of relationship with the heroes depicted [in this chapter].

———

A particular feature and distinction of Lermontov's ["Princess Mary"] is that it is constructed according to the rules of drama. At the beginning is the exposition: Pechorin examines and studies, with the aid of Dr. Werner, "spa society," in which he becomes engaged. Next comes the complication. The relationships of Pechorin, Grushnitsky, Vera, and Princess Mary become bound in a single knot. On the sixteenth of May, the dramatic struggle begins. Pechorin enchants Princess Mary, makes a fool of Grushnitsky, and captivates Vera. Next we have the expansion of dramatic effect: Princess Mary becomes infatuated with Pechorin; Grushnitsky becomes angry; Vera is overcome by jealousy; Grushnitsky concocts a plot against Pechorin, Pechorin says to Princess Mary, "I don't love you," and Vera [fears that] her relationship with Pechorin might be exposed. The crisis approaches – the duel. Grushnitsky perishes, glimmerings of hope are aroused in Princess Mary, and Vera gives away her secret to her husband. The denouement arrives: Pechorin disposes of Mary, parts with Vera, alienates Werner, and takes his leave. Both the development and denouement gather all of the characters into one knot. This narrative drive, similar to the drama, distinguishes "Princess Mary" and anticipates Dostoevsky's novel-dramas.[2]

NOTES

Reprinted from V. Fisher, "Poetika Lermontova," *Venok M. Iu. Lermontovu: Iubileinyi sbornik* (Moscow-Petrograd, 1922), 196–236.

1. Note the end of "Bakhchisarai Fountain" (*Bakhchisaraiskii fontan*) and the poems "Desire" (*Zhelanie*) and "The 19th of October" (*19 oktiabria*), 1825, 1831, and 1836, respectively.

2. The full text of Fisher's article may be found at http://www.uwyo.edu/lermontov.

# The Caucasus and Caucasian Peoples in Lermontov's Novel

SERGEI DURYLIN

Translated by Matthew Feeney

The action of the novel takes place in the northern Caucasus in the mid-1830s. The historical background, against which Lermontov develops episodes from the life of Pechorin, involves the war with the inhabitants of the mountains. Pechorin himself, along with other notable characters in the novel – including Grushnitsky, Maksim Maksimych, Vulich, the anonymous author of the "travel notes," and many others – are officers who are direct participants in the war tsarist Russia was waging against the mountain tribesmen. The story, "Bela," portrays a series of Caucasian mountain people from the tribes against which the war in the northern Caucasus was then being fought. In the character Kazbich, Lermontov depicts an *abrek* (a warrior shaped by historical events fighting against the Russian conquerors). In "Bela" Lermontov portrays, on the one hand, the life and daily routine at a Russian fortress on the so-called "Caucasus Line," and, on the other hand, a mountain *aul* [village]. In the story "The Fatalist," a large Cossack village is depicted on that same line. In "Bela" and "Maksim Maksimych," the author portrays the Georgian Military Road with all of the peculiarities of movement along it in a time of war. In the story "Taman," a small naval port is depicted by Lermontov. The society of officers, relaxing and "taking the cure" at the waters after their military expeditions, is portrayed in the story "Princess Mary." Stories, arguments, and opinions about the mountain tribes of the Caucasus, who find themselves at war with Russia or who have recently been conquered by its forces, are continually discussed by the novel's characters. Information is scattered here and there in the course of the novel about the life, national peculiarities, and military characteristics of the Circassians, Chechens, Kabardinians, Ossetians and Shapsugs, along with information about so-called "peaceful mountain peoples," *abreks*, and others.

To understand the conditions of life under which the action of Lermontov's novel proceeds and in the midst of which all of the peculiarities of Pechorin's character are revealed, it is necessary to compare them to those aspects of historical reality, the northern Caucasus of the 1830s, that deliver up an authentic vision of reality in Lermontov's novel.

It was as far back as the time of Peter I that the conquest of the shores of the Black and Caspian Seas had begun with the aim of annexing the rich lands of the Caucasus to Russia. In 1801 under Alexander I, Georgia, exhausted by devastating raids by Turkey and Iran, was annexed to Russia. Thereafter, Mingrelia (1803) and Imeretia (1804) followed. Azerbaijan also came under the power of Russia during the reign of Alexander I. Under Nicholas I, Armenia was annexed, and in this way "tsarist Russia consolidated its rule in the Transcaucasus. The high Caucasian Mountains separated the new possessions from the rest of Russia. Warlike mountain people lived in these mountains. No one could subdue them."[1]

In establishing and protecting routes into the new Transcaucasian possessions, tsarist Russia inevitably had to enter into battle with the mountain tribes whose land the routes crossed. "Hiding in the gorges and forests, knowing perfectly their native mountain territory, the freedom-loving mountain people tenaciously fought for their independence and step by step defended their land" (ibid). The war of tsarist Russia with the Caucasian mountain tribes lasted over sixty years, required incalculable sacrifices, and concluded with the victory of the Russian forces only in 1864.

The tsarist Russian offensive against the mountain peoples from 1816 to 1827 was notable for its intensity. The "Commander-in-Chief of Georgia" and the commander of the forces in the Caucasus was then a well-known field general, a participant in Suvorov's campaign into Italy and in the war of 1812, Aleksei Petrovich Ermolov (1772–1861), "the furious *shaitan* [devil]," as the mountain people called him.

The era of the greatest of Russia's successes occurred "under Ermolov," or "under Aleksei Petrovich," to use Maksim Maksimych's expression. In the 1830s, when the action of *A Hero of Our Time* takes place, the Russian offensive into the depths of the mountains had come to a halt. In some places it became quite paralyzed due to the successful and fierce actions of the mountain tribesmen, who, to repulse tsarist Russia at the beginning of the decade, gathered around Gazi Mukhamed, and then, from the middle of the decade, around the figure of Shamil. Shamil was able to unite the mountain tribes closely and for twenty-five years waged systematic and often victorious battle against the Russian forces. It is quite understandable, therefore, that in the 1830s in Russian officers' circles, the "Ermolov epoch" was remembered as a longed-for time of military prowess.

Ermolov's plan to subjugate the Caucasus required steady penetration into the depths of the mountains, but with forward advance occurring only after a decided "pacification" of specific districts and peoples had been achieved. Ermolov energetically built the Caucasus Line, which, with a chain of fortresses, Cossack villages, fortifications, cordons, and guard posts, was to link the Black Sea with the Caspian. Passing along the banks of the Kuban, Laba, Malka, Terek and Sunzha rivers, it was to overcome all of the tribes of the Caucasus by means of a continuous assault. Ermolov began the "pacification" of the Caucasus in 1818 in Chechnya, on the eastern flank of the line that he created. He conducted a military terror against the mountain tribes. First, he summoned the elders of the Chechens above the Terek and declared to them that if they allowed thieves and brigands to pass through the territory, their *amanaty* [hostages – S. D.] would all be hanged to the very last man. He announced to them, "I do not need peaceful swindlers. Choose either obedience or complete and utter destruction."[2]

Ermolov's methods of subjugation of the Caucasus elicited approval not only in military-gentry circles of the 1820s to the 1830s but also from a representative of [an emergent] liberal bourgeoisie, N. A. Polevoi. He wrote of his approval in his journal, *The Moscow Telegraph:* "Bloodthirsty animals can be kept in obedience only by fear. . . . In the rocks of the Caucasus, wild laughter and the death-rattle of the throttled victim can be the only answer to the protests that come from our gentlemen philanthropists."[3]

Voices of opposition were heard only rarely and weakly in the 1830s. To the voices of Lorer and of Pushkin, [the latter] who spoke out in *A Journey to Arzrum* of the need to introduce the rudiments of enlightenment and culture into the mountains, we may add the voice of the Decembrist Baron A. E. Rozen, a soldier who fought in the Caucasus and equated Ermolov's military-administrative methods to those of the conquerors who destroyed the populations of Central and South America. "We were imitating the old former line of action. Like Pissarro and Cortés, we transported only armaments and fear to the Caucasus and made our enemies still more wild and warlike, instead of luring them to the conquered plains and to the banks of the rivers with [the enticement of positive] benefits, such as flowering settlements."[4] These individual voices of protest were drowned out by a choir of bourgeois landed gentry, who recognized the Ermolov terror as the only reliable means of asserting Russian sovereignty in the Caucasus. In the 1830s, that the Caucasus should be conquered and annexed to Russia became an unquestionable truth for the government, all political leaders, the gentry, and the bourgeoisie. General Ermolov, who governed the Caucasus from 1816 to 1827, was the earliest and the most straightforward champion of applying brutal pressure on the free Caucasus. [His policy was the] result of the dictates of Russian tsarism.

Tsarist Russia, intruding into the depths of the Caucasus, clashing with its many peoples, and giving no consideration to the peculiarities of their history, nationality, or culture, strove to transform them into a faceless, systematically exploited human mass of colonial possessions. In addition, among Russian officers the widespread attitude toward the mountain tribes was the same as that toward savages, who they saw as standing either outside culture altogether or at its lowest level. Their attitude conformed completely with the aims of tsarist policy in the Caucasus.

Lermontov gives his Maksim Maksimych an unreserved admiration for Ermolov, which is historically accurate and allows him to express the dominant attitude toward the Caucasian natives that was natural to all Ermolov's followers. The Russian junior captain has only one general definition for all of the greater and lesser peoples of the conquered Caucasus: "these Asiatics are terrible rascals" (4). According to Maksim Maksimych's vulgarized qualification, all of the natives of the Caucasus are divided up into "an exceedingly stupid people" and "robbers." To the first group, for example, belong the Ossetians, while to the second group belong the Kabardinians. Both the one and the other, however, he considers equally "cheats" and "swindlers."

In the "Bela" chapter's description of the poor dwellings and the meager mode of life of the Ossetians made by Maksim Maksimych, the author of the memoirs reinforces the junior captain's all-too-common judgment of the Ossetians as nonentities. This attitude is full of the new colonial conquerers' arrogance in regard to the peoples of the Caucasus. The [traveling] narrator's labeling of the Ossetians as "wretched people" (8) yields only a little to the round condemnation the junior captain makes of the whole people: "An extremely foolish people . . . they don't know how to do anything and are incapable of any education" (8).

---

Speaking with contempt about the Ossetians, Lermontov's junior captain is reluctantly forced to acknowledge the military valor of some of the other mountain peoples. But in all other categories, he equates them to those same Ossetians he believes are doomed to historical nonexistence. He says, "Our Kabardians or our Chechens, although they may be robbers and paupers, are at least reckless daredevils" (8). Maksim Maksimych's opinion of the fighting abilities of the Kabardinians is similar to that of the model officer of the

Caucasus described by Lermontov in his essay, "The Caucasus Veteran" ["*Kavkazets*"]. There he says, "About the mountain people this is how he talks 'A good people; only they are really such Asians! The Chechens, it is true, are scoundrels, but to make up for it, the Kabardinians are really simply fine people. Well, there are also people among the Shapsugs who are fairly good, only they do not at all compete with the Kabardinians, either in dress, as they are not able to, or in skill at riding horseback, although they also live cleanly, very cleanly.'"5

———

Any recognition of the mountain peoples' courage cannot, however, completely alter the basic opinion of the junior captain that his enemies are some kind of rabble among humanity. The same Maksim Maksimych, despite acknowledging the military prowess of the Kabardinians, pronounces a judgment under which he, in general, subsumes all mountain peoples: "Well, you see, it is a known fact that these Circassians are a bunch of thieves. They cannot help filching anything that is within reach; they may not need the thing, and yet they will steal it . . . " (45). The opinion of the junior captain about the "thieving" of the Circassians represents the collective opinion of the conqueror's camp. It is defamation of a whole nationality, a deliberate method used in the battle against other nationalities. We find an example of such condemnation in *Travels to Georgia*, a travelogue in which the author says, "The Circassian has all the cruelty of a bloodthirsty animal, surpassing it in cunning. A tiger that is not hungry does not throw itself onto a man. It seeks to hide itself from the enemy, which it hates. The Circassian is the opposite. He attacks suddenly, steals everything he can from the victim, and if the captive does not represent anything that he is greedy for, i.e., cannot offer him any great price for his ransom or cannot work in the *aul*, the Circassian kills him, regardless of age or sex. Does the tiger kill for the pleasure of killing? Only the Circassian is capable of such a useless, evil deed."6 In similar opinions and judgments of the Russian military, gentry, and bourgeoisie, guilt for their lot was placed on the mountain peoples. This, as it were, authorized the conquerors to condemn whole nationalities of the Caucasus to punishment.

―――

Where does the action of "Bela" take place? To which mountain tribe do Bela, Azamat, and Kazbich belong?

To the [traveling narrator's] question "And have you been long in the Chechen region?" (8), Maksim Maksimych gives an affirmative reply: "Yes, I was stationed there for about ten years with my company in a fort near *Kamenniy Brod* [Stone Ford]" (8). In another statement Maksim Maksimych says that he was once situated "in a fort beyond the Terek" (10). This points to the *left*, eastern flank of the Caucasus Line, to Chechnya. The fortress "beyond the Terek" could only be on the Sunzha line or still farther south into the depths of Chechnya. This identification of the location is confirmed by Pechorin's words to Bela: "You are not in love with some Chechen, are you? If you are, I'll let you go home immediately" (25), i.e., to the Chechens, since the native home of Bela was in all "about four miles from the fort" (11). Bela herself, worrying about Pechorin as he leaves to go hunting, fears a "Chechen [will carry] him off to the mountains" (36).

It is clear, too, from Bela's brother, that the action of the story takes place in Chechnya on the Sunzha line, for he says, "Now, my father is afraid of the Russians and won't let me join the mountain bands" (16). This is a clear indication that the *aul* of Azamat's father is located in the foothills of Chechnya and that the boy longs to go to free, mountainous Dagestan, to Shamil. In fact, all of the natives, the heroes of "Bela," speak about their lives from the perspective of Chechens.

Maksim Maksimych describes an occurrence in the home of Bela's father as an event at the home of *Circassians* and objects to Pechorin's remark to him about Bela: "You don't know these Circassian girls" (26). The Circassian tribes, however, did not live "beyond the Terek" but beyond the Kuban, not on the left (or eastern) but on the right flank of the Caucasian Line. The geographical description by the junior captain sharply contradicts his ethnographic description.

This contradiction is permitted by the fact that "Circassian" in the usual sense of the word in the 1820s and 1830s is often understood to mean in general all mountain peoples of the Northern Caucasus with whom the war was fought, just as "Tatar" implies, in general, all Caucasians of the Islamic religion. In this sense Pechorin too, knowing correctly the nationality of the Chechen girl Bela, nevertheless calls the female inhabitants of her native *aul* "Circassian girls."

———

Maksim Maksimych's years of service were passed in a combat infantry battalion. He had been stationed in one of the forts along the Sunzha line during the most tumultuous time of Ermolov's battle with the Chechens. The old field officer, despite his contempt toward these "Asiatics," was sympathetic to them as "daredevils" because of their courage and stubborn fortitude in the war against the Russians. In 1838 the junior captain says, "Nowadays, thank goodness, things have quieted down" (8). The post-Ermolov decade (1827–37) was indeed not accompanied by any conspicuous "affairs" with the Chechens. This lull continued until the end of 1839. The demand by Russia for mass payment in the form of weapons caused extreme agitation among the warlike Chechen people. Imam Shamil raised the separate tribes of Chechens against Russia, and toward autumn of 1840, all of Chechnya was enveloped in rebellion. Mikhail Lermontov had to personally participate in action against them in Lesser and Greater Chechnya in the summer and autumn of 1841, including the bloody battle at the Valerik River on the eleventh of July (described in his letter to V. A. Bakhmeteva).[7]

The fortress, in which Maksim Maksimych's company was situated and where Pechorin was sent after the duel with Grushnitsky, was built in the middle of the recently subjugated Chechen population for the purpose of maintaining Russian authority. At the same time, it was to provide a secure base for further advances into the depths of Chechnya.

Maksim Maksimych notes that "About four miles from the fort there lived a [peaceful] prince" (11). The Chechens, Circassians, and other mountain peoples who had recognized the authority of the Russians were called "peacefuls." But because the mountain people's oath of allegiance to the Russian government was always compelled by force and never given freely, a clear distinction between "peaceful" and hostile populations did not really exist.

-----

Lermontov portrayed three "peaceful" Chechens with historical accuracy. The most loyal of them and, by all appearances, the most "peaceful," was the old prince, Bela's father. The prosperous stratum of the population, as everywhere, reconciled itself best with foreign rulers, for they suffered less from the conquerors, who preserved for the upper stratum of the subjugated population its dominion over the working people. Russia secured power over the mountain princes, *khans* and *beks*, by preserving their titles and possessions and bestowing on them "favors" from the tsar. Thus, the "peacefulness" on the part of the upper stratum of the Chechen people was bought. As we have seen, Azamat, the son of the so-called "peaceful prince," confesses to Kazbich, "My father is afraid of the Russians and won't let me go to the mountain bands" (16). Being a bold youth, Azamat easily changes his status from that of a "peaceful" to that of an *abrek*, a title of significance throughout the mountains. Kazbich, however, is an enemy of the Russians and uses the label "peaceful" only as a cover. He both participates in raids on Cossack villages and conducts trade with the Russians in their fortresses.

Lermontov portrays the "old prince," the father of the Chechen girl, Bela, as the *kunak* [patron] of the Russian junior captain Maksim Maksimych, who commands the fortress on the Sunzha line. Maksim Maksimych says, "We were *kunaks* . . ." (11). The custom of *kunachestvo* [patronage] was widespread throughout all of the Caucasus as a quasi-life insurance policy in an era of interminable intertribal warfare, when "every Circassian, who crossed into lands foreign to him was considered an enemy or an alien. [If he did] he ran the risk of being killed, robbed, or sold as a slave somewhere. To avoid this danger, he had to have in the foreign society an influential patron, a *kunak*, on whom he could rely. No one could harm a person protected by *kunachestvo* without the threat of the *kunak*'s vengeance."8

Receiving its original meaning from the widespread mountain custom of hospitality, the word *kunak* acquired the further sense of "friend" or "good acquaintance." Maksim Maksimych uses it in this sense, calling both the "old prince" and Kazbich *kunaks*. In his essay "The Caucasus Veteran," Lermontov describes the friendship of the Russian officers with "peaceful" Circassians and Chechens as an everyday occurrence: "He made friends with a peaceful Circassian and started to go to visit him in his *aul*. A stranger to the refinements of city life, he came to love the locals' plain and wild ways. Ignorant of Russian history or of European politics, he gave himself up to the poetic traditions of the warrior nations. He fully understood the morals, manners, and customs of the mountain peoples, learned by name their epic heroes, and memorized the genealogies of the key families. He knows which prince is trustworthy and which is a swindler, who is friends with whom, and between whom there is blood. He speaks Tatar well."9 Maksim Maksimych proves to be just such a Caucasus veteran. He is a *kunak* both to the "peaceful prince," the father of Bela, and to the *abrek*, Kazbich, who is considered to be one of the "peacefuls" as well. Such *kunachestvo*, simply the maintenance of good relations with different elements of the surrounding native population, was a sound political device for a commander, like Maksim Maksimych, of the garrison.

NOTES

Reprinted from S. N. Durylin, *Geroi nashego vremeni M. Iu. Lermontova* (Moscow, 1940; reprint, Ardis, 1986).

1. Cf. *Kratkii kurs istorii SSSR*, ed. A. V. Shestakov (Moscow, 1938), 89.

2. P. I. Kovalevskii, *Kavkaz: Istoriia zavoevaniia*, 3d ed., vol. 2 (St. Petersburg, 1915), 153.

3. *Moskovskii telegraf*, no. 15 (1833): 337.

4. A. E. Rozen, *Zapiski dekabrista* (St. Petersburg, 1907), 261.

5. *Minuvshie dni*, no. 4 (1928): 23.

6. *Moskovskii telegraf*, no. 15 (1833): 336.

7. See http://www.uwyo.edu/lermontov for this and other Lermontov letters.

8. N. Dubrovin, *Istoriia voiny i vladychestva russkikh na Kavkaze* (St. Petersburg, 1871), vol. 1, bk. 1, 78–79. Cf. vol. 2, bk. 2, 44–45.

9. *Minuvshie gody*, no. 4 (1928): 23.

# Lermontov's Fate

EMMA GERSHTEIN

Translated by Dawn Moser

The tsar took with him Lermontov's book and said good-bye to his sick wife in Ems. Accompanying him on the ship to Peterhoff on the twelfth of June 1840 were Benckendorf and Orlov. On 12/24 June,[1] Nicholas I began writing his letter to the emperoress and continued it the entire time he sailed. On 13/25 June we find the first mention of Lermontov's novel: "I worked and [then] read the entire [first part of] *Hero*, which is well written. Later we drank tea with Orlov and chatted all evening. He is one of a kind!"

On the morning of 14/26 June, the travelers once again proceeded to read. At three in the afternoon, the tsar writes, "I worked and [then] continued to read Lermontov's composition. The second volume I find [so far] to be less successful than the first.[2] The weather became marvelous and we were able to eat lunch on the upper deck. Benckendorf was terribly afraid of the cat, so Orlov and I tormented him. We have a cat on board and it is our main focus during our leisure hours."

At seven in the evening, the novel had been read to the end. "During this time," Tsar Nicholas I wrote,

I completed *Hero* and find the second part disgusting and completely worthy of being [considered] entirely fashionable trash! It is the same portrayal of despicable and incredible characters like the ones met in modern foreign novels. These types of novels spoil dispositions and developed embittered personalities. And although one reads these cat sighs [sentimental nonsense] with repulsion, they still have a painful effect because in the end you become accustomed to believing that the whole world consists only of such [abhorrent] characters [as Pechorin]. Even the deeds that appear at first glance to be good are committed out of vile and impure motives. What kind of results can this produce? Hatred and disgust for humanity! But is this the purpose of our existence on earth? People are entirely too inclined to become hypochondriacs or misanthropes; so, why then write such drivel and arouse suspicion or develop such tendencies! Thus, I repeat, in my opinion, this is a pitiful talent, indicating an author with a disturbed mind.

The character of the captain is portrayed successfully. I began reading the tale and I hoped to myself and was pleased to think that he would somehow be the hero of our days, because this type of person is usually found to be more real compared to those who are so indiscriminately accorded the epithet [hero]. Undoubtedly, the Caucasian corps consists of many of them, but rare is the person who is able to discern them. The captain himself, however, appears in this work as an embodiment of hope, albeit an unrealized one, and Mr. Lermontov did not succeed in developing this noble and simple character. He replaces [Maksim Maksimych] with despicable, very uninteresting characters, who, better than boring us, had best remain anonymous if only not to cause disgust! Bon voyage Mr. Lermontov; let him, if it is at all possible, clear out his head in those surroundings [the Caucasus] where he can complete the portrait of the captain [firsthand]; that is, if he has the slightest capability of understanding and portraying the character clearly.

We know now that previously, in the palace, the [Imperial family] had read [Lermontov's] "The Demon." We understand there was disagreement for a long time between the tsar and tsarina about Lermontov's significance [as a writer]. Nicholas I and Benckendorf followed the poet's publications. That Lermontov's short poem "January 1st" aroused indignation serves as proof of this. The poem "In Memory of A. I. Odoevsky" hardly passed unnoticed [in the palace] when it was printed in the December 1839 edition of *Notes of the Fatherland*, for it mourned the death of [the Decembrist] A. I. Odoevsky, one of Nicholas I's "friends of December 14." The tsar clearly did not understand [Lermontov's poems] "Meditations," "The Poet," and "Bored and Sad." He found them no less boring than Pechorin's diary [in part 2 of the novel]. But in all of Lermontov's poetry published in *Notes of the Fatherland*, Nicholas I instinctively felt the strength of Lermontov's hostility toward him, a strength that would yield Nicholas I no authority.

The beginning of Nicholas I's letter to the emperoress allows one to wonder about Benckendorf's participation in discussions of *A Hero of Our Time*. Fooling around on the deck of the ship, the Bogatyr,[3] the chief of secret police [Benckendorf] most likely succeeded in sharing with the tsar his point of view on Lermontov's novel. This conclusion is supported by the resemblance of the tsar's letter to the Third Section's [secret police's] censorship of Lermontov's "The Masquerade," in Benckendorf's response to which the young writer is compared to a French *Book of Horrors*. In content, Nicholas I's comments about *A Hero of Our Time* seem inspired by Benckendorf's personal review of "The Masquerade." Its style too resembles Benckendorf's message to the tsar about Lermontov's poem on the death of Pushkin: "Taking up this theme is itself an act of provocation and in the end an expression of shameless freethinking well beyond criminal in nature," [Benckendorf wrote in response to that poem].

At three in the afternoon on the fourteenth of June 1840, the tsar announces to the tsarina that in the morning he had read "Princess Mary" and "worked," which means he was busy with Benckendorf. After lunch they cavorted with the cat and read *A Hero of Our Time* to the end. This is where the comparison of Pechorin's ideas and passions to "cat sighs" [may have been] born. The mockery of Lermontov's hero, Pechorin, is saturated with the tsar's and Benckendorf's personal hatred of the author.

NOTES

Reprinted from E. Gershtein, *Sud'ba Lermontova* (Moscow, 1986), 100–3.

1. The two dates reflect Old and New Style calendars (the reason behind the October Revolution of 1917 being celebrated in November).

2. The 1840 edition of *Hero* appeared in two volumes.

3. A *bogatyr* is a Russian epic hero (here, used ironically).

# The Genuine Meaning
# of Pechorin's Monologue

V. LEVIN

Translated by Katrina Jones

The question [addressed] here concerns the interpretation of Pechorin's famous monologue:

> Yes, such was my lot from my very childhood! Everybody read in my face the signs of bad inclinations, which were not there, but they were supposed to be there – and so they came into existence. I was modest – they accused me of being crafty: I became secretive. I felt deeply good and evil – nobody caressed me, everybody offended me: I became rancorous. I was gloomy – other children were merry and talkative. I felt myself superior to them – but was considered inferior: I became envious. I was ready to love the whole world – none understood me: and I learned to hate. My colorless youth was spent in a struggle with myself and with the world. Fearing mockery, I buried my best feelings at the bottom of my heart: there they died. I spoke the truth – I was not believed: I began to deceive. . . . (126–28)

Students of Lermontov's work invariably examine this monologue as one of the key passages in the novel. Some have named it "Pechorin's confession," others "the epitaph of a lost spirit," and to a third group, it comes as an illustration of Lermontov's response to Russian higher society of the 1830s. In a word, when the question is about how Pechorin "came to such a pass in life," without fail this monologue is brought to the forefront. The force of this inertia has had a great power. These three interpretations of the monologue have become almost axiomatic. However, an attentive investigation of this passage indicates that the monologue plays a completely different and far from vital role in understanding Pechorin [as victim]. There is no basis whatsoever for attaching a literal meaning to his words.

In "Pechorin's Journal," this monologue is delivered up in the entry for June 3. It begins with the following: "I often wonder, why do I so stubbornly try to gain the love of a little maiden whom I do not wish to seduce, and whom I shall never marry?" (122). This question and the answer that follows disclose the purpose behind Pechorin's ensuing monologue. All the conversations Pechorin has with Princess Mary are subordinated to this purpose. They are all links in a continuous chain, the splendid moves of a chess master. Let's look at the phrase that precedes it: "I thought a moment, and then said, *assuming a deeply touched air*" (126; the emphasis is mine – V. L.). If one *assumes* a certain air, it means one is playing a role; and thus we have reason to disbelieve him. Pechorin delivers his touching monologue, watching to see what impression his words make on the princess. With this passage, will he arrive at his goal and win the contest? Yes, his tactical move is magnificent and he hits the mark – the princess is amazed and touched. Immediately after the monologue we read, "At that moment, I met her eyes; tears danced in them; her arm leaning on mine, trembled; her cheeks glowed; she was sorry for me! Compassion – an emotion to which all women so easily submit – had sunk its claws into her inexperienced heart" (128). How cold and calculated these phrases are. How contrary they are to the tones and sounds of Pechorin's own high-flown and passionate confession! Note too that the entry is completed in Pechorin's journal that very same day. Pechorin has not had time to gain a new perspective on this event. He has written it down immediately – hot on the heels, so to say. Pechorin does not win the contest with this one move. He methodically, precisely, and with a great deal of forethought, enacts his role. Earlier, on May 22, he had written: "After several moments of silence, I said to her, *assuming a most submissive air* . . . " (113). For May 29 we read: "every time that Grushnitsky comes up to her, I *assume a humble air* and leave them alone together" (121). And further: "I looked at her intently and *assumed a serious air*" (121). In the game Pechorin plays, there is a third party – Grushnitsky. In conversations with him (as on May 16), Pechorin also "*assumed a serious air*" (101) (all of the previous emphases are mine – V. L.). By the fifth repetition of "I assumed . . . an air," Lermontov shows that, in the spectacle this superior actor performs, the monologue in question serves as only one of the techniques (perhaps the most effective and decisive) in Pechorin's "assault" on Princess Mary. There is yet another small monologue by Pechorin that consists of the same style. It also is directed at Princess Mary (from the June 7 entry, i.e., about four days after the first monologue): "Forgive me, Princess, I have acted like a madman. . . . This will not happen again: I will see to it. Why must you know what, up to now, has been taking place in my soul? You will never learn it, and so much the better for you. Adieu" (138). At the beginning of "Princess Mary," we encounter almost exactly these same words. It occurs after Pechorin describes Grushnitsky and the romantic air he affects, something that amuses not only Pechorin but Lermontov too:

> His coming to the Caucasus is likewise a consequence of his fanatic romanticism. I am sure that on the eve of his departure from the family country seat, he told some pretty neighbor, with a gloomy air, that he was going to the Caucasus not merely to serve there, but that he was seeking death because . . . and here, probably, he would cover his eyes with his hand and continue thus: "No, you must not know this! Your pure soul would shudder! And what for? What am I to you? Would you understand me? . . . " and so forth. (85)

Twice Pechorin stands before Princess Mary in the pose of a Grushnitsky. This does not occur by chance. Always the psychologist, Pechorin calculates that by wrapping himself up in a halo of romance, he will all the more quickly achieve his aim. Pechorin *consciously* imitates a person at whom he scoffs.

But if we discount what purpose Pechorin pursues in his monologue, if we discount the melodramatic form of the monologue, might not Pechorin be conveying the truth [about his upbringing]? Perhaps he had decided beforehand to tell the princess about his past, assuming that the truth would have a better effect here than any fabrication. But this is doubtful. From Maksim Maksimych's narrative, we find that there never had been a conflict between young Pechorin and society. Pechorin was sufficiently rich and wellborn that society opened its wide and hospitable arms to him. Pechorin was hardly an outcast (as one would conclude from his monologue). On the contrary, he enjoyed great success in society. This is confirmed by the relationship between Pechorin and Mary's mother, Princess Ligovskaya, who from the very beginning looks upon him as a man of her own circle. Some kind of unpleasantness, a duel perhaps, had occurred that caused his exile to the Caucasus – certainly [this unpleasantness] does not compromise him at all in the eyes of society, and the doors of the drawing rooms, as usual, are opened wide to him.

Pechorin deceives not only the gullible Princess Mary – which once again shows Lermontov's genius. The monologue seriously deceives many an experienced critic. But not all of them. Belinsky, for example. It is not easy to gloss over this first, inimitable student of *A Hero of Our Time*. Belinsky immediately understood that Pechorin's words were not entirely truthful and that the monologue is not a tale about his past at all. The purpose of the monologue was clear to him: "Poor Mary! How methodically, and with such calculated accuracy, his evil soul leads her on the road to ruin!"[1] In this way the great critic summarizes his impression of the monologue. This observation (as well as a later remark, "she accepted everything for ready coin") certifies that Belinsky did not believe Pechorin at all. At least he didn't take Pechorin's "confession" for "ready coin."

Another [Belinsky] remark should not mislead us either: "Did Pechorin speak sincerely or did he dissemble? It is difficult to make up one's mind definitely, for it appears to be both" (240). As we shall see, we can be certain that Belinsky did not doubt the monologue's veracity. He doubted something else. When a great actor enters a scene, he forgets that he is playing some kind of role. He *sincerely* believes that he is Lear, Othello, or [Gogol's] Khlestakov. It is precisely this type of sincerity Belinsky had in mind [in regard to Pechorin].

Belinsky distinguished the concepts "truth" and "sincerity" carefully. The critic proposes that Pechorin, while pursuing specific goals and uttering undoubted lies, in his own remarkable improvisation, inspired as it is, at some point begins to believe in its truth and consequently *lies* with absolute *sincerity:* "It is not only that [types of the Pechorin stripe] remember well their deepest sufferings," [Belinsky] writes, but that "they are also inexhaustible in their invention of the *imaginary*" (240). With these words Belinsky conveys clearly his disbelief in the *veracity* of Pechorin's words. But with the greatest subtlety, the critic reveals the *sincerity* within *deceit:* "They do not care if the cause of the complaint is true or false, and their bilious sorrow is, in like manner, candid and genuine. Moreover, they begin with a *conscious lie* . . . and continue it until they can finish in utter sincerity. They do not know when they lie or when they tell the truth, when their words are a cry of the soul, or when they are [empty] phrases" (241). Unfortunately, later critics of the novel have not understood what was utterly clear to Belinsky – with genuine artistic inspiration and talent, Pechorin plays his joke on Princess Mary, who herself has created the role of the romantic hero for him, [and comes to believe it himself].

NOTES

Reprinted from V. Levin, "Ob istinnom smysle monologa Pechorina," *Tvorchestvo M. Iu. Lermontova* (Moscow, 1964), 276–82.

1. V. G. Belinskii, *Polnoe sobranie sochinenii*, 13 vols. (Moscow, 1953–59), 4:241.

III  PRIMARY SOURCES

# Reviews of *A Hero of Our Time*
## circa 1840

S. P. Shevyrev

Translated by Lisa Holte and Matthew Feeney

Since the death of Pushkin, not one new name has, of course, shone as brightly on our literary firmament as that of Mr. Lermontov. A decisive and multifaceted talent, he commands both poetry and prose almost equally well. It usually happens that poets begin with lyric verses. Their dream floats about at first in the uncertain ether of poetry. Some remain in it always, while others proceed into the lively and varied world of the epic, of drama, and of the novel. Lermontov's talent was evident in both genres from the very beginning. He was both an inspired lyric poet and a remarkable narrator. Both worlds of poetry, our inner (spiritual) and outer (real) world, were equally accessible to him. It seldom happens that life and art appear in such close and inseparable friendship in such a young talent. Almost every work of Mr. Lermontov is an echo of some strongly lived moment. At his very entry into the literary arena, the keen observation, the lightness, and the skill with which the narrator captures whole characters and reproduces them in art are remarkable. Experience cannot already be so strong and rich in these years, but in gifted people it is replaced by some kind of presentiment through which they comprehend in advance the secrets of life. Fate, alighting upon such souls, which acquire at their birth the gift of foreseeing life, immediately opens unto them the source of poetry. Thus lightning, striking by chance a rock that conceals in itself the source of the water of life, opens an outlet for it, and a new freshet bursts forth from the open lap of nature.

A true feeling for life combines harmoniously in the new poet with a true feeling for the refined. His creative energy readily subdues images taken from life and lends them a living personality. In his writing, the stamp of an austere taste is apparent. There is no sugary exquisiteness of any kind, and from the beginning we are struck by his soberness and his fullness and conciseness of expression, which belong to more experienced talents. In youth they indicate the power of an unusual gift. In a poet, in a lyric poet still more than in a writer of prose, we see a connection to his predecessors. We observe their influence, an influence that is highly understandable, for a new generation has to begin where the former generation has left off. In poetry, in all the suddenness of its most brilliant occurrences, there has to be a memory of tradition. The poet, no matter how original, still has his teachers. But we note with particular pleasure that the new poet underwent various influences, and that he did not have any teacher who was exclusively his favorite. This itself already speaks in favor of his originality. But he himself is also visible in many of his works by virtue of his style. His remarkable uniqueness is apparent.

With particular pleasure we are prepared on the first pages of this critical review to greet a fresh new talent upon his first appearance, and we dedicate this detailed and sincere critique to *A Hero of Our Time* as one of the most remarkable works of our modern literature.

———

All of our poets of genius were conscious of the splendid variety of Russian localities. Pushkin, after his first work, which had its birth in the open domain of fantasy, fed on Ariosto, began with the Caucasus to create his first picture of real life. Then the Crimea, Odessa, Bessarabia, the interior of Russia, St. Petersburg, Moscow, and the Urals followed in turn to feed his rakish muse.

It is remarkable that our new poet also begins with the Caucasus. It is not through any gift of fantasy that many of our writers have been enamored of this land. Here, apart from the magnificent landscapes of nature that seduce the eyes of the poet, Europe and Asia come together in eternal, irreconcilable enmity. Here Russia, organized in a civil manner, repulses the streams of mountain peoples that eternally burst forth, not knowing what a social contract is. Here lies our eternal battle, insignificant to the giant Russia. Here a duel takes place between two forces, the civilized and the savage. Here there is life! How can the imagination of the poet not long to be here?

This striking opposition of two peoples was alluring to him. The life of one of them is cut from European cloth and knit together by the [thread] of decent society, while the life of the other is wild, unrestrained, and recognizes nothing except freedom. Here our artificial, overly delicate passions, cooled by society, meet the stormy natural passions of men who are not subservient to any reasonable restraints. Here curious and striking extremes are encountered by the observer-psychologist. This world of a people that is completely different from ours is already poetry in itself. We do not love that which is ordinary to us, that which always surrounds us, that which we have seen enough of and heard much about.

From this we understand why the poet's gift, of which we speak, revealed itself so quickly and freshly in view of the mountains of the Caucasus. Pictures of majestic nature acted strongly upon his receptive soul, born for poetry, and it opened up quickly, like a rose when struck by the rays of the morning sun. The landscape was spread out before him. Vivid images of the life of the mountain tribesmen struck the poet. These were mixed with memories of life in the capital. In an instant, society was transported to the gorges of the Caucasus, and all of this animated the artist's thoughts.

Having explained some of the background for the stories of the Caucasus, we move to the details. We turn our attention one after another to pictures of nature and locale, to characters, and to the life of society. We then fuse all of this together in the character of the hero of our stories. Here we will also try to grasp the author's main idea.

Marlinsky schooled us in the brightness and colorfulness of the paints with which he loved to create pictures of the Caucasus. To the ardent imagination of Marlinsky, it did not seem like much to humbly observe the splendid nature of the region and convey it with a true and apt word. He was disposed to force images and language. He threw the paints wholesale from his palette in any manner at all and thought the more colorful and varied it was, the more of a likeness the copy would have to the original. Pushkin did not paint in this way. His brush was true to nature and at the same time ideally fine. In his "Prisoner of the Caucasus," the landscape of snow-covered mountains and *auls* enclosed, or better, constrained all of the events. Here people are present for the landscape, as in [the paintings of] Claude Lorrain, and not the landscape for the people, as in [the paintings of] Nicolas Poussin or Domenicino. But "Prisoner of the Caucasus" has already been forgotten by readers, that is, since the time that [Marlinsky's] "Ammalat-Bek" and "Mulla Nur," with the varied colorfulness of their paints, all generously splashed together, grabbed their attention.

That is why we can say with special pleasure in praise of the new painter of the Caucasus that he was not keen on the colorfulness and brightness of his paints but was true to the taste of the refined. He subdued his sober brush in pictures of nature and copied them without any exaggeration or sugary exquisiteness. The road across Gud-Gora and Krestovaya and the Koishaur Valley are described accurately and vividly. Anyone who has not been in the Caucasus but has seen the Alps can tell that this has to be true. Nevertheless, it should be remarked that the author does not like to remain too long on the pictures of nature that only occasionally flash before his mind. He prefers people and hurries past the gorges of the Caucasus, past the wild streams, to the living person, to his passions, to his joys and grief, to his cultured or nomadic way of life. That is what is better. It is a favorable sign of a developing talent.

Pictures of the Caucasus have, moreover, been described to us so often that it is good to wait a little to repeat them in all their detail. The author has very skillfully put them in the far distance, and they do not obstruct his view of events. It is curious to us to see pictures of the life of the mountain tribesmen or of the lives of members of our society in the middle of this splendid natural setting. That is how the author has done it. In his two main stories, "Bela" and "Princess Mary," he has painted two pictures. The first of these was taken more from the life of the tribes of the Caucasus. The second was taken from the worldly life of Russian society. There are a Circassian wedding ceremony with its rituals; the dashing surprise raids of horsemen; dreadful *abreks* with their lassos; and Cossacks with theirs; constant danger, the trading of cattle, theft; vengeful urges, and the breaking of oaths. There is Asia, of which the people and the rivers, according to the words of Maksim Maksimych, are such that "there is absolutely no depending on them!" (34). But all the more vivid, all the more striking is the story of the stealing of the stallion Karagyoz, which is part of the plot of the story. This story is taken accurately from the life of the mountain tribesmen. The horse is everything for the Circassian. On it he is tsar of the world and laughs softly at fate. Kazbich owned the horse Karagyoz, jet black, with legs like steel wires and eyes as good as those of a beautiful Circassian girl. Kazbich has fallen in love with Bela but does not want to exchange his horse for her. Azamat, Bela's brother, gives up his sister, if only to take the horse away from Kazbich. This story is all drawn directly from the customs of the Circassians.

In the second picture, we see Russia's educated society. It brings to these splendid mountains, which are the nest of a wild and unrestricted way of life, both its physical ailments, the fruits of an artificial life, and its psychological ailments, imparted to it by strangers. Here there are cold, empty passions. Here there is the intricateness of emotional depravity. Here there are skepticism, dreams, scandal, intrigues, a ball, a contest, and a duel. Like chalk, all of this world is at the foot of the Caucasus! People in fact appear as ants when you look at their passions from the heights of the mountains that touch the sky.

This world is all a true copy of our lively and empty reality. It is one and the same everywhere, both in St. Petersburg and Moscow and at the waters of Kislovodsk and Ems. It spreads its empty idleness, slander, and petty passions everywhere. To show the author that we have followed with all due attention the details of his pictures and have compared them with reality, we will take the liberty of making two observations that concern Moscow.

The novelist, in depicting characters borrowed from the life of high society, blends with them the traits normally common to the whole estate. He introduces Princess Ligovskaya from Moscow and characterizes her with the words "She likes risqué anecdotes and sometimes, when her daughter is not in the room, says improper things herself" (96). This trait is totally untrue and sins against the locality. It is true that Princess Ligovskaya spent only the last half of her life in Moscow, but since she is forty-five years old in the story, we think that in twenty-two and a half years, the tone of Moscow society would have broken her of this habit if she had ever acquired it in the first place. For some time it has been fashionable for our journalists and authors to attack Moscow and to impute to it terrible tales. Everything that could not be true in another city is sent off to Moscow. Under our authors' pens, Moscow appears not just as some kind of China, for thanks to travelers, we have accurate information about China. No, it is sooner some kind of Atlantis, a storehouse of fables where our novelists pile up whatever whim their wayward imagination allows.

————

But in our author's stories, we do not encounter any slander of our princesses in the person of Princess Ligovskaya. She may however be an exception. No, there is an epigram on Moscow princesses that purports they look upon young people with some contempt, that this is a habit in Moscow, and that they only feed on forty-year-old wits there. All of these remarks, it is true, were put in Dr. Werner's mouth, who, according to the author, is distinguished by an observer's keen eye. But not in this case. It is apparent that he has not lived for long in Moscow. It was only during his youth, and he took some event that pertained to him personally for a general habit [of Moscow society]. He noticed after all that young ladies in Moscow pursue learning, and he adds that they do that well. And we agree with him. To study literature, however, does not guarantee deep erudition. Nevertheless, let the young ladies of Moscow study it. What on earth is better for men of letters, not to mention society itself, which can only gain from such pursuits on the part of the fair sex? Is this not better than cards, than scandal, than chatter, than gossip? But we will return from an episode permitted by our local relationships to the subject itself.

From a sketch of the two main pictures consisting of Caucasian life and the life of Russian society, we turn to the characters. We will begin with the secondary characters, not with the hero of the stories, about whom we are obliged to speak in more detail later, for the main connections between the novel, our life, and the main idea of the author lie in him. From among the secondary characters, we must give first place, of course, to Maksim Maksimych. What a whole-hearted character, a native Russian. What a good soul. The subtle infection of Western education has not penetrated here. Under the false outward coldness of a soldier who has seen plenty of danger, he has preserved all of the ardor and all of the life of the soul. He loves nature inwardly but is not enraptured by it. He loves the music of the bullet because his heart beats more strongly upon hearing it. How he takes care of the sick Bela! How he comforts her! With what patience he waits for his old acquaintance, Pechorin, after hearing of his return! How sad he feels when Bela does not remember him before her death! How pained his heart is when Pechorin indifferently extends his cold hand to him! How he still believes in feelings of love and friendship! Fresh, untouched nature! A clean, childlike soul in an old soldier! Here is the sort of character in whom our Old Rus speaks! And how he is elevated by his Christian humility when, upon denying all of his better qualities, he says "And in truth who am I to be remembered by anybody before death?" (47). We have not met such a dear and vivid character in our literature for a very long time. This is a character who is more pleasant to us because he is taken from native Russian life. We must even complain somewhat to the author that it is as if he does not share our righteous indignation with Maksim Maksimych when "Pechorin out of absentmindedness or for some other reason proffered his hand while Maksim Maksimych wanted to throw himself on Pechorin's neck" (62). After Maksim Maksimych, we look at Grushnitsky. His personality, of course, is unattractive. He is truly a frivolous person. He is vain. Without anything to be proud of, he is proud of his gray cadet overcoat. He loves without love. He plays the role of the disillusioned, and herein lies the source of Pechorin's dislike for him. Pechorin does not like Grushnitsky due to the very same feeling that is peculiar to us when we do not like a person who imitates us, who turns into an empty mask that which in us is living essence. He does not even have the feeling that distinguishes our veterans, the feeling of honor. This is some degenerate from among [military] society, capable of the basest and blackest deed. The author reconciles us somewhat to his creation not long before the latter's death, that is, when Grushnitsky confesses that he despises himself.

Dr. Werner is a materialist and a skeptic, like many doctors of the new generation. Pechorin was bound to like him because they both understood each other. A vivid description of his character is especially memorable (92). Both of the Circassians in "Bela," Kazbich and Azamat, are described by traits common to all of their tribe, in which the individual differences between characters cannot yet have reached the degree that exists in educated society.

We will turn our attention to the women, especially to the two heroines, who both fall victim to the hero. Bela and Princess Mary form between themselves two firm opposites, like the two societies from which each comes. They belong among the poet's most wonderful creations, especially the first. Bela is a wild, timid child of nature, in whom the feeling of love develops simply, naturally, and, once having developed, becomes an unhealed wounded heart. The princess is no such person. She is the product of an artificial society, in whom fantasy is discovered before the heart. She is a person who beforehand imagined for herself the hero of a novel and wants by force to embody him in one of her admirers. Bela very readily comes to love the person who has even abducted her from her parents' house. But he did this out of passion for her. As she believes, he at first devotes himself only to her. He loads the child with gifts. He charms her every minute. Seeing her coldness, he feigns despair and is ready to do anything.

The princess is no such person. All natural feelings are quelled in her by some kind of harmful dreaminess, by some kind of artificial upbringing. We love the warm human gesture in her that makes her lift the glass to the ailing Grushnitsky when he, leaning on his crutch, bent forward in vain to pick it up. We understand also that at this time she blushed, but we are annoyed at her when she glances back at the gallery afraid that her mother might have noticed her kind deed. We do not complain at all about this to the author. On the contrary we render full justice to his power of observation, which skillfully captures a prejudice that does not bring honor to a society that calls itself Christian. We also forgive the princess when she takes a great interest in Grushnitsky's gray overcoat and concerns herself with him as an imaginary victim of the persecutions of fate. In Princess Mary this scarcely springs from a natural feeling of compassion, of which, like a pearl, a Russian woman can be proud. No, in Princess Mary this is the impulse of an overly delicate feeling. Her love for Pechorin proves this. She comes to love in him the unusual, which she seeks, that ghost of her imagination by which she is carried away so thoughtlessly. Here the dream passes from her mind to her heart, for even Princess Mary is capable of natural sensations. Bela, through her terrible death, dearly atoned for the thoughtlessness of her memory of her dead father. But by her fate the princess gets what she deserves. A harsh lesson to all princesses whose natural feelings are repressed by artificial upbringing and whose heart is spoiled by fantasy! How dear, how graceful this Bela is in her simplicity! How saccharine the princess is, with all her calculated glances, in the company of men! Bela sings and dances because she feels like singing and dancing and because she amuses her friend by doing so. Princess Mary sings so that she will be listened to and is annoyed when she is not. If it were possible to combine Bela and Mary into one person, we would have an ideal woman in whom nature would be preserved in all its charm but in whom a secular education would not be only an outward gloss but something more essential in life.

We do not consider it necessary to mention Vera, who is inserted by the author as a secondary character. She is not attractive to anyone. She is one of the victims in the stories and still more a victim of the author's need to complicate the intrigue. We will not turn our detailed attention to the two short sketches "Taman" and "The Fatalist" either, in the presence of two of the most significant. They only serve as supplemental stories that are there to better develop the character of the hero, especially the last story, where Pechorin's fatalism is evident. (It is consistent with all his other characteristics.) But in "Taman" we cannot omit the smuggler without some mention. She is a fantastic creation in which both the airy uncertainty of the outlines of Goethe's Mignon, to whom the author himself alludes, and the gracious wildness of Hugo's Esmeralda are partly combined.

Just as the threads of a web, weighed down by brightly winged insects, are linked to an enormous spider that has entangled them in its net, all of the novel's events, characters, and details are intertwined with the hero of the story, Pechorin. We will go into the character of the hero of our story in detail. First, we will address the main relation of the work to life, and second, discuss the author's main idea.

Pechorin is twenty-five years old. In appearance he is still a boy. You would believe him to be no more than twenty-three, but looking more intently, you would, of course, also think he was thirty. His face is pale but still fresh. Upon lengthy observation you notice traces of wrinkles intersecting one another. His skin has a feminine delicacy. His fingers are pale and thin. There are signs of a nervous weakness in all the movements of his body. When he laughs, his eyes do not laugh, because his soul burns in his eyes. But Pechorin's soul has already shriveled up. What kind of dead person is this who has withered before his time? What kind of a boy is this, covered with the wrinkles of old age? What is the reason for such an incredible metamorphosis? Where is the inner root of the malady that has consumed his soul and weakened his body? Let us listen to him and hear what he has to say about his youth.

In his early youth, from the minute that he left the guardianship of his relatives, he began to furiously enjoy all of the pleasures that could be obtained by money, and, of course, he became fed up with these pleasures. He entered high society, but he became sick of it too. He fell in love with social beauties and was loved in return. But their love only upset his imagination and self-respect, and his heart remained empty. He began to study but grew tired of it. Then he became bored. In the Caucasus he wanted to dispel his boredom by facing Chechen fire, but he became still more bored. His soul, he says, has been spoiled by society. His imagination is restless. His heart is insatiable. Nothing is enough for him, and his life becomes more futile with every passing day.

There is a physical illness that bears among the common people the foul name "dog's old age." It indicates a perpetual hunger of the body nothing can satisfy. This physical illness corresponds to the psychological disease of boredom, which is the perpetual hunger of a depraved soul that seeks strong sensations and cannot be satiated by them. This is the highest degree of apathy in a human being, resulting from early disillusionment, from a depressed or dissipated youth. In souls born without energy, what becomes mere apathy rises, in strong souls called to action, to a level of hungry, unsatisfied boredom. It is an illness with a pathology all its own, even if it differs according to the temperament of the person that it afflicts. This illness kills all human feeling, even compassion. We remember how Pechorin was on the point of rejoicing once when he detected this feeling in himself after his parting with Vera. We do not believe that the love of nature the author attributes to this living corpse could be preserved in him. We do not believe that he could be lost in reverie. In this case the author spoils the wholeness of [Pechorin's] portrait and attributes, as it were, his own feeling to his hero. Can a person who loves music only for the sake of digestion also love nature?

Eugene Onegin, who participated to an extent in the birth of Pechorin, suffered from the same illness. But it remained at a lower level in him, the level of apathy, for Eugene Onegin was not endowed with emotional energy. In addition, he did not suffer from the pride of spirit and thirst for power that plague the new hero. Pechorin was bored in St. Petersburg, and he was bored in the Caucasus. He goes to Persia and gets bored. But his boredom affects those around him. [With the boredom] he cultivates an invincible pride of spirit that knows no barriers and sacrifices whomever he comes across, if only so he can be amused if only momentarily. He has a natural inclination to contradict, as do all people who suffer from the drive for power. He is not capable of friendship because friendship demands concessions that offend his self-respect. He looks on all events in his life as antidotes to his gnawing boredom. His greatest merriment is to disappoint others! It is an immense delight for him to pick a flower, smell it, then cast it away! He himself confesses that he feels this insatiable greediness that devours everything he encounters on his way. He looks upon the sufferings and joys of others only in relation to himself, as upon food that sustains his emotional strength. Ambition in him is suppressed by circumstances, but it reveals itself in another form, the thirst for power, the pleasure of subordinating all that surrounds him to his will. In his opinion, happiness is only fulfilled pride. [Any personal] suffering brings to mind the pleasure of tormenting another. There are moments when he understands the vampire. Half his soul has withered, but the other half remains only to deaden the souls of those around him. We have condensed here all of the features of this terrible character [that appear in the novel], and it is dreadful to us!

Who in the world has he attacked in his fits of indomitable ambition? On whom does he test the excessive pride of his soul? On poor women whom he disdains. His view of the fair sex reveals in him a materialist who has read many French novels of the modern school. He notices breed in a woman as he would in a horse. All of the features he admires in them concern physical appearance alone. He is preoccupied with a regular nose, velvety eyes, white teeth, or some kind of delicate fragrance. In his opinion the first touch decides everything in love. If a woman makes him feel that he should marry her, then good-bye love! His heart turns to stone. Only obstacles [to love] arouse in him a false feeling of tenderness. We remember that at the possibility of losing Vera, she becomes more dear to him than anything else. He throws himself onto his horse and flies after her. The horse dies on the way, and he cries like a child but only because he cannot achieve his goal, only because his sense of inviolable power is thwarted. But he remembers this moment of weakness with vexation and says that anyone who would have looked at his tears would have turned away from him in contempt. How these words speak of an unbending pride!

This twenty-five-year-old sensualist has come across many women in his life, but two, Bela and Princess Mary, are especially remarkable. The first, he corrupts sensually as he is carried away by his feelings. The second, he corrupts emotionally but only because he cannot succeed in corrupting her sensually. Feeling no love in him, he can only joke and play at love. He merely seeks diversion from his boredom. He amuses himself with the princess the way a cat, once satisfied, amuses itself with a mouse. But he does not escape boredom in this way because, as a person experienced in the ways of love, as an expert in the hearts of women, he has foreseen the entire drama he is about to perform on a whim. After he has upset the dreams and chafed the heart of the unfortunate [Princess Mary], he finishes her off with the words "I do not love you."

We do not in any way believe that the past acts strongly upon Pechorin or that he does not forget anything (as he says in his journal). [Pechorin's self-assessment] does not follow from anything we know about him; again the wholeness of his portrait is broken by [such remarks]. Any person who could, on the same day, both bury Bela and laugh [at her death], who years later, upon Maksim Maksimych's mention of her, can only grow slightly pale and turn away, such a person is not capable of submitting to the power of the past. This is a strong, but hard-hearted, soul. All impressions slip by him almost imperceptibly. This is a cold and calculating *esprit fort* who is not capable either of being captivated by nature, which demands real feelings, or of retaining in himself traces of the past, a past that is too

painful and delicate for his petulant selfishness to recall. These ego-
ists usually spare themselves and try to avoid unpleasant sensations
altogether. We remember how Pechorin closes his eyes after notic-
ing between the crevices of the rocks Grushnitsky's bloodied corpse,
the man whom he has killed. He did this only to avoid experiencing
an unpleasant impression. If the author ascribes to Pechorin such
vulnerability in relation to the power of the past, he does it only to
rationalize, to some extent, the fact that Pechorin keeps a journal.
We do not believe, however, that people like Pechorin can keep
journals. This claim is a major mistake the novel makes. It would
have been far better had the author narrated all of these events from
his own perspective. He could have done so more skillfully both in
an artistic sense and in relation to the fiction, for by his personal
participation as narrator, he could have softened, if only slightly, the
unpleasantness the immoral impression the hero of the novel makes.
Such a mistake entails yet another. The story of Pechorin does not at
all differ from the story of the author himself, and, thus, [Pechorin's
distinct] character features should have been reflected in unique
characteristics of his journal's style, an effect it does not achieve.

Let us summarize briefly all we have said about the character of
the hero. Apathy, the consequence of a corrupted youth and of all of
the defects of his upbringing, made Pechorin feel a deadly boredom.
Boredom, combined with the excessive pride of his ambitious spirit,
made Pechorin into a scoundrel. And the main root of all evil is a
Western upbringing, alien to any sense of our [Russian] beliefs.
Pechorin, as he himself says, is convinced of only [three things] –
that he was born on an exceedingly nasty evening; that, other than
death, nothing can be worse than having nothing happen [in one's
life]; and that death cannot be avoided. These words are the key to
all of his exploits. The solution to the riddle of his life lies in them.
Nevertheless, his was a strong soul, a soul that could have accomplished something higher.

In one place in his journal, he recognizes a higher calling. He
says, "why did I live, for what purpose was I born? . . . And yet that
purpose must have existed, and my destination must have been a

lofty one, for I feel, in my soul, boundless strength. But I did not divine that destination, I became enticed by the lure of hollow and thankless passions. From their crucible, I emerged as hard and cold as iron, but lost forever the ardor of noble yearnings – the best blossom of life" (158–59). When you look at the strength of this lost soul, you begin to feel sorry for him as for one of the victims of this harsh malady of the century.

After examining in detail the character of the hero of the story in whom all of the events are focused, we come to two main questions, the answers to which conclude our discussion [of the novel]. First, what is the relationship of this character to contemporary life? Second, is such a character plausible in the world of fine art?

Before resolving these two questions, we turn to the author himself and ask him what he thinks about Pechorin. Does he not hint at his main idea and at its relation to contemporary life?

The author says, "Perhaps some readers will want to know my opinion of Pechorin's character. My answer is the title of this book. 'But this is wicked irony,' they will say. I wonder" (64). In the author's opinion, then, Pechorin is a hero of our time. Both [Pechorin's] view of life, as contemporary as it appears to be to us, and the basic idea of the work are reflected in this [auctorial] remark.

If this is so, it follows that our century is terribly ill. But what exactly does its basic ailment consist of? To judge by the sick person through whom the fantasy of our poet makes its [prose] debut, the ailment of our century consists both of pride of spirit and of the baseness that derives from satiated flesh! And, indeed, if we turn to the West, we will find that the author's bitter irony is a painful truth. A century of proud philosophy thinks it can understand all the secrets of the world merely through the questing of the human spirit; a century of vain industry pleases ceaselessly and in every way all of the whims of the flesh, thus weakened by pleasure. Through these two extremes, such a century expresses in itself the ailments that have overcome it. Is not the pride of the human spirit (apparent in these abuses of personal freedom, of will, and reason) noticeable too in France and Germany? Is not the moral depravity, which abases the body, an inevitable evil – acknowledged as such by many in the West – that has entered into their customs? If one lacks a nourishing love and has neither the faith nor the hope through which our earthly existence is supported, how can one not perish, how can the soul not wither?

———

The ailment, reflected in the century's great works of poetry, was in the West the result of [these] two maladies. But how did this ailment that the West suffers from [infect us]? Do we deserve it? We can respond to this query with an example. It sometimes happens that after a long or even a brief contact with a dangerously ill person, we imagine we ourselves have contracted the same disease. This, in our opinion, is how we might best understand the development of the character we are examining.

Pechorin, of course, has nothing in himself that is titanic. Furthermore, he is not able to achieve anything of this stature either. He belongs to those pygmies of evil that are now so abundant in narrative and dramatic literature of the West. But this is not even his main shortcoming. Pechorin does not have anything substantial within himself that derives from a purely Russian way of life, a life that could not disgorge such a character. Pechorin is only a ghost, thrown off by the West on us. He is only the apparition of an ailment, appearing for a moment in the fantasy of our poets, *un mirage de l'occident*. There, he is a hero of the real world, while for us he is only a hero of fantasy, and in this sense a hero of our time. Here is an essential shortcoming of the work. With the very same sincerity with which we at first greeted the brilliant talent of the author for the creation of his many wholesome characters, for his descriptions, for his talent in developing his narrative, with the same sincerity, we reproach him for the main idea of his work personified in the character of the hero. Yes, in the work we encounter magnificent landscapes of the Caucasus, the beautiful sketches of life in the mountains, the gracefully naive Bela, the artificial princess, the fantastic and frolicsome girl of Taman, the glorious and kind Maksim Maksimych, even the frivolous Grushnitsky, and all of the fine traits of society in Russia. But everything, everything in these stories is chained to the ghost of the main character, who does not seem to emanate from this life at all. Everything is sacrificed to him, and in this lies the main and essential shortcoming of what the author has invented.

Nevertheless, this new work of the poet, even with this shortcoming, has a deep meaning for our Russian life. Our existence is divided, so to speak, into two sharp, almost opposite, halves, of which one abides in the material world, in the truly Russian world, while the other abides in some abstract world of ghosts. We live *in fact* within our Russian way of life but still think and dream of living in the life of the West, with which we do not have any essential contiguity in our past. In our native, in our real, Russian life, we preserve a rich seed for our future development. This seed can grow into a splendid tree on our fresh soil, but only if we nourish it with the useful fruits of the West, never with its harmful poisons. But in our dreamy life, which the West casts upon us, we nervously, it would seem, suffer its ailments and, like children, try on the mask of disillusionment that does not have its origins in anything of our own. This is precisely why in our dream, in this terrible nightmare, through which a Mephisophelean West stifles us, we seem to ourselves to be rather worse off than we, in fact, are. Apply this to the work we are examining, and it will be perfectly clear to you. All of Mr. Lermontov's stories, excepting Pechorin, belong to our vital Russian life. But Pechorin himself, with the exception of his apathy alone, which was only the beginning of his moral malady, belongs to the dreamy world, produced in us by a false reflection from the West. He is a ghost, having substance only in the world of our fantasy.

And in this regard, the work of Mr. Lermontov in itself conveys a deep truth of moral importance. He gives us this ghost, who belongs not to him alone, but to many from this generation, as someone real. To us he is frightful, but from his terrible image, something useful can be derived. The works of poets such as Mr. Lermontov, who have received from nature the gift of foresight, can be studied with great benefit for the moral edification of our society. Such poets provide reflections of contemporary life in their works without their own knowledge. They, like an airy harp, tell us in their music about the secret motions of the atmosphere our dull senses cannot even begin to perceive.

We will indeed put to good use the lesson offered by the poet. There are maladies in a person that begin with the imagination and then turn little by little into substance. We will put ourselves on guard so that the ghost of [Pechorin's] ailment, so strongly depicted by the brush of this new talent, does not cross from the world of empty dreaming into the world of harsh reality.

NOTE

Reprinted from S. P. Shevyrev, "*Geroi nashego vremeni*. M. Lermontov. 2 parts, Spb., 1840," *Moskvitianin* 1, no. 2 (1841): 515–38.

## S. O. Burachok

Translated by Andrew Swensen

*A conversation in a drawing room:*

"My lady, you have read *Hero* – what did you think of it?"

"Ah, an incomparable thing! . . . the likes of which has never been seen in Russian . . . everything is so alive, so tender, so new . . . with such lightness of style! . . . it simply captivates one's interest."

"And you, my lady?"

"Never have I read such a work, and I was so sorry when it ended so quickly. Why only two parts and not twenty?"

"And you, my lady?"

"It reads . . . well, what a delight! You do not want to let it slip from your hands. If only everyone wrote like this in Russian, we would not read a single novel in French."

"What of you, Ivan Ivanovich, what would you say?"

"It seems to me that the appearance of *A Hero of Our Time* and its reception demonstrate more strikingly than anything the general decline of our literature and of our readers' tastes."

*All* (in unison): Ah! How could that be?! Ah! Who is offering such a vulgar critique?! Ah! This is simply envy! Ah! This is how they kill off talent! Ah! Ivan Ivanovich, be so kind!

*I*: Mesdames, messieurs – Why fight and cause a stir? Would it not be better to disassemble the entire novel, examine its springs, its nuts and bolts, and its parts, and then discuss it?

*They*: Examine, discuss . . . What a man! Who analyzes when one need only delight in it? *Hero* is a true delight! Its precious soul, how sweet! Its horror, how sweet!

*I*: As you like, mesdames, and so this is what I will do, if only for myself, while you have your delight.

Getting inside the thing itself, I disassembled *Hero*, and here is what I found: the external construction of the novel is good, and the style is good; the contents are romantic to the extreme, i.e., fundamentally false; there is not the slightest harmony between causes, means, events, consequences, and goals – in other words, the internal construction of the novel is not fit whatsoever: the idea is false, and its execution is misdirected. The external appearance of a society man has been captured quite well, but the qualities of the human spirit and heart have been distorted to the point of being ridiculous. The entire novel is an epigram composed of unceasing sophistries, and so it entirely lacks any trace of philosophy, religiousness, or Russian national spirit.[1] There is more than enough to satisfy the tastes of the "heroes of our time," but at the same time, for the more sensible man, for the mere layman in the ways of contemporary heroism, it is all too joyless. From the depths of his soul, he laments over why Pechorin, the real author of the novel, so maliciously employs his wonderful gifts, and thanks to this nonentity, the praises of people arise, people who are somnolent due to their emptiness of mind, heart, and soul. It is a shame that he died and left on his grave this monument of "light reading," resembling a grave: gleaming with gilt on the outside but decaying and putrid within.

"Who will unseal the grave?"

"In truth it would not usually be appropriate, but for the sake of medical-literary [research] it now becomes necessary."

Here are the *contents* of the grave: for his distinguished service the "hero of our time" is exiled to the Caucasus, to one of the frontier forts. He appears before the fort commander, one Captain Maksim Maksimych. Maksim Maksimych is a hero of past times: simple, kindhearted, somewhat educated, a servant of the tsar and the people for all of his life and to his death – these days many Maksim Maksimyches have been reborn as "heroes of our time." Retired on their farms and stationed in the forts of the Caucasus, their fragments remain intact. Here is Maksim Maksimych in his entirety! A living character, and he would be the single pleasing character in the whole book if only the painter had not, for the benefit of his "hero," chosen to shade the good-natured captain in hues of *un bon homme*, a humorous eccentric. Such are the laws of light reading! In goodness one should find only the amusing and the humorous, for otherwise it would be dry and boring. Thus, how tender and great is our "hero," standing next to Maksim Maksimych, Maksim who, like a friend, has taken him in, who, like a brother, has comforted him, and who, like a father, has tended to him. And the other? He finds all this only funny or unbearable – and deigns only to spare Maksim Maksimych from a few thumps on the nose for his love. It is a shame the author did not use [such thumping] to round out his high-flown effects.

The "hero" is a true hero![2] In the rain and cold, on the hunt all day, all others grow cold and tired, but he cares not at all. On another occasion the wind blows in the room, the shudders bang, and we are certain that he has caught cold – he trembles and has grown pale! Yet still he goes out to battle the boar, face to face. A peaceful Circassian prince lives near the fort, and he has a wonderful daughter, Bela, and a ne'er-do-well son, Azamat. The hero and Maksimych are invited to a celebration at the prince's. The daughter, a beauty, of course, has danced, and now she approaches the hero, sings him a song, and in her song expresses her love for him. The hero falls in love, but his rival, the Circassian Kazbich, sees this and grows jealous. He has a magnificent steed. The heroine's brother, Azamat, is terribly fond of this steed. The Circassians start cutting and hacking at one another with their sabers, and meanwhile, our hero and the captain, thanks to their soundness of mind, gallop off to the fort. The hero conceives a plan for the abduction of Bela. Her brother Azamat appears:

"You like Kazbich's steed?" asks the hero.

"Terribly so, and there is nothing I would not sell for it!"

"Would you like me to get it for you? What would you give for it?"

"Anything you like!"

"Bring me your sister."

"Very well."³

Said and done! The hero steals the steed from Kazbich, gives it to Azamat, and gets Bela. Then Kazbich kills Bela's father, and Azamat disappears without a trace. Maksim Maksimych learns of this on the first day of the abduction, and as the commander of the fort, he comes to deliver an order to the hero, "You have done a loathsome deed. Turn in your sword."

"Mitka, my sword!" says the hero, not rising from his bed.

"Why have you taken Bela?"

"Because I like her."⁴

Faced with this logic, the commander is at a loss and merely waves his hand. The hero begins to live with the heroine as if with a wife, but after four months he grows tired of her. He has become bored and spends entire days on the hunt. Bela begins to wither and cry, and this too frustrates him. The commander begins to feel sorry for her and attempts to reason with the hero. The hero replies to him in heroic language:

"I have an unfortunate disposition: whether it is my upbringing that made me thus or whether God created me so, I don't know: I only know that if I am a cause of unhappiness for others, I am no less unhappy myself. Naturally, that is poor comfort for them, neverthe-less, this is a fact" (39–40). The hero rhetorically expands on this theme, adducing numerous facts to justify himself and to provide justification for all similar heroes of the present and future. This is beyond eloquence! Maksim Maksimych can utter nary a peep! Here even Cicero, with all of his obligations as man and citizen, would find himself at a dead end.

"The love of a wild girl was little better than that of a lady of rank; the ignorance and naïveté of one pall on you as much as the coquetry of the other. I still like her, I suppose; I am grateful to her for several rather sweet moments; I am ready to die for her – only I find her company dull. Whether I am a fool or a villain, I don't know. . . ." (40).

"I know indeed," M. Maksimych should have responded. "You are two things: as dull-witted as a stump, even with all of your cleverness, and as mean as a hungry wolf." But the author would not permit him to respond in this way, and the hero, conscious that he is growing more shallow because of his brand of heroic nonsense, comes to his end a few pages later, "from boredom."

"The junior captain," says the author – which is to say the hero himself, Pechorin – "did not understand these subtle distinctions." He shook his head and smiled slyly.

"It was the French, was it, who introduced the fashion of being bored?"

"No, the English."

"Ah, that's how it is!" he answered. "Well, they have always been inveterate drunkards!" (41–42).

The junior captain's remark is pardonable – in order *to abstain from liquor, he naturally tried to convince himself that all misfortunes in the world come from drinking.*

This, *of course*, is nonsense, in the author's opinion.

Based on the "legal foundation" of his justifications, the hero falls out of love with Bela. He begins to grow bored more freely and wanders off on the hunt ever more often and for longer periods of time. Once he even entices the junior captain to accompany him. They ride along and see Kazbich galloping with something white across his saddle. The hero gives chase, fires, and shoots the horse. Kazbich falls with Bela in his arms, plunges his dagger into her back, and hides in the bushes. Bela is dying, but before her death she wants to become a Christian so that she will not be parted from [Pechorin] in the next world. But she changes her mind. The junior captain says a few feeble words over her, but from the hero – not a word! Bela dies. The junior captain weeps. But the hero? He chuckles!

In sum: theft, robbery, drunkenness, the abduction and seduction of a young woman, two murders, loathing for everything holy, apathy, paradoxes, sophistries, and atrocities of spirit and body. These are all the elements of the first act of our hero's travels. In fact, one should be horrified! How light and tender! Everything is so sweet. These are the tastes of educated society, especially those of the fairer sex! How natural, a nature so alive!

By this I do not mean to suggest that it is necessary to expunge every little sin, filth, and vice from fine literature or that it is necessary to lull the reader only with charitable, bright, high-minded, and pure deeds, which, in fact, are so rare in base humanity. No, I only want all the colors of a painting of the human heart to be true to the original, showing both its light and dark sides. I want readers not to be led into a study filled with idealized monsters that have been neatly tidied up. I want the rendering of the dark side to serve some purpose and not merely to disgust the reader. And I want the *author not to slander an entire generation of people, offering a monster and not a man as a representative of that generation.*

The hero heroically spent three months in boredom at the fort and then was transferred to a regiment in Georgia, and news of him ceased. Five years later, Maksim Maksimych arrives at Kobi and learns that his hero is in the same place as the commander. The old man is happy beyond belief – any wait for an old friend is too long! "He will be delighted to see me!" he thinks to himself. The hero's lackey is "a hero of our lackeys," and the junior captain asks him to report Maksimych's presence to his master. The hero-lackey does not even honor him with an answer, much less a glance, but nonetheless makes the announcement. So Maksimych sits on a bench alongside a hut and awaits the hero. He is called to tea, then to supper, and finally to bed. Maksimych sits and waits, but the hero never comes. Finally, the object of his longing appears. The old man wants to throw himself onto his heroic neck, but the other rather coldly extends his hand.

"How glad I am, dear Maksim Maksimych! Well, how are you?"

"And thou? . . . And you?" stammered the old man with tears in his eyes. "All those years . . . all those days . . . but where are you off to?"

"I am going to Persia, and then further on. . . ."

"Not right now? . . . Oh, but wait, my dearest friend! . . . We aren't going to part right now, are we? We have not seen each other in such a long time."

"I have to go right now, Maksim Maksimych," answered the hero – and he left (58).

Struck with grief Maksim Maksimych exits the stage and does not appear again in the entire novel.[5] Only Pechorin's journal remains. Pechorin has forgotten about it, and, in the excitement of the chance encounter, [Maksim Maksimych] does not manage to return it to him. Maksim Maksimych hands over the journal to Mr. Lermontov.[6] These very writings, or journal, of Pechorin are published. [The journal] is truly natural, so natural, but it is a shame that everything that is natural is not necessarily refined, and not everything merits publication or the trappings of biting sophistries and pointed epigrams. It is not so bad to keep silent about many things, about many very natural things. However, freedom is the watchword of romanticism! There is no need to jump in with antiquated, worn-out theories.

The hero's second adventure occurs in Taman. A rotten little town where no one grants the hero accommodations. Barbarians! Cretins! Not granting accommodations to the hero of our time! Such is the state of things among our educated and enlightened class. Not only are all boudoirs wide open to him – live and sleep wherever you like – but indeed what could be sweeter than having him as a boarder! Perhaps the single honest family to be found in Taman resides on the edge of town – an old woman, a blind son, and a darling little daughter – but then these are smugglers, heroes worthy of the hero of our time.

On the first night, the hero notices that the old woman is not deaf, the blind boy is not blind, and the little daughter is an evil young woman. He begins to investigate the young beauty and then lets on to her that he has observed their scheme. The young woman-heroine does not alter her expression but rather feigns that she has fallen in love, and she embraces and kisses the hero and then arranges to meet him that night on the shore of the sea. The hero fixes his pistol to his belt and sets off. The woman meets him, gets [him] into a boat, and then pushes off to sea. As the boat sails along, the heroine embraces the hero tenderly and sweetly, and his pistol plunks into the water. The hero realizes her plans for him, and she attempts to throw him into the water. The hero battles, the boat rocks; she is after him, he is after her. It ends as it should, and having defeated her, he throws her into the water, where she disappears among the waves. The hero somehow reaches the shore, and as he is walking along, he sees his undine to the side, wringing out her hair. A boat bearing a smuggler approaches. The blind boy brings some sort of bundle onto the boat. The undine jumps in, the blind boy is thrown off, and off she goes. The boy cries. The hero enters his hut. His Cossack guard is sleeping, and his box and all of his heroic things are gone. He rages at humanity more bitterly than ever.

"What happened to the old woman and the blind boy?"

"I don't know," the hero answers, "What are human joys and sorrows to me?"[7]

Thus ends this fine adventure and part one with it.[8]

The second part contains the hero's adventure at a spa. A magnificent creation! All romantic elements are present without exception, and so let us hear them in order.

The hero has come to the waters – apropos, he is a wealthy man – has let a savage's quarters in this savage place, has dressed himself up in savage emotions, and has taken up living as a savage. He records his impressions in his journal, and you read his journal. It begins with a description of the local surroundings. Then he describes the inhabitants, the locals, and those passing through, the men and the women. "The wives of the local officials, the hostesses of the waters, so to speak, were more favorably disposed; they have lorgnettes, they pay less attention to uniforms, they are used to encountering in the Caucasus an *ardent heart* under a numbered army button and a *cultivated mind* under a white army cap" (82). The hero, being a hero indeed, feigns having both a heart and a mind, but why touch on such banal things? One wonders what ignites his heart, which has dried out into a scrap of leather? One wonders how this mind has been educated, a mind that is but an empty mill of apt epigrams on and about everything, a mind to which black seems white and white seems black? Whatever the case may be, there is no doubt that the hero maintains a fine opinion of himself.

These ladies are very charming, and remain charming for a long time! Every year, their admirers are replaced by new ones. Very well, enough of that. Next the hero comes to a well and describes that [scene]: "In the avenues of vines, one could glimpse now and then the variegated bonnets of ladies partial to shared isolation, since I would always notice, near such a bonnet, either a military cap or one of those round civilian hats that are so ugly" (83). Next he meets the cadet Grushnitsky, an acquaintance from his travels in the Caucasus. Grushnitsky also belongs to the species of hero, and therefore the Hero General describes him in most malicious epigrams. They then meet an elder princess and her daughter, Mary. Grushnitsky, in his soldier's coat, falls in love with the young princess, and she with him, for she assumes him not to be a cadet but rather one suffering punishment for a duel, for an insult – basically for his heroic adventures. What poetry this is: the young princess falls deeply in love, and they are enamored with one another.

The hero overhears them, observes them, and finds it necessary to have the young princess fall in love with him. The heroic assault begins with rude and indecent actions. This draws attention to him and, quite naturally, attracts the secret affections of the young princess. She now falls deeply in love with him and loses her mind – she also comes from the stock of [run-of-the-mill] heroines. The mother also comes from such stock: "She likes risqué anecdotes and sometimes, when her daughter is not in the room, says improper things herself. She announced to me that her daughter was as innocent as a dove. What do I care? I was on the point of replying that she need not worry, I would not tell anybody" (96). Yet another hero appears: Werner, a doctor at the spa. A description of the surgical hero follows, for much the same reason: "He had a caustic tongue: under the label of his epigram, many a kindly man acquired the reputation of a vulgarian and a fool. . . . We soon came to understand each other and became pals – for I am not capable of true friendship" (91–92). The pals begin to talk, and within a verst they are divining one another's thoughts. All this, of course, is horrifying, but more important, it bears witness to the astute nature of their minds.

"As for me, I am convinced of only one thing," says the hero-medic, "that, sooner or later, one fine morning, I shall die."

"I'm better off than you," answers the Hero General, "I've one more conviction besides yours, namely, that one miserable evening I had the misfortune to be born."[9] From this moment on, the heroes "distinguished each other in the crowd."

"Observe, my dear doctor," says the Hero General, "that without fools, the world would be a very dull place. . . . Consider: here we are, two intelligent people; we know beforehand that one can *argue endlessly about anything, and therefore we do not argue*; we know almost all the secret thoughts of each other; one word is a whole story for us; we see the kernel of our every emotion through a triple shell. [Naturally, all of this is utter nonsense, but how sweet it sounds in this tale! – S. B.] Sad things seem to us funny, funny things seem to us melancholy, and generally we are, to tell the truth, rather indifferent to everything except our own selves" (93). In a word, when it comes to being open, the hero has quite a fine opinion of himself, and with good reason; otherwise, he would begin writing similar banalities and would present them as wonderfully intelligent things.

Only one more heroine is missing from our complete set, the married woman, and so she too appears at the waters:

"Vera!" the hero cried. "We have not seen each other for a long time."

"Yes, a long time, and we have both changed in many ways!"

"So this means that you do not love me any more?"

"I am married!" she answered.

"Again? Several years ago, however, the same reason existed, and yet . . ." (103).

In a word you understand our heroine. Her husband is a kind and respected old man. "I did not allow myself a single jibe at him," says the author-hero. "She respects him as a father – and will deceive him as a husband. The thunderstorm caught us in the grotto and detained us there for an extra half hour" (104–5).

Now the drama has taken shape. Vera, living in the same building as the princess, wants to play the role of the good wife. The hero is in love with the princess, and she with him. Vera is wasting away from jealousy, and the cadet Grushnitsky, having been made into an officer, loses all of his charm and the princess's love along with it – she cuts herself off completely. He conceives a plan for a duel to ward off the hero and confers with a few other similar heroes, but the Hero General overhears their scheme. In the meantime a cavalcade is formed to go riding, and all the heroes gallop off, with the princess and the Hero General riding alongside one another. They are crossing a fast-flowing stream when the princess's head begins to spin; the hero heroically catches her by the waist and gives her a fleeting kiss – the princess utters not a word! Then the princess, like a true heroine, confesses her love to him, and our selfless hero confesses to her . . . that he does not love her. The princess falls ill. Meanwhile, Vera, softened by her jealousy and in the absence of her husband, arranges to meet him in her quarters that night. Grushnitsky learns of this and keeps watch for the hero who, wrapped in two shawls, begins to descend from the window after his tryst, and when he is opposite the princess's window, his rival and a comrade try to catch him. He knocks them off their legs, and one of them fires a shot. The residents take this as an attack by Circassians. Grushnitsky says that the hero has been with the princess that night. The hero steps forward and challenges him to a duel: they will fire at one another on the edge of an isolated cliff at a distance of six paces so that the one killed will fall into the chasm, thus averting possible suspicion. The hero kills Grushnitsky, who tumbles down the cliff. *"Finita la comedia,"* (171) says the hero to his second, the doctor-hero.

The events are discovered. Everything is clear, yet there is no evidence. The old man, Vera's husband, realizes what is wrong, puts her on a coach, and sets off. The hero wants to kiss her one more time and gallops off on his exhausted steed. He drives it to death, and, not able to continue on foot, the hero falls to the wet grass and begins to sob like a child. The description of this failed mission is most impassioned: "All my firmness," writes the hero-author, "all my coolness vanished like smoke; my soul wilted, my reason was mute and if, at that moment, anyone had seen me, he would have turned away in contempt" (175).

What an astonishing thing it is for these heroes to consider themselves so highly! Committing murders of both body and morals, they consider themselves to be steely and cool under duress. Their souls are steely, particularly when they are rolling around in the filth of vicious romantic cruelties. Their reason speaks well, particularly when they blather nonsense in the highest of styles. And they think to themselves that no one could possibly turn away from them in disgust and loathing! You go there and talk to them.

All the while, the military command, apparently unable to comprehend the nuances and charms of contemporary heroism, assigns the hero to Maksim Maksimych's fort [in punishment] for all of his adventures. The hero makes his preparations and comes to the elder princess to bid her farewell. She says to him, "My daughter is dying because of her love for you; what is holding you back? Marry her."[10] The hero requests permission to speak with the young princess herself, and she enters: "Princess, I laughed at you. I do not love you and will not marry you," the hero says, then he bows respectfully and leaves.

There is no sin here that needs concealing. Pechorin so wishes to display his heroism in the most colossal dimensions, and he, as they say, has *overseasoned the broth.* All the heroes and heroines without exception, no matter how much they feign the tone and manners of high society, nonetheless appear from under their masquerade costumes as barracks heroes and heroines. [There is] not one proper and tolerable person among them. They are all utterly intolerable because they are false and exaggerated.

The final tale is "The Fatalist," also from Pechorin's journal. He is serving in some battalion. The officers gather at a certain major's quarters and begin to talk of predestination. The hero here wishes to shine with philosophical audacity. Lieutenant Vulich, a Serb, rises and says, "You are blathering nonsense!" – and, in fact, they are blathering nonsense, albeit blathering in the finest of literary styles [as they] propound something we might call heroic philosophy. Vulich removes one of many pistols hanging from the wall, and he asks his host:

"Is it loaded?"

"I don't know."

"All the better."[11]

He then places the pistol to his forehead, "I am taking bets that I will not kill myself." The hero pulls out his money and takes the bet. All are numb except the hero. He sprinkles some powder into the pan, raises the pistol to his forehead, and – bang! . . . a misfire. He powders the pan once again, aims at someone's army cap, and fires a bullet right through it. Everyone gasps.

"You see," says Vulich, "this is what predestination means."

"You will die today; I see it in your eyes," the Hero says to him.

Vulich departs for home, and along the way he encounters an armed and drunken Cossack, bared saber in hand, who has just hacked apart a pig out of simple cruelty. Vulich asks him, "Whom are you looking for?"

"You," the Cossack says and then hacks into Vulich, cleaving him from the shoulder to the heart. Naturally, he dies, and the hero, promising a "continuation to follow," lapses into a discussion on moral philosophy, saying something about the superstitions of our ancestors, then adding, "But we, *we, their miserable* descendants, who roam the earth without convictions or pride, without rapture or fear (except for that instinctive dread that compresses our hearts at the thought of the inevitable end), we are no longer capable of *great sacrifice*, neither for the good of mankind nor even for our own happiness, because we *know* its *impossibility* [a sophistry – S. B.] and pass with indifference from doubt to *doubt*, just as our ancestors rushed from one delusion to another [a sophistry and a lie – S. B.]. But we, however, do not have either their *hopes* or even that indefinite, albeit *real*, rapture that the soul encounters in any struggle with men or with *fate* [a sophistry and nonsense – S. B.]. And many other similar thoughts passed through my mind (N.B. and set themselves to the pages of my journal). I did not detain them, since I *do not care to concentrate on any abstract thought*; and indeed what does it lead to?" [a sophistry and nonsense of the highest order – S. B.] (188).

Such is the way throughout the entire book, and not one line soothes your heart. All of this is essentially derived from contemporary examples of light reading, and as has been said correctly, "No great wisdom enters into the soul of a cruel artist." Truth is a gift and is the blessing of God. It is given only to those who are worthy, gentle, and humble. The embittered and self-confident man speaks only a lie when thinking he speaks the truth. In every place where Pechorin philosophizes, he is, in this regard, remarkably true to the character of those who are embittered, and such is the case in the passage here cited.

It is impossible to conceive a better epitaph for the graves of all the "heroes of our time"! – sophistry upon sophistry, lie upon lie, absurdity upon absurdity – this is what they are. Herein lies the motif of the whole novel, and it develops this theme precisely in its characters and its words. At every step the mentality of this raving literature threads a psychological incongruity throughout the novel. More briefly stated, this book is the ideal of light reading. It should have great success! All of the characters, except Maksim Maksimych with his shading ever so ridiculous, are remarkable and choice heroes, and for all of their optical diversity, all are cast in the same mold – from the author himself, Pechorin, the Hero General, to the various others in their masques, one in a uniform, another in a skirt, and still another in an overcoat. All bear one and the same face, and all are just a group of junior barracks officers who have not yet had their fill of childish antics. A fine bundle of switches, and how they would glisten in your hand! However, Pechorin himself simply dreams all of this up for the sake of "greater effect." Such people who completely lack feeling and conscience are not possible in nature. [The folk villain and hero type like] Vanka Kain, and there have been such, cuts the throat of some man, and then his conscience torments him. But apparently these ladies and gentlemen have never had any conscience. There are many egotists and rogues who in the presence of others seem to hold nothing sacred, but in their souls and in their journals, they feel and write completely otherwise. Here we have a hero, somewhat like a blank slate. To that blank slate is attached a device for [recording] thoughts. The device turns with the wind, and yet nothing is generated within – no reason, no feeling, no conscience. Psychologically speaking, this is impossible.

I will not begin to repeat what has already been said about light reading, for the absurdity of this theory is all the more obvious in practice. Insofar as literature should be *the service of God in the guise of humanity*, I ask then: What service to humanity does the portrait of such a hero offer? That after him the number of heroes should multiply? For surely they will not diminish, for the book reads such that the hero is tender, intelligent, and sharp-witted, and, in his most horrific deeds, he still seems a victim of fate. He so naively white-washes all of his deeds, or rather misdeeds, though they are seemingly shaded in black. I am not only troubled that this light reading has no religious or national spirit, but it also lacks philosophy, that is, good sense – it has but an accumulation of sophistries. Take the commonplaces of good sense, turn them inside out, and you will get the newest, most sharp-witted sophistries that, in the heat of the moment of reading, will strike you with their intoxicating spirit and will seem to be worth something.

Many in this world are intelligent [*umno*] but not wise [*razumno*]. An angel of light on the outside but a devil within. Even a devil is smart but is not wise, and thus he is falsehood. Our *mental* powers – intelligence, sensuality, and desire – do not endure without the support of the spiritual powers – reason, feeling, and will. Intelligence is capable of logically and mathematically analyzing truth and falsehood in the same way, and thus we see the foundation and point of departure for giving it reason as well. But when reason is clouded, intelligence blathers nonsense. *Aesthetic feeling*, the element of sensuality, is the most self-serving feeling, and in everything it seeks only pleasures for itself, and it takes as much pleasure in a painting of evil as in a painting of good. However, in the light of spiritual feeling, the aesthetic taste will not tolerate paintings of evil, hideousness, and rage. *Desire* strives equally toward both evil and good, as if all were desirable. But guided by the disciplined will of the spirit, it chooses only the good and veers away from evil – and if this order is broken, the soul suffers.

Therefore, to those whose spiritual powers have grown dull, the hero of our times will seem a magnificent thing, despite the aesthetic and psychological absurdity. For those possessing even the slightest trace of spiritual powers, this book will be dreadfully unbearable. It is a terrible shame to devote a good artistic gift to such revolting absurdities, with the certainty that they will meet with great success. The task of quickly pleasing weak people is simple and well known, but is it the artist's task to exploit that weakness in people? Is the artist not called to cure that weakness rather than compound it? Where true labors are, there too is true art! Everything contrary to this is simply sleight of hand, worthy of the complete loathing of well-intentioned criticism. I admit that I would have no reason to mention this hero if he were not deemed indispensable as a model of light reading, as a clearly evident explication of the absurdity of romantic theories on light literature.

That class of people who find their own company suffocating and unbearable, who seek the company of many, who say and listen to virtually anything just so that they can talk and listen to others (rather than to themselves and to the inner reproaches of their feeling and conscience when necessity keeps them home), for these the hero of our time is a discovery: without leaving their homes, they feel as though in the company of their friends, and they stifle the feeling of their loneliness – how happy are they, and for them this book is a marvel! Naturally, all such individuals will not agree with me, and I shall not bother trying to pursue this. Thank God that the world is a big enough place to have good, sensible people in it as well – though not one such soul has come across our hero, this most recent deviation from nature.

I ask once again: do we really need a tale that, in offering to portray natural man to us, portrays the play and struggle between his mental side and his spiritual? The hero has none of this, and you see only his mental side – and of this only its outer shell – untruthful, immature, but well dressed. It succeeds in all things and conquers in all places, and all that is lofty, noble, and delightful falls prostrate before it. This mental juvenility, this contemporary pseudoheroism, besmirches everything spiritual. Wicked people can besmirch the good – such is the order of things – but wicked feelings can never overcome spiritual feelings. For so long as a man lives, they will constantly fight their way through to him, and they will give him not a moment of respite from their moans, especially in moments of solitude. I want to show [elsewhere] how the conditions of the true novel have been realized in [the recent novel] *Meshchanin* [*The Petty Bourgeois* by Bashutsky].[12] Our taste depends greatly on the form our thoughts take.

NOTES

Reprinted from S. O. Burachok, "*Geroi nashego vremeni. Sochineniie M. Lermontova.* 2 parts, Spb., 1840," *Maiak,* no. 4 (1840): 210–19.

1. The word here translated as "national spirit" is *narodnost'* and is alternately translated "nationality," "nationhood," and even "nationalism."

2. Throughout his review Burachok plays on the dual meanings of the Russian word, *geroi,* which denotes both "hero" – it is the word used in the title of *A Hero of Our Time* – and "protagonist" when speaking of a narrative. "Hero" is used throughout this translation because of the deliberate irony and wordplay on the title of Lermontov's novel.

3. Burachok gives an inexact rendering of the transaction (Cf. Lermontov, *A Hero of Our Time,* trans. Nabokov, 20).

4. Burachok gives an inexact rendering of the dialogue between Maksim Maksimych and Pechorin (Cf. Lermontov, 23–24).

5. Burachok is in error – Maksim Maksimych appears again in "The Fatalist."

6. Burachok does not distinguish Lermontov and his traveling narrator.

7. Burachok does not quote the text but cites from memory and/or for pejorative rhetorical effect.

8. The 1840 edition of the novel appeared in two volumes, the first concluding with "Taman."

9. Burachok's quotation is inexact (Cf. Lermontov, 92).

10. Burachok summarizes the mother's conversation with Pechorin (Cf. Lermontov, 178).

11. Here and elsewhere in relation to "The Fatalist," Burachok composes his own dialogue (Cf. Lermontov, 184–86). The emphases, too, are Burachok's.

12. Bashutsky's lame novel is mentioned in a negative light in Bulgarin's review of *A Hero of Our Time.*

## Faddei Bulgarin

Translated by Matthew Micheli

Prejudice is one of the most harmful dispositions in a human being. Much rides on it. Each must bespeak his judgments and opinions no matter what they might be. Under the influence of this disposition, even the smartest and most honest of men can act foolishly, be unjust, and thus consign even the innocent man to a life of misery. Only a strong will, aimed at doing what is right, can save us from this damaging disposition, which so skillfully catches our mind and our heart in its nets. I almost fell into its snare . . . listen.

Once, a certain gentleman came to me at eight in the morning. His kind did not usually visit me. A pleasant man, like a three-ruble piece, a man not caught up in dreams, poetry, impulsiveness, and so forth. He had performed for me several of those unimportant services that cultured people exchange, but I had not yet had the occasion to repay him in kind. "I came to you to ask a favor," he said.

"Your wish is my command! I am happy to serve you."

"Please print an announcement about a book that will soon be published. Here it is!"

I looked at the announcement and smiled involuntarily, knowing by its exaggerated, unrestrained, and fulsome praise that the announcement had been cast in the foundry of the "absolute subjective-objective" literary camp.[1]

The visitor noticed my ambivalent smile and said, "Although the author of the book I am asking you to announce has works printed in journals that are armed against you, I give you my word that this young author in no way belongs to that group."

I could only conceal my annoyance at his words. "Dear gentleman," I replied, "you don't even know me and yet you speak to me in such a way! In literature I know only two parties: the party of good writers and the party of foolish ones. Whether an author is an enemy or a friend, I couldn't care less. If he writes well, I will praise him, but if he writes poorly, I will proclaim it and provide proof of it as well. This is my unalterable rule! I will print your announcement but soften it, of course. When the book is published, I will give my unbiased opinion of it." The visitor left me, having planted in my mind a firm prejudice against the book.

Then the book burst forth into the world. In the journals where the author usually prints his works, they started to praise it in the most amusing fashion, defaming all other writers in the process. My prejudice began to ripen. I didn't have the stomach even to take it into my hands. Their peculiar praise damaged the book to such an extent that a rather unfavorable opinion of it arose in me. I unwittingly succumbed to it. So as not to waste time or money on an inanity, I didn't even buy the book. My prejudice had already brought forth such fruit!

Finally, a critique of the book by S. O. Burachok appeared in the journal *Maiak*. It led me to conclude that the novel, *A Hero of Our Time*, is not more nor less than a sweetened, aromatic [liqueur] poured into a delightful glass cut from mountain crystals. I was about to take fright, but when I noted that in the same Burachok article, he considered A. P. Bashutsky's *Meshchanin* an example of a real novel, and that the worth of *A Hero of Our Time* was measured on its scale, I decided to read it at bedtime, hoping that it, like many of our great creations these days, would put me to sleep according to Griboedov's recipe:

> You get no sleep from French books;
> But from Russian ones I get nightmares.[2]

Suddenly it was 11:30. I read and read, and the reading captivated me. I wanted to lay it down, extinguish the light, and go to sleep. Impossible! The book had fixed itself to my will, my mind, my heart, and all of the feelings of my soul. I read, and when I had read to the final page, it was six o'clock in the morning. At my age!? It was embarrassing to admit that I had spent the entire night without sleep. And for a novel! The next day I couldn't work at all. I sat around with a headache but was not annoyed. On the third day, I read *A Hero of Our Time* again and found myself angry with the author that the book was so short. All this happened to me for the first time in a professional life spanning twenty years. For no other Russian novel had I ever sacrificed a whole night's sleep, and for the first time ever, I read a book twice in a row and complained that it wasn't longer.

I don't know the author at all. I have never met him. I have never read any of his works, because I don't read the journals that publish his verse. I don't know, and don't want to know, what opinion he has of me. But having read *A Hero of Our Time*, I lay down before the author my literary banner and give him a full salute.

Tell me, for God's sake, where did this talent ripen and develop? By what magic power has this young mind been bestowed with the ability to penetrate the depths of the human soul? What incomprehensible power has torn the mask from society's face to explain to him the disease from which it suffers in "our time," in this nineteenth century of ours? All of this is miraculous to me. *A Hero of Our Time* is the young author's first attempt at prose! Do you understand what this means? The minds of geniuses rise to great heights in their first poetic flights, but examples of the same in prose are extraordinarily rare. Prose requires deep science and much careful consideration. Victor Hugo wrote many poor novels and stories before he wrote *Notre Dame de Paris*. For a long time, Balzac struggled before he rose to the quality of *Eugenie Grande, Pere Goriot*. Walter Scott didn't begin to write novels until his mature years, that is, only after he had had many experiences in life and in the arts. The author of *A Hero of Our Time*, with his first try, is on the same level that these other authors, and after many unsuccessful attempts, expended so much time, experience, and labor to reach.

O Rus, Mother of all Slavic peoples! How much talent, how much wisdom and moral power are nurtured in thy womb! Other peoples have already exhausted their literary gift, yet we have hardly scratched the surface of our own deep mines. So let us now turn to the novel.

*A Hero of Our Time* is a work of high artistry, well thought out, and executed with consummate artistry. The predominant idea is the resolution of a great moral question of our time: what do a resplendent upbringing and all the refinements of high society lead to if there are no positive guidelines, no faith, hope, or love? With this novel the author provides answers – [they lead] to egoism, satiation early in life, spiritual emptiness, and ultimately the grave. The main character of *A Hero of Our Time*, Pechorin, is not a new, unheralded personage among us. He is a brother of Zafa, the egoist of the genius Eugenie Sue's *Salamander*. However, all of the details, all the accessories, all the episodes and secondary characters are entirely Russian and are completely original. All of the characters, except for the main one (Pechorin), represent types taken from Russian life and Russian society. Pechorin himself couldn't be completely original. He had to be similar to a Western European, because Western Europe has printed its stamp on this modern generation. The West has created these cold beings and infected them with the plague of egoism at the very time when we should be glowing with love, friendliness, and selflessness.

The story takes place in the Caucasus. On a trip through the mountains, the author[3] meets an old army officer, Maksim Maksimych, whom he asks to tell about life there. Maksim Maksimych, a person drawn by Vernet, but with the colors of a Tenier or van Dyck,[4] tells about Lieutenant Pechorin, who had been under his command in one of his outposts in the Caucasus. The tale is astonishing, perfect in its own way. Pechorin, a man from the upper crust of St. Petersburg society, well educated and wealthy, has an amazing influence on the old captain. This influence, you could say, conquers him.

Maksim Maksimych's story goes as follows: They set out for a wedding at a mountain prince's. The prince's [younger] daughter, a half-wild Circassian of unusual beauty named Bela, catches Pechorin's eye. The prince also has a son, Azamat, a fifteen-year-old youth, a daring horseman, and a genuine *gorets* (mountain warrior). Azamat is fond of a steed that belongs to Kazbich. During the wedding party, Maksim Maksimych overhears Azamat begging Kazbich for his steed, promising him in exchange all the earth holds, even his sister, Bela, whom he rashly decides to steal from his father and present to Kazbich. When Pechorin hears about the conversation, he promises Azamat Kazbich's horse if only Azamat will bring him his sister. They agree. Azamat steals his sister from his parents' home and brings her to the fort to Pechorin, who gives the horse to Azamat while Kazbich sells sheep to Maksim Maksimych. Azamat climbs on and rides off into the mountains, joining a marauding band and never returning to his parents' home. Kazbich is Asiatic! Out of revenge he kills Azamat's father, the prince (suspecting him of collaborating with his son). One day while Pechorin is out hunting, Kazbich kidnaps Bela, who has momentarily left the confines of the fort. Pechorin races after Kazbich and wounds him, but Kazbich kills Bela. Here we engage a real picture, so to speak, the details of which are very gripping.

In the mountains the author and Maksim Maksimych separate, but they meet up again in Vladikavkaz where they await a convoy so they can continue their journey. The convoy arrives – a carriage of another traveler attracts their attention. The carriage belongs to none other than Pechorin! Imagine the joy of the good-hearted Maksim Maksimych, who considers Pechorin a true friend, for he lived with him for so long in a mountain fort, who catered to him as if he were his own son! Pechorin sends the carriage on to his lodgings but stays behind with the colonel. Maksim Maksimych sends for Pechorin, letting him know that he is there, imagining that Pechorin will immediately come running and embrace him. This is not exactly how things transpire!

They call Maksim Maksimych to drink tea and have dinner, but he cannot leave the gates of the lodge and continues to wait for his dear Pechorin. He doesn't come! A forlorn Maksim Maksimych spends the entire night waiting. The next day, after the horses have been readied, Pechorin appears. Maksim Maksimych, forgetting all his sorrow, rushes to embrace his old comrade, but Pechorin casually takes off his glove and puts his hand out coolly to greet the friendly captain. Maksim Maksimych's spirits fall. His soul and pride suffer from Pechorin's rebuff. This even causes Maksim Maksimych to shed tears. Pechorin leaves, saying he is going on to Persia and even further. Maksim Maksimych is surprised that he does not ask about the papers Pechorin has left with him since the days at the fort. The author requests them, and with annoyance Maksim Maksimych throws them out, like they were trash. These are the notes of "Pechorin's Journal." From this time forward, the author, acting as narrator, exits the stage. You read "Pechorin's Journal." (He dies while returning from Persia.) These are the notes of an egoist satiated by life.

The second picture is set in Vladikavkaz, and although, at first, it is not rich in events, it is painted with the same skillful hand. The anticipation of the good-hearted Maksim Maksimych, his impatience to see Pechorin, their meeting, the portrait of Pechorin, the captain's sorrow, his vexation – delight, delight, delight! Only a most uncommon gift could have delivered up this chef d'oeuvre from such a simple incident.

"Pechorin's Journal" provides an entire course on the anatomy of the human heart and exposes a cold mind, which in some people takes the place of the soul. What a terrible and instructive spectacle! Parents, young men, and women! Read it, study it, and learn from it! What is the significance of a person who possesses all charms and intellectual gifts but lacks a soul? This is a plague-infested person, who destroys everything he touches, destroys all who want to love, comfort, and help him! A terrible situation, a bitter and pitiful lot in life!

The third picture is "Taman." Pechorin travels to the Caucasus and stops for a time in Taman, where he awaits transport by sea. He takes lodging in a room in a crippled old woman's hut. The family consists of the landlady, who pretends to be deaf, a blind orphan, and the landlady's daughter who, judging by her manner, is half-wild and half-crazy. A wonderful setting and remarkable characters! Victor Hugo, we respect your great gift. But in this particular instance, we ask you to lay down your pen before our young novelist! That's right, you have not painted anything better than Lermontov's picture! So as not to destroy it, I will not tell you any more about this tale. It is a wonderful drama! The fourth picture belongs to the type [of painting] we encounter in Briullov's *The Last Day of Pompeii*,[5] not by similarity of content but by composition, that is, by the abundance of separate scenes on one canvas. And all of these separate scenes lead us to a single theme. In Briullov's painting, a flaming Vesuvius dominates, destroying the entire population of the city. But in Lermontov's painting, what dominates is Pechorin's icy soul. It brings destruction upon everything exposed to its deadly influence. The action takes place at the spa in Pyatigorsk and in Kislovodsk. The portrait includes a Princess Mary, whom Pechorin pursues for the sake of passing the time and whom Pechorin convinces to fall in love with him. This portrait is quite charming. The princess is a flirt and somewhat sentimental, nourished as she is by the romanticism of our time. She is kindly disposed toward a certain young man who wears a soldier's greatcoat, a cross, and who is wounded besides. She imagines to herself that this man is some poor, unfortunate soul reduced in the ranks. When this very youth, whom she has listened to so attentively before, appears to her as a dandy in an officer's full-dress uniform and perfumed to high heaven, she discovers that he was merely a cadet after all, and his charm disappears. Here at the spa as well, we meet Vera, a married woman, who has loved Pechorin for a long time. He is more attached to this woman than to any other in the novel. Vera's character is described best: it is really perfect. Grushnitsky, the cadet who becomes an officer and who is in love with the princess and dies at Pechorin's hands in a duel, the Dragoon Captain, and Dr. Werner are new prototypes, unique creations one and all. Life and high society at the spa are depicted with amazing authenticity, truthfulness, and artistry. A significant part of "Pechorin's Journal" is filled with judgments of himself, people, society, and women. The judgments of an egoist satiated by life are naturally caustic and ironic – this is the mind of a Mephistopheles presented from the point of view of a fallen soul, for whom the secrets of the human heart and all human wisdom have been opened. My God! How much wisdom, erudition, observation, and truth are all here! The fifth and final picture is "The Fatalist." This is an episode that many readers consider extraneous. I think the opposite. Everything in this book has been thought out and laid out in such a way that the novel, composed as it were from fragments, represents an elegant whole and links cause and effect successfully. Pechorin sees the evil nesting in his heart, feels that he is unhappy, and turns away from all fellow feeling (from love, friendship, and compassion for others) and seeks justification in fatalism. He does not believe in fatalism but presents events, not as proof or disproof of fatalism, but as mundane events in and of themselves. Yet in his tale one can see a desire to have others believe that he is heartless only because of the powers of fatalism. Asking whether we should believe in fatalism, like the people of ancient time, present-day pagans, and Moslems, Pechorin asks the kind Maksim Maksimych what his opinion is on the matter and recounts to him the incident from which the query has arisen, an incident that is both miraculous and unusual. It is about an officer who is killed by a drunk on the street. At first Maksim Maksimych does not understand the question, but then, after thinking it through, says, "Yes I'm sorry for the poor fellow.

Why the devil did he talk to a drunk at night! However, this must have been assigned to him at birth." Pechorin continues, "Nothing more could I get from him: He does not care, generally, for metaphysical discussions" (194). The author uses Russian superstition to solve the problem and thus ends his book. We will repeat for the hundredth time – the novel is a marvel, from the first page to the last. The scenes, portraits, and the characters are drawn with a master's brush. The style is lively and fascinating. The Russian language is superb, pure, clear, and correct, without floweriness or excessiveness. Its wisdom is immense! Its ability to capture the reader's interest is strong in each sketch. Its aim is high! You, you so-called lions, bearded and shaggy, you copiers of Byron's coldness and the pride of satraps, you, who are hastily trying to imbibe life wholly but without studying it, here is a mirror for you.

I have yet to read a better novel in Russian. This is a real novelist, a real narrator, and a real critic speaking to you. Yet many feel him to be inexorable, merciless, and even annoying, for he openly tells the truth to our bombastic critics, to the impudently self-assured, and to the sneaky literary egotists who vainly attempt to conceal their foolish arrogance. Here is a young author, with whom I am not acquainted, who more than likely does not think favorably of me, judging by the literary circles into which he has perchance fallen. This is a young author who possesses genuine and authentic gifts, and I praise his composition with such joy, as if I were sharing in the glory with him. And I will share it with him, because the glory of Russian literature redounds to all of us, to all of Russia, and we can congratulate [Russia] sincerely for such an author, for the creator of *A Hero of Our Time*. From this time forward, the author must arm himself with courage and patience. There will be many talented, envious imitators who will follow him. But a genuine writer does not know envy. Such a writer dedicates an entire life to literature, and all of his time, sacrificing ambition and social gain to it. Envy is the fate of those impostors in literature who use art as a means to achieve other aims. An authentic writer is a slave to art's demands. Even if his worst enemy were to accomplish something really fine, he would praise it so as not to lower himself to the level of slanderer. Writers, like a judge, should not look at the person, but at his work.

## NOTES

Reprinted from F. V. Bulgarin, "*Geroi nashego vremeni. Sochineniie* M. Lermontova. Dve chasti. Spb., 1840," *Severnaia pchela* (October 30, 1840): 981–83.

1. A broadside at the vogue of German romantic philosophy current at the time.

2. Alexander Griboedov is famous for his drama "Woe from Wit," which was not published in his lifetime. He was killed by a mob while serving as ambassador to Iran.

3. Bulgarin mistakes Lermontov for the traveling narrator.

4. Claude-Joseph Vernet, an eighteenth-century preromantic painter; David Teniers, The Younger, a seventeenth-century genre painter; Sir Anthony van Dyck, a seventeenth-century Flemish baroque artist best known for his portraits.

5. Karl Pavlovich Briullov was the most outstanding painter of the romantic period in Russia. His chief work is *The Last Day of Pompeii* (1830–33), which made his fame.


## L. Brant

Translated by Victoria Klein

Without question this work numbers among the best of the past year's belles lettres and in general deserves an honored place in our literature: if not in every detail, then absolutely for style and expository skill. When a book's debut creates a stir and a powerful impression, the critic must not write immediately upon its publication. A balanced opinion is needed, one attained by attentive listening to the rumblings in the journals and discussions in the public, an opinion that balances negative bias and excessive enthusiasm by taking a dispassionate, calm view. Finally, taking as a starting point the laws of taste and common sense, the critic delivers a verdict – if not an infallible one, than one close to the truth, or at least one striving toward it. [With this said], we will give our candid opinion of Lermontov's noteworthy work. Readers of reviews published in *Russian Invalid* during the past year might have noticed that this critic's diligent aim has been moderation removed from any polemics. (Moderation is entirely necessary in our literature today, where the rare book receives a fair and impartial hearing.) Various reasons have impeded this reviewer from giving his opinion of every notable work of the past year, so now we will examine a few works worthy of the title page for 1840. First place goes to Lermontov.

*A Hero of Our Time*? What must await the reader of a book with a title so specific and, one might add, so categorical? Quite naturally [we expect to meet in the work] a man who represents his time, his age, and who reflects within him, as in a mirror, the epoch's spirit, ideas, and distinctiveness. This being the case, [I must submit that] the author slanders our time a bit. We are far from accepting [Lermontov's] representative of the contemporary age simply as a narcissist and egotist, completely indifferent to good, not knowing happiness, and willing to deprive his fellow man of it. In our opinion such is Lermontov's hero, *Pechorin*. We also think that no single individual can represent the diverse types of a specific time in society or that all kinds of virtues, vices, merits, and shortcomings converge readily in that single person. In defense of the author, it is best to surmise that he named his work [*A Hero of Our Time*] only because he wished to avoid the worn-out and thousand-times-repeated title "The Story of Mr. So-and-So or Mrs. Such-and-Such" [so common in the press today]. True, this work by Lermontov is on the order of a "Story of Mr. So-and-So." But some critics think otherwise [about its genre] and attribute to the author's separate sketches a general connection, labeling the whole if not an inseparable story, then a novel. This is incorrect. At least we do not see between Lermontov's tales any correlation other than that the same personage, Pechorin, appears in each. Each tale or story represents a separate episode from his life, but in content they are completely independent from one another. "Bela" and "Princess Mary" are the two principal sketches; the story called "Maksim Maksimych" comprises a type of epilogue to "Bela." It would be unintelligible and incomprehensible on its own. Whereas "Taman" is a truly artistic, deeply poetic episode, "The Fatalist" weakens the impression made by the story preceding it ["Princess Mary"] and in general has no great interest or artistic merit.

The action of Lermontov's stories occurs in the Caucasus, a place of temptation for many of our writers, beginning with Marlinsky and ending with the author of the novelette, *The Seeker of Intense Feelings* (*Iskatel' sil'nykh oshchushchenii*), which discovered neither the secret of the novel nor of its parody. Long ago Marlinsky's imitators had already bored the public with pompous and pseudorapturous descriptions of the Caucasus. Even in the original [Marlinsky tales], the descriptions of the Caucasus were excessively elaborate. By refusing to follow the path of these bards of the Caucasus, Lermontov spares us from superfluous, unnaturally embellished descriptions of its nature. Under Lermontov's pen, pictures of the Caucasian lands become simple and natural. It is evident that Lermontov wrote under the genuine influence of spontaneous impressions, for much strength and poetry lie in his short sketches.

We must give the context of Lermontov's two main stories to the reader in order to lay out Pechorin's character, the fictional hero of our time who is portrayed masterfully in an artistic sense, but who, in a moral sense, provides little comfort to our age.

On the road from Tiflis, the author meets an elderly officer, staff captain Maksim Maksimych, who began his service in the Caucasus under A. P. Ermolov.[1] The staff captain is simple, even a bit rough, yet good-natured and upright. He lacks the benefit of an education but is warmed through and through with a basic goodness of heart. Although not developed poetically, the character of this staff captain may serve as an excellent example of several of our Caucasus veterans, who have become reconciled to their wild military life and, consequently, remain foreigners in the stylish atmosphere of high society in the capital's salons. It is a shame that the author did not introduce Maksim Maksimych to Pechorin in the story about

Princess Mary rather than Bela. The fashionable society figures (or at least ones with pretensions to worldliness) who sparkle in this tale would have become more nuanced had the original character of Maksim Maksimych been presented alongside them. In [Maksim's] stead, we have Dr. Verner, which is unfortunate because Werner is an unoriginal character, more contrived than our Maksim Maksimych, who is as alive as one can imagine.

Despite opposite personalities and variations in age and education, meeting on the road brings people closer. The author quickly stirs Maksim Maksimych to be open, leading him to tell the story of Bela:

A peaceful Caucasian prince invites Maksim Maksimych and Pechorin, a young officer who is serving under his command, to the wedding of his oldest daughter. She has a charming sister, Bela, and a brother, Azamat, a wild and impulsive youth and cutthroat. The fact that he was only fifteen does not matter, for the Asiatic nature develops earlier in life than it does in the European. Among the guests feasting at this wedding is a daredevil, a mountain horseman, or, more simply put, a bandit named Kazbich, who owns an incredibly fast horse. Azamat has coveted Kazbich's horse for a long time. He would give anything for the racer, but Kazbich can be tempted by nothing in exchange for his priceless Karagyoz, not even the beautiful Bela, whom the obliging brother has offered Kazbich for the horse. Do not be surprised by this offer given by an Asiatic mountain warrior [gorets] who is as wild himself as a steppe steed.

Kazbich replies to Azamat's offer to steal his sister with a song:

> We have many beautiful girls in our villages,
> Stars are ablaze in the dark of their eyes.
> Sweet is to love them – an enviable lot;
> Bold freedom, however, is merrier still.
> Gold can purchase you a foursome of wives,
> But a spirited steed is a priceless possession:
> He will not be outstripped by the wind in the steppes,
> He will never betray, he will never deceive (18).

The European [Pechorin's] subtle, refined taste is not as passionate about horses – he prefers something more deserving of human love. Pechorin finds out about Azamat's offer to Kazbich, and the idea awakens in the enlightened European's heart to use to his advantage the weakness of the Tatar stripling (as Maksim Maksimych calls Azamat). Pechorin will obtain Kazbich's horse for Azamat and in return will himself get Bela from Azamat.

After putting up a weak resistance, which suggests no coquetry, but virginity's involuntary and newly awakening feelings, the poor girl falls for Pechorin with all the fervor of an Eastern passion. Soon thereafter, however, in response to her tender, ardent caresses, Pechorin's coldness becomes apparent, and he leaves her alone at home while he spends whole days hunting. Melancholic from unrequited love, she wanders alone around the fortress walls. During one of these outings, she becomes the victim of Kazbich's well-aimed shot.[2] The unhappy Bela dies with an enduring love for Pechorin in her heart and with the naive hope of meeting him in her heaven.

As for Pechorin this was far from the first woman whom he had loved and ceased to love. Life had become boring long before for Pechorin, but this does not prevent him from seizing all possible pleasure from it. By his own confession, Pechorin despises both himself and others. What can be expected from one who does not respect himself? He surely must be a pitiful narcissist and, if one may say so, a sensualist. This is the reason why the kind Maksim Maksimych pities poor Bela, as a father would a daughter. From the very first, Maksim Maksimych disapproves of Pechorin's abduction and, as his superior, wants to restrain him from this ignoble and reprehensible act. Pechorin, however, succeeds in persuading the compliant Maksim Maksimych otherwise. After all, Maksim Maksimych admits how deeply he loves Pechorin.[3]

When the staff captain interests the author in Bela's touching story, Pechorin himself appears [on the scene]. Kind Maksim Maksimych suffers an indescribable joy at meeting his former colleague, but the latter responds to the staff captain's open embrace with a cold and inattentive handshake. [Pechorin's] insulting rebuff almost makes kind, simple-hearted Maksim Maksimych cry. Clearly, Pechorin is the same kind of friend as he is a lover. Nevertheless, incessant, nagging recollections of conscience hide behind [Pechorin's] mask of indifference and coldness: a conscience before which the shadows of Bela and others like her loom. The author does not describe [Pechorin's conscience]. In an attempt to delay, if only for a moment, Pechorin's departure, Maksim Maksimych offers to return to Pechorin the papers he has been keeping for him. Pechorin says that he does not need them. In this way the author succeeds in obtaining Pechorin's journal. The author extracts the remaining three tales [of *A Hero of Our Time*] from them, including the episode "Princess Mary."

Pechorin meets the princess at the spa in Pyatigorsk. Around her hovers a crowd of ill and healthy admirers, among whom it seems she has singled out a cadet. With Pechorin's appearance, however, the cadet loses the princess's favor. At one time Pechorin had belonged to the highest society, through which he had acquired his aristocratic ways and habits. This, combined with his intellect and education, plus the advantage of his personal appearance, allows Pechorin to quickly dislodge the cadet. The cadet is a shallow young man, who struts about in a soldier's greatcoat, which he has pulled from his heavily laden trunk for the purpose of impressing Princess Mary. Pechorin, utilizing practiced and clever methods of seduction, quickly gains power over the princess's heart. He compels her to say "I love you" first. When this tender word, which has brought happiness to so many, flies from Mary's pretty, rosy lips, Pechorin announces indifferently that he does not love her but has merely played a trick on her. The trick cuts deeply into the poor girl's heart and she sinks into a profound illness. Her mother, in tears, offers Pechorin the princess's hand. A tête-a-tête between Pechorin and Mary (that unfortunate girl) follows. Pechorin, like a true hero, remains intransigent and departs.

Such a demonic character [as Pechorin appears to be] is hardly even plausible. Let us assume, however, that such a man really exists. Then why is he a hero and a representative of our time? For we see in his character only an exception [to the rule, not a representation of it], a moral monstrosity who arouses only one thing: indignation. He is like one of the products of the young French school that seems already out of fashion. Would [Lermontov], in fact, take upon his conscience a morally uncertain youth, who seeks to imitate this Pechorin [in real life]?

Pechorin remains a puzzle. The author did not impart one noble trait to his character. Neither did he speak of him with contempt. By the way, we forgot to mention that in the process of ruining Princess Mary, Pechorin had also renewed an old love affair with a married lady [Vera]. She was also at the spa and was, in fact, quite ill. She suffers from an unshakable, illicit, but all the same tender and passionate love for Pechorin. We also forgot to mention that Pechorin has a duel with the aforementioned cadet and kills him. The cadet, no matter how the author tries to abase him, invites our sympathy far more than Pechorin can, for he is conscious of his misdeed [in challenging Pechorin to a duel] and [for this reason] his woeful death redeems his insignificance and pettiness.

It is also true that Pechorin dies, according to the author, who promises us a continuation of Pechorin's adventures at another time. If the author, however, intends to keep his promise, then we dare ask from him two things: to recount if only one incident that might somehow reconcile us to this strange man and to explain the idea of the work. We, in our simplicity, absolutely do not understand it, even though some critics have placed the idea above that of Pushkin's Eugene Onegin! Allow me to say, out of respect for the memory of our immortal poet, that Pushkin's imagination never gave rise to such a creation as Pechorin, who should never be compared with the likes of Eugene Onegin. We, however, truly admire Lermontov's talent. He is one of the best of our writers, and we value him even more as a poet and a crafter of verse. But we think (together with the majority of our enlightened public) that for now Pushkin's position in Russian literature remains unchallenged.

Having laid out our opinion of the content of Lermontov's work, we will give him his due and praise his style and expository skill, as we stated at the beginning of our article. His skill at using language brings new turns of phrase, freedom from elaborateness and pomposity, an artistic simplicity of expression, a master's touch in nature description, an authenticity in the development of dialogue with its witticisms, cleverness in the development of his story lines, originality in the depiction of character, and a plethora of ideas, which are often true and profound. All this belongs to Mr. Lermontov's pen, from whom our literature rightly expects great things. As for the hero in *A Hero of Our Time*, let us conclude with his own words: "All my life has been a chain of sad and unsuccessful contradictions of heart and mind."[4]

NOTES

Reprinted from L. V. Brant, "Geroi nashego vremeni. Sochinenie M. Lermontova. Spb., 1840," *Russkii invalid*, nos. 17–18 (January 22, 1841): 71–72.

1. Brant confuses the traveling narrator's identity with Lermontov's. General Ermolov was commander of the Russian army in the Caucasus roughly in the second and third decades of the nineteenth century.

2. This is a misreading of the plot by Brant.

3. It is logical, Brant argues, that Maksim Maksimych would be hospitable to Pechorin's "prank" because of that love.

4. Some critics, foreseeing that the character of Pechorin was bound to be denounced, try to find excuses for him through various rationalizations. Those who are against this truly satanic character are called oafs, preachers, and tedious moralists. We count ourselves willingly among the number of dolts who do not understand Pechorin. Be that as it may, we also wash our hands of approval for any similar creations, even though they be wrapped within the most artistic and masterful forms (as almost all of Lermontov's characters are, for he has an uncommon gift for character depiction). We have heard that one journal shares our opinion, although we confess to not having read its criticism of Lermontov's work [Brant's note].

# Select Bibliography

## Primary Sources

Lermontov, Mikhail. *The Demon and Other Poems*. Trans. Eugene M. Kayden. Yellow Springs, Ohio, 1965.

———. *A Hero of Our Time*. Trans. Paul Foote. New York, 1974.

———. *A Hero of Our Time*. Trans. Philip Longworth. London, 1975.

———. *A Hero of Our Time*. Trans. Vladimir and Dmitri Nabokov. New York, 1958.

———. *M. Iu. Lermontov v vospominaniiakh sovremennikov*. Ed. V. A. Manuilov and M. I. Gillel'son. Penza, 1960.

———. *Major Poetic Works*. Trans. Anatoly Liberman. Minneapolis, 1984.

———. *Masquerade*. Trans. Roger W. Phillips. *Russian Literature Triquarterly* 7 (1973): 67–116.

———. *Polnoe sobranie sochinenii v 5-i tomakh*. Ed. B. M. Eikhenbaum. Moscow/Leningrad, 1935–37.

———. *Polnoe sobranie sochinenii v 6-i tomakh*. Ed. N. F. Belchikov, B. P. Gorodetskii, and B. V. Tomashevskii. Moscow/Leningrad, 1934–37.

———. "Princess Ligovskaya." In *A Lermontov Reader*. Trans. Guy Daniels, 117–213. New York, 1965.

———. *Selected Poetry*. Trans. C. E. L'Ami and Alexander Welikotny. Winnipeg, 1965.

———. *Selected Works*. Trans. A. Pyman and Irina Zheleznova. Moscow, 1976.

———. *Sobranie sochinenii v 4-kh tomakh*. Ed. V. A. Manuilov et al. Leningrad, 1981.

———. *Vadim*. Trans. Helena Goscilo. Ann Arbor, Mich., 1984.

## Secondary Sources

Aizlewood, Robin. "*Geroi nashego vremeni* as Emblematic Prose Text." In *From Pushkin to Palisandriia: Essays in the Russian Novel in Honor of Richard Freeborn*, 39–51. New York, 1990.

Alekseev, M. P., A. Glasse, and V. E. Vatsuro, eds. *M. Iu. Lermontov: Issledovaniia i materialy*. Leningrad, 1979.

Andrew, Joe. "'The Blind Will See': Narrative and Gender in 'Taman,'" *Russian Literature* 31, no. 4 (1992): 449–76.

————. "Mikhail Lermontov." In *Writers and Society during the Rise of Russian Realism*, 42–75. Atlantic Highlands, 1980.

————. "Mikhail Lermontov and *A Rake's Progress*." In *Women in Russian Literature, 1780–1863*, 53–78. New York, 1988.

Angeloff, A., and Pr. Klingenburg. "Lermontov's Uses of Nature in the Novel *Hero of Our Time*." *Russian Literature Journal* 88 (1970): 3–12.

Arian, I. "Some Aspects of Lermontov's *A Hero of Our Time*." *Forum for Modern Language Studies* 4 (1968): 22–32.

Baak, Joost van. "Sub'ekt i mir u Lermontova. Opyt semanticheskogo obobshcheniia." *Russian Literature* 34, no. 1 (1993): 1–20.

Bagby, Lewis. "Inscription in 'Fatalist.'" *Romantic Russia* 2 (1998): 35–47.

————. "Narrative Double-Voicing in Lermontov's *A Hero of Our Time*." *Slavic and East European Journal* 22 (1978): 265–86.

Barratt, Andrew, and A. D. P. Briggs. *A Wicked Irony: The Rhetoric of Lermontov's "A Hero of Our Time."* Bristol, 1989.

Briggs, A. D. P. "Lermontov in the Negative." *New Zealand Slavonic Journal* (1986): 11–24.

————, ed. *Mikhail Lermontov: Commemorative Essays.* Birmingham, 1992.

————. "'Pikovaya Dama' and 'Taman': Questions of Kinship." *Journal of Russian Studies* 37 (1979): 13–20.

Brodskii, N. L., et al. *Zhizn' i tvorchestvo M. Iu. Lermontova: issledovaniia i materialy.* Khudozhestvennaia literatura, 1941.

Brown, Edward E. "Mikhail Lermontov: Dramas and Narrative Prose." In *A History of Russian Literature of the Romantic Period*, 4:217–61. Ann Arbor, Mich., 1986.

Chistova, I. S., et al. *Lermontovskii sbornik.* Leningrad, 1985.

Cox, Gary. "Dramatic Genre as a Tool of Characterization in Lermontov's *A Hero of Our Time*." *Russian Literature* 11–12 (1982): 163–72.

Debreczeny, P. "Elements of the Lyrical Verse Tale in Lermontov's *A Hero of Our Time*." In *American Contributions to the Seventh International Congress of Slavists.* Vol. 2 of *Literature and Folklore*, ed. Victor Terras, 93–117. The Hague, 1973.

D'iakonova, Nina. "Byron and Lermontov: Notes on Pechorin's Journal." In *Lord Byron and His Contemporaries*, ed. Charles E. Robinson, 144–65. Newark, Del., 1984.

Durylin, S. N. *"Geroi nashego vremeni" M. Iu. Lermontova.* Moscow, 1940; reprint, Ann Arbor, Mich., 1986.

————. *Kak rabotal Lermontov.* Moscow, 1934.

Eagle, Herbert. "Lermontov's 'Play' with Romantic Genre Expectations in *A Hero of Our Time*." *Russian Literature Triquarterly* 10 (1974): 299–315.

Egolin, A. M., et al. *Literaturnoe nasledstvo: Pushkin, Lermontov, Gogol.* Vol. 58. Akademiia nauk, 1952.

Eikhenbaum, B. M. *Lermontov.* Trans. Ray Parrott and Harry Weber. Ann Arbor, Mich., 1981.

———. *Lermontov: Opyt istoriko-literaturnoi otsenki.* Leningrad, 1924. Also in *O literature,* 140–287. Moscow, 1987.

———. "Literaturnaia pozitsiia Lermontova." In *Literaturnoe nasledstvo.* Moscow, 1941, 43–44:3–82.

———. *O proze.* Leningrad, 1969.

———. "O smyslovoi osnove *Geroia nashego vremeni*." *Russkaia literatura* 3 (1959): 8–27.

———. *Stat'i o Lermontove.* Moscow/Leningrad, 1961.

Entwhistle, W. J. "The Byronism of Lermontov's *A Hero of Our Time*." *Comparative Literature* 1 (1949): 140–46.

Etkin, Efim, ed. *Mikhail Lermontov: 1814–1989.* Norwich, 1992.

Faletti, H. "Elements of the Demonic in the Character of Pechorin in Lermontov's *Hero of Our Time*." *Forum for Modern Language Studies* 14 (1978): 365–77.

Fisher, V. M. "Poetika Lermontova." *Venok M. Iu. Lermontovu.* Moscow, 1914.

Fokht, U. R., ed. *Lermontov: logika tvorchestva.* Moscow, 1975.

———. *Tvorchestvo M. Iu. Lermontova.* Moscow, 1964.

Freeborn, R. "*A Hero of Our Time*." In *The Rise of the Russian Novel,* 38–73. Cambridge, 1973.

Fridlender, G. M. "Lermontov i russkaia povestvovatel'naia proza." *Russkaia literatura* 1 (1965): 33–49.

Garrard, John. *Mikhail Lermontov.* Boston, 1982.

———. "Old Wine in New Bottles: The Legacy of Lermontov." In *Poetika Slavica: Studies in Honor of Zbigniew Folejewski,* 41–52. Ottawa, 1981.

Gershtein, Emma. *Sud'ba Lermontova.* Moscow, 1986.

Gillel'son, Iu. I., and Manuilov, V. A., eds. *M. Iu. Lermontov v vospominaniiakh sovremennikov.* Moscow, 1972.

Gilroy, M. *The Ironic Vision in Lermontov's "A Hero of Our Time."* No. 19. Birmingham, 1986.

Ginzburg, L. Ia. "*Geroi nashego vremeni*." In *M. Iu. Lermontov,* 207–29. Leningrad, 1941.

———. *Tvorcheskii put' Lermontova.* Leningrad, 1940.

Golstein, Vladimir. *Lermontov's Narratives of Heroism.* Evanston, Ill., 1998.

Goscilo, Helena Irena. "The First Pečorin: En Route to *A Hero of Our Time.*" *Russian Literature* 11–12 (1982): 129–62.

———. "Gilded Guilt: Confession in Russian Romantic Prose." *Russian Literature* 14 (1983): 149–82.

———. "Lermontov's Debt to Lavater and Gall." *Slavonic and East European Review* 59 (1981): 500–15.

Gregg, R. "The Cooling of Pechorin: The Skull beneath the Skin." *Slavic Review* 43 (1984): 387–98.

Grigor'ian, K. N. *Lermontov i ego roman "Geroi nashego vremeni."* Leningrad, 1975.

———. "Pechorin and Hamlet: Towards a Typology of Character." Trans. C. Roberts. *Canadian Review of Comparative Literature* 1 (1974): 235–52.

Grigorovich, D. V. *Literaturnoe vospominaniia,* 171. Leningrad, 1928.

Gurevich, I. "Zagadochen li Pechorin?" *Voprosy literatury* 2 (1983): 119–35.

Halpert, E. "Lermontov and the Wolf Man." *American Imago* 32 (1975): 315–28.

Harvie, J. A. "The Vulture and the Dove." *Comparative Literature Studies* 18 (1981): 15–32.

Heier, E. "The Second *Hero of Our Time.*" *Slavic and East European Journal* 2 (1967): 35–43.

Heldt, Barbara. "Misogyny and the Power of Silence." In *Terrible Perfection: Women and Russian Literature,* 25–37. Bloomington, Ind., 1987.

Holk, A. G. F. van. "O gulbinnoi strukture Pechorina." *Russian Literature* 31–34 (1992): 545–54.

Karlinsky, Simon. "Misanthropy and Sadism in Lermontov's Plays." In *Studies in Russian Literature in Honor of Vsevolod Setchkarev,* 166–73. Columbus, Ohio, 1986.

Kelly, Lawrence. *Lermontov: Tragedy in the Caucasus.* New York, 1977.

Kessler, R. L. "Lermontov's *A Hero of Our Time.*" *Texas Studies in Literature and Language* 32–34 (1990): 485–505.

Kotliarevskii, N. M. Iu. *Lermontov: lichnost' poeta i ego proizvedeniia.* St. Petersburg, 1909.

Lavrin, Janko. *Lermontov.* New York, 1959.

———. "Some Notes on Lermontov's Romanticism." *Slavonic and East European Review* (1957–58): 69–80.

Layton, Susan. "Lermontov in Combat with *Biblioteka dlia Chteniia*." *Cahiers du Monde russe* 35, no. 4 (1994): 787–802.

———. "Nineteenth-century Russian Mythologies of Caucasian Savagery." In *The Russian Orient, Imperial Borderlands and Peoples, 1750–1917*, ed. Daniel Brower and Edward J. Lazzerini, 80–99. Bloomington, Ind., 1997.

———. *Russian Literature and Empire: Conquest of the Caucasus from Pushkin to Tolstoy.* Cambridge, England, 1994.

———. "Some Notes on Lermontov's Romanticism." *Slavonic and East European Review* 36 (1958): 11–20.

Lebedev-Polianskii, P. I., et al. *Literaturnoe nasledstvo: M. Iu. Lermontov.* Vol. 2. Akademiia nauk, 1948.

Levin, V. I. "'Fatalist': Epilog ili prilozhenie?" In *Iskusstvo slova*, ed. D. D. Blagoi, 161–70. Moscow, 1973.

———. "Ob istinnom smysle monologa Pechorina." In *Tvorchestvo M. Iu. Lermontova. 150 let so dnia rozhdeniia*, 276–82. Moscow, 1964.

———. "Problema geroia i pozitsiia avtora v romane *Geroi nashego vremeni.*" In *Lermontov i literatura narodov Sovetskogo Soiuza*, 104–26. Erevan, 1974.

Lisenkova, N. A. "Motivatsionnaia sfera romana M. Iu. Lermontova *Geroi nashego vremeni*. Povest' 'Kniazhnia Meri.'" In *Tvorchestvo M. Iu. Lermontova. Sbornik statei, posviashchennykh 150-letiiu so dnia rozhdniia M. Iu. Lermontova*, 170–224. Penza, 1965.

———. "Vliianie romanticheskoi motivirovki na formirovanie zhanrovoi struktury istoricheskogo romana Lermontova 'Vadim.'" In *M. Iu. Lermontov: voprosy traditsii i novatorstva*, 38–45. Riazan', 1983.

*Literaturnoe nasledstvo: M. Iu. Lermontov*, 1, vols. 43–44. Moscow, 1941.

Magogonenko, G. P. *Lermontov i Pushkin: problemy preemstvennogo razvitiia literatury.* Moscow, 1987.

Makhlevich, Ia. L. "Rasshifrovka nekotorykh sokrashchenii v *Geroe nashego vremeni.*" *Voprosy literatury* 4 (1976): 209–18.

Manuilov, V. A. *Geroi nashego vremeni: Kommentarii.* Moscow/Leningrad, 1966.

———. *Lermontov: Zhizn' i tvorchestvo.* Leningrad, 1939.

———, ed. *Lermontovskaia entsiklopediia.* Moscow, 1981.

———, ed. *Letopis' zhizni i tvorchestva M. Iu. Lermontova.* Moscow/Leningrad, 1964.

Manuilov, V. A., and M. I. Gillel'son, eds. *M. Iu. Lermontov v vospominaniiakh sovremennikov.* Moscow, 1972.

———. *Roman M. Iu. Lermontova "Geroi nashego vremeni."* Moscow/ Leningrad, 1966.

———. *Roman M. Iu. Lermontova "Geroi nashego vremeni." Kommentarii.* Leningrad, 1975.

Markovich, B. M. "O znachenii nezavershennosti v proze Lermontova." *Russian Literature* 33–34 (1993): 471–94.

Marsh, Cynthia. "Lermontov and the Romantic Tradition: The Function of Landscape in *A Hero of Our Time*." *Slavic and East European Review* 66, no. 1 (1988): 35–46.

Mersereau, John, Jr. "'The Fatalist' as a Keystone of Lermontov's *A Hero of Our Time*." *Slavic and East European Journal* 4 (1960): 137–46.

———. *Mikhail Lermontov.* Carbondale, Ill., 1962.

Michailoff, Helen. "The Death of Lermontov (The Poet and the Tsar)." *Russian Literature Triquarterly* 10 (1974): 279–98.

Mikhailova, E. N. *Proza Lermontova.* Moscow, 1957.

Miller, O. V., ed. *Bibliografiia literatury o M. Iu. Lermontove: 1917–1977.* Leningrad, 1980.

Milner-Gulland, R. "Heroes of Their Time? Form and Idea in Buchner's *Danton's Death* and Lermontov's *Hero of Our Time*." In *The Idea of Freedom: Essays in Honour of Isaiah Berlin*, ed. A. Ryan, 119–37. Oxford, 1979.

Nakhapetov, B. A. "Obraz doktora Vernera iz romana M. Iu. Lermontova *Geroi nashego vremeni* kak ob"ekt psikhologicheskogo eksperimentirovaniia." *Voprosy psikhologii* 11: 91–97.

Peace, Richard A. "The Role of 'Taman' in Lermontov's *Geroy nashego vremeni*." *Slavonic and East European Review* 45 (1967): 112–29.

Powelstock, David. "Living into Language: Mikhail Lermontov and the Manufacturing of Intimacy." In *Russian Subjects: Empire, Nation, and the Culture of the Golden Age*, eds. Monika Greenleaf and Stephen Moeller-Sally, 297–324. Evanston, Ill., 1998.

Reed, W. L. *Meditations on the Hero: A Study of the Romantic Hero in Nineteenth-Century Fiction.* New Haven, Conn., 1974.

Reeve, F. D. "*A Hero of Our Time*." In *The Russian Novel*, 45–63. London, 1967.

Reid, Robert. "Eavesdropping in *A Hero of Our Time*." *New Zealand Slavonic Journal* 1 (1977): 13–22.

———. "Ethnotope in Lermontov's Caucasian *Poemy*." In *Mikhail Lermontov: Commemorative Essays (1991)*, ed. A. D. P. Briggs, 89–106. Birmingham, 1992.

———. *Lermontov's "A Hero of Our Time."* Bristol, 1997.

Richards, D. J. "Lermontov: *A Hero of Our Time.*" In *The Voice of a Giant: Essays on Seven Russian Prose Classics*, ed. Roger Cockrell and David Richards, 15–25. Exeter, 1985.

———. "Pechorin and the Art of Seduction." *Journal of Russian Studies* 22 (1971): 3–9.

———. "Two Malicious Tongues – the Wit of Chatsky and Pechorin." *New Zealand Slavonic Journal* 11 (1973): 11–28.

Ripp, V. "*A Hero of Our Time* and the Historicism of the 1830s." *Modern Language Notes* 92 (1977): 969–86.

Rowe, W. W. "Deadly Joking in Pushkin and Lermontov." In *Patterns in Russian Literature II: Notes on the Classics*, 140–46. Ann Arbor, Mich., 1986.

———. "The Motif of Falling in *A Hero of Our Time.*" In *Patterns in Russian Literature II: Notes on the Classics*, 134–39. Ann Arbor, Mich., 1986.

Schmid, Wolf. "O navatorstve lemontovskogo psikhologizma." *Russian Literature* 34, no. 1 (1993): 59–73.

Scotto, Peter. "Prisoners of the Caucasus: Ideologies of Imperialism in Lermontov's 'Bela.'" *Publications of the Modern Language Association of America* 107, no. 2 (1992): 246–60.

Serman, I. *Mikhail Lermontov: 1836–1841.* Verba Publishers, 1997.

Shepard, Elizabeth C. "The Society Tale and the Innovative Argument in Russian Prose Fiction of the 1830s." *Russian Literature* 10, no. 2 (1981): 111–62.

Slonim, Marc. *An Outline of Russian Literature*, 37–45. New York, 1958.

Spector, I. "The Death of Lermontov." *Slavia* 16, no. 4 (1941): 98–102.

Stenbock-Fermor, E. "Lermontov and Dostoevskij's Novel *The Devils.*" *Slavic and East European Journal* 3 (1959): 219–30.

Sukhotin, V. P. "Znachenie predlozhenii v 'Tamani' M. Iu. Lermontova." In *Sobranie nauchnykh trudov Piatigorskogo pedagogicheskogo instituta*, 206–34. Piatigorsk, 1948.

Todd, William Mills III. "*A Hero of Our Time*: The Caucasus as Amphitheater." In *Fiction and Society in the Age of Pushkin*, 137–63. Cambridge, Massachusetts, 1986.

Tomashevskii, B. V. "Proza Lermontova i zapadnoevropeiskaia literaturnaia traditsiia." In *Literaturnoe nasledstvo.* Moscow, 1941, 43–44:137–63.

Tsybenko, E. Z. "Osobennosti pol'skoi i russkoi romanticheskoi prozy 1830–1840-kh godov. K probleme geroia i printsipov ego

204 : Select Bibliography

izobrazheniia." In *Romantizm v slavianskikh literaturakh*, 110–53. Moscow, 1973.

Turner, C. J. G. *Pechorin: An Essay on Lermontov's "A Hero of Our Time."* Birmingham, England, 1978.

———. "The System of Narrators in Part I of *A Hero of Our Time.*" *Canadian Slavonic Papers* 17 (1975): 617–28.

Udodov, B. T. M. Iu. *Lermontov: Khudozhestvennaia individual'nost' i tvorcheskii protsess.* Izdatel'stvo voronezhskogo universiteta, 1973.

Ulph, O. "Unmasking the Masked Guardsman." *Russian Literature Triquarterly* 3 (1972): 269–80.

Umanskaia, M. M. "'Roman sud'by' ili 'roman voli.'" *Russkaia literatura* 1 (1967): 18–28.

Van der Eng, Jan. "The Character of Maksim Maksimyč." *Russian Literature* 34, no. 1 (1993): 21–36.

*Venok M. Iu. Lermontovu: Iubileinyi sbornik.* Izdanie V. V. Dumov, 1914.

Vinogradov, A. M. Iu. *Lermontov.* Moscow, 1932.

Vinogradov, B. S. "Gortsy v romane Lermontova *Geroi nashego vremeni.*" In *M. Iu. Lermontov. Voprosy zhizni i tvorchestva*, ed. A. N. Sokolova and D. A. Gireev, 54–66. Ordzhonikidze, 1963.

———. "O *Geroe nashego vremeni.*" In *M. Iu. Lermontov: Materialy i soobshcheniia*, 20–34. Stavropol', 1965.

Vinogradov, V. V. "Iazyk Lermontova." In *Ocherki po istorii russkogo literaturnogo iazyka XVII–XIX vv*, 269–301. Moscow, 1938.

———. "The Language of Lermontov." In *The Russian Literary Language.* Trans. Lawrence L. Thomas, 158–77. Madison, Wisc., 1969.

———. "Stil' prozy Lermontova." In *Literaturnoe nasledstvo.* Moscow, 1941, 43–44:517–628. Also in *Stil' prozy Lermontova.* Ann Arbor, Mich., 1986.

Vishevsky, Anatolii. "Demonic Games, or the Hidden Plot of Mixail Lermontov's 'Knjazna Meri.'" *Wiener Sawistischer Almanach* 27 (1991): 55–72.

Viskovatyi, P. A. *Mikhail Iurievich Lermontov: zhizn' i tvorchestvo.* Moscow, 1891.

Warner, N. O. "The Footnote as a Literary Genre: Nabokov's Commentaries to Lermontov and Pushkin." *Slavic and East European Journal* 30 (1986): 167–82.

Zholkovskii, A. "Semiotika 'Tamani.'" In *Lotman-70: sbornik statei k 70-iiu prof. Iu. M. Lotmana*, 248–56. Tartu, 1992.

Zhuravleva, A. I. "Poeticheskaia proza Lermontova." *Russkaia rech'* 5 (1974): 21–27.

# Contributors

Lewis Bagby is a professor of Russian and the director of International Programs at the University of Wyoming. He is author of *Alexander Bestuzhev-Marlinsky and Russian Byronism.*

Jane Costlow is a professor of Russian and the Christian A. Johnson Professor of Interdisciplinary Studies at Bates College. She is the author of *Worlds within Worlds: The Novels of Ivan Turgenev* and coeditor of *Sexuality and the Body in Russian Culture.*

Matthew Feeney graduated from the University of Wyoming in Russian in 1980 and from the State University of New York at Albany in Russian in 1988 and 1994. He is completing his doctorate in Slavic linguistics at the University of Kansas, where he is an instructor of Russian.

Lisa Holte graduated from the University of Wyoming in Russian in 1997 and entered the graduate program in the Department of Slavic Languages and Literatures at the University of Indiana.

Katrina Jones graduated from the University of Wyoming in Russian in 1995 (and again in 1997 in secondary education). She is working in the Technical Services Department of the Laramie County Library System and pursuing a master's degree in library science.

Victoria Klein graduated from the University of Wyoming in Russian in 1993 and is completing her doctorate in Russian history at Princeton University.

Joseph Krafczik graduated from the University of Wyoming in Russian in 1983 and with a master's degree in Russian and East European studies from the University of Michigan in 1986. He is an instructor of Russian at the University of Wyoming.

Susan Layton teaches at Strathclyde University, Glasgow, and is an associate of the Centre d'études du monde russe in Paris. She is the author of *Russian Literature and Empire: Conquest of the Caucasus from Pushkin to Tolstoy*.

Matthew Micheli graduated from the University of Wyoming with honors in Russian in 1999 and from Brigham Young University's law school in 2002 cum laude.

Dawn Moser graduated from the University of Wyoming in Russian and zoology and physiology in 1998 and is in her second year of veterinary school at Colorado State University.

Joseph Peschio graduated from the University of Wyoming in Russian in 1996 and is completing his doctorate at the University of Michigan in the Department of Slavic Languages and Literatures.

Andrew Swensen is an assistant professor of Russian at Brandeis University. He teaches courses in Russian literature and is preparing a book on romantic aesthetics.